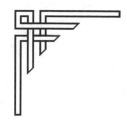

ANALYZING SOCIAL PROBLEMS
Essays and Exercises

Dana Dunn and David V. Waller, Editors

University of Texas at Arlington

Prentice Hall, Upper Saddle River, New Jersey 07458

Library of Congress Cataloging-in-Publication Data

Analyzing social problems : essays and exercises / Dana Dunn and David
  V. Waller, editors
      p.   cm.
   Includes bibliographical references.
   ISBN 0-13-346537-3
   1. Social problems—United States.   2. Social problems.
3. Critical thinking.   I. Dunn, Dana.   II. Waller, David V.
HN59.2.A52   1997
361.1′0973—dc20   96-23250
                                                                      CIP

Editorial Director: Charlyce Jones Owen
Editor in Chief: Nancy Roberts
Marketing Manager: Chaunfayta Hightower
Acquisitions Editor: Fred Wittingham
Editorial/production supervision
   and interior design: Serena Hoffman
Buyer: Bob Anderson
Cover design: Wendy M. E. Alling

This book was set in 11/12 Times Roman
by The Composing Room of Michigan, Inc.,
and was printed and bound by Semline.
The cover was printed by Semline.

© 1997 by Prentice-Hall, Inc.
Simon & Schuster/A Viacom Company
Upper Saddle River, New Jersey 07458

Printed in the United States of America

10 9 8 7 6 5 4 3

ISBN 0-13-346537-3

Prentice-Hall International (UK) Limited, *London*
Prentice-Hall of Australia Pty. Limited, *Sydney*
Prentice-Hall Canada Inc., *Toronto*
Prentice-Hall Hispanoamericana, S.A., *Mexico*
Prentice-Hall of India Private Limited, *New Delhi*
Prentice-Hall of Japan, Inc., *Tokyo*
Simon & Schuster Asia Pte. Ltd., *Singapore*
Editora Prentice-Hall do Brasil, Ltda., *Rio de Janeiro*

CONTENTS

Preface   ix

Introduction
Analyzing Social Problems:
Issues and Approaches   1

Part I
Troubled Social Institutions   5

1   I Need a (Traditional) Wife!: Employment-
Family Conflicts (*Janet Saltzman Chafetz*)   6
Exercises   13

2   Domestic Violence: Hitting Us Where We Live
(*Linda Rouse*)   17
Exercises   23

3   Social Concern About Teen-age Pregnancy
(*Monica A. Longmore*)   25
Exercises   29

4   The Achievement Crisis and School Reform:
From "Basics" to "Excellence" (*Dorothea
Weir*)   31
Exercises   37

5   Your Money or Your Life: Access to Medical
Care as a Social Problem (*Robert A.
Hanneman*)   39
Exercises   45

6   Aging and Health Care (*Jan W. Weaver
and Stanley R. Ingman*)   47
Exercises   53

7   The Problems of U.S. Workers
in a Restructuring Global Economy
(*Ramona Ford*)   57
Exercises   63

8   Is the Criminal Justice System Biased?
(*Carol Y. Thompson*)   65
Exercises   71

Part II
Social Inequalities   79

9   Inequality and Stratification (*Jonathan H.
Turner*)   80
Exercises   87

10   Poverty in the United States (*Leonard
Beeghley*)   89
Exercises   97

11   Racist and Egalitarian Ideologies in Modern
American Culture (*Charles Case*)   99
Exercises   105

12   Racism, Capital Punishment, and the U.S.
Supreme Court (*Adalberto Aguirre, Jr.,
and David V. Baker*)   107
Exercises   115

13   Who's the Boss? Race, Ethnicity, and Gender
in Managerial Jobs (*Elizabeth M. Almquist*)
117
Exercises   123

14   The Feminization of Poverty (*Dana Dunn
and David V. Waller*)   125
Exercises   129

15 Constructing Children's Problems (*Joel Best*)
131
Exercises 135

16 Sexual Orientation and Inequality (*Kenneth Allan*) 137
Exercises 143

17 Disability (*Richard K. Scotch*) 145
Exercises 149

Part III
Social Deviance 153

18 Is America Becoming More Violent?
(*Robert L. Young*) 154
Exercises 159

19 Delinquency and Youth Gangs (*David MacKenna*) 163
Exercises 169

20 Chemical Dependency: Is It Disease or Symptom? (*Gregg Dockins*) 171
Exercises 177

21 The Myths and Realities of Homelessness and Mental Health (*Dee Southard*) 179
Exercises 183

Part IV
Global Social Problems 187

22 Will There Be Another Nuclear War?
Social Behavior and Nuclear Weapons
(*Lloyd J. Dumas*) 188
Exercises 199

23 The Environment as a Social Issue (*Ray Darville*) 195
Exercises 199

24 Gender Inequality in Developing Societies (*Dana Dunn*) 201
Exercises 207

25 Global Population, Poverty, and Child Labor
(*Elizabeth D. Leonard*) 209
Exercises 213

Conclusion
Addressing Social Problems 217

CONTRIBUTING AUTHORS

Adalberto Aguirre, Jr., is a professor of sociology at the University of California at Riverside. His research interests include sociolinguistics, the sociology of education, and race and ethnic relations. His research publications have appeared in *Social Problems* and the *Social Science Journal.* His most recent book publications are *American Ethnicity: The Dynamics and Consequences of Discrimination; Race and Ethnicity in America; Criminal Justice;* and *Racism and Bigotry in Higher Education: A Perilous Climate for Minorities.*

Kenneth Allan is an assistant professor of sociology at the University of North Carolina at Greensboro. His areas of research and teaching interest include gender, theory, and stratification. He has published on gender inequality.

Elizabeth M. Almquist, Regents Professor of Sociology at the University of North Texas, teaches and does research on the intersections of race, class, and gender, and is currently studying these issues in a Wyoming ranching community. She is past chair of the Section on Sex and Gender of the American Sociological Association, past president of the Southwestern Sociological Association, and current president of the Southwestern Social Science Association.

David V. Baker is an associate professor of sociology at Riverside Community College. His research interests are race and ethnic relations, inequality in criminal justice, and immigration. His research publications have appeared in such journals as *Ethnic Studies, Social Justice,* and *The Justice Professional.* His publications include *Sources: Notable Selections in Race and Ethnicity.*

Leonard Beeghley is a professor of sociology and graduate coordinator at the University of Florida. He is the author of several books, among them *Living Poorly in America* (1983), *The Structure of Stratification,* 2nd ed. (1996), and *What Does Your Wife Do: Gender and the Transformation of Family Life* (forthcoming).

Joel Best is professor and chair of the Sociology Department at Southern Illinois University at Carbondale. His research focuses on deviance and social problems. His books include *Threatened Children* (1990) and the collections *Troubling Children* (1994) and *Images of Issues* (1995).

Charles Case is an associate professor of sociology at Augusta College. His areas of research include race and ethnicity and stratification. He has published several research articles in recent years on these and other topics.

Janet Saltzman Chafetz is a professor of sociology at the University of Houston. Over the past 25 years she has written extensively in the area of the sociology of gender, focusing primarily on developing theoretical understandings of stability and change in systems of gender inequality. Her most recent research concerns the impact on family structure of changes in women's relationships to the labor force in advanced industrial nations.

Ray Darville is an associate professor of sociology at Stephen F. Austin State University. His research interests include the environment, inequality, and gender. He has published articles in *Sociological Spectrum, Sociological Inquiry, Family Perspec-*

tive, *International Journal of Aging,* and *Human Development.*

Gregg Dockins has directed alcohol and drug abuse programs for the past six years. He is currently running a program for adolescents in Dallas, Texas. He is also an M.A. student in sociology at the University of Texas at Arlington.

Lloyd J. Dumas is a professor of political economy at the University of Texas at Dallas. He has published four books and numerous articles on issues related to the international arms race and its impacts on global security and economic well-being. His latest book, currently in preparation, *Threatening Ourselves: Dangerous Technologies in an Error-Prone World,* deals with the security implications of human fallibility and technical failure.

Dana Dunn is an associate professor of sociology and director of women's studies at the University of Texas at Arlington. Her research focuses on gender inequality and women and work. She is currently co-authoring a social problems textbook (with Robert Heiner) and editing a forthcoming book with Roxbury Publishers titled *Workplace/Women's Place.*

Ramona Ford is an associate professor of sociology at Southwest Texas State University at San Marcos. She is the author of *Work, Organization, and Power: Introduction to Industrial Sociology.*

Robert A. Hanneman is an associate professor of sociology at the University of California at Riverside. His research interests include simulation methods and health care delivery systems. He has published numerous books and articles on these topics.

Stanley R. Ingman is a professor and director of the Texas Institute for Research and Education on Aging at the University of North Texas. His publications include *Elder Abuse: Practice and Policy* (1989); *Eldercare, Distributive Justice, and the Welfare State: Retrenchment or Expansion* (1994); and *An Aging Population, an Aging Planet, a Sustainable Future* (forthcoming). Dr. Ingman is the principal investigator for two projects funded by the Administration on Aging: "Gerontology in Education: Teaching the Teachers" and "Seniors for Childhood Immunizations."

Elizabeth D. Leonard is a Ph.D. candidate at the University of California at Riverside. Her areas of interest include children, stratification, and family violence.

Monica A. Longmore is an associate professor of sociology at Bowling Green State University. Her areas of research include the family, socialization, and processes of self-concept development. Her research publications have appeared in such journals as *Social Forces, Journal of Marriage and the Family, Sociological Perspectives, Social Psychology Quarterly,* and *Teaching Sociology.*

David MacKenna is an associate professor of criminal justice at the University of Texas at Arlington. His research has focused primarily on police operations and governmental and private security. During 1992–1994 he was co-investigator in a major project funded by the U.S. Department of Health and Human Services which compared social and behavioral characteristics of gang and nongang members in Forth Worth, Texas.

Linda P. Rouse is an associate professor in the Department of Sociology and Anthropology at the University of Texas at Arlington, where she teaches social psychology, sociology of the family, and social statistics. Her research in the area of domestic violence focuses on male assailants in cases of women battering and abuse in dating relationships. She has also worked with shelters for battered women and is the author of *You Are Not Alone: A Guide for Battered Women.*

Richard Scotch is an associate professor of sociology and political economy at the University of Texas at Dallas. He has published numerous articles and monographs on social policy reform and social movements in disability, health care, education, and human services. His current research interests include the implications of federal HIV/AIDS programs for local service systems addressing other chronic health conditions and the implications of alternative paradigms of disability for employment and public policy.

Dee Southard is a sociology Ph.D. candidate at the University of Oregon and a National Science Foundation Graduate Fellow (1992–1995). Her work has established a global electronic archive and database on homelessness on the Internet. She is currently the founding coordinator of the only Internet discussion list dedicated to issues involving the homeless: Homeless@csf.colorado.edu. She may be contacted directly at Southard@oregon.uoregon.edu.

Carol Y. Thompson is an associate professor of sociology and criminal justice at Texas Christian University. Her research has focused on gender and cultural influences on crime and victimization, and on the reaction to crime. Her current research focuses on images of deviance among women in film.

Jonathan H. Turner is a professor of sociology at the University of California at Riverside. His areas of interest include theory, stratification, and race and ethnic relations. He has published two dozen books and is the author of dozens of research articles.

David V. Waller is an assistant professor of sociology at the University of Texas at Arlington. His areas of interest are theory, sociology of science, formal organizations, and stratification. He has published several articles and book chapters on these topics.

Jan W. Weaver is a candidate for a Ph.D. and a research associate at the Texas Institute for Research and Education on Aging at the University of North Texas. Her research interests include adult day care, gerontology, and education. Recent publications include "Temporary Housing: Adult Day Care and Respite Services" in *Housing and the Aging Population: Options for the New Century,* W. E. Folts and D. E. Yeatts, eds. (New York: Garland, 1994), and "Adult Day Care: State Regulatory and Reimbursement Policy" in *Perspectives on Aging* (April–June 1995). Weaver is the associate editor for the *Southwest Journal on Aging.*

Dorothea Weir is principal evaluator in the Office of Evaluation and Testing in the Dallas Independent School District. Her research interests include educational achievement among inner-city minorities and educational stratification.

Robert L. Young is an associate professor of sociology at the University of Texas at Arlington. His research has focused on the public perceptions of and reactions to crime, with special emphasis on private firearm ownership and attitudes toward the death penalty. His current research focuses on the construction and negotiation of interpersonal accounts.

PREFACE

We conceived of this book because we feel that when students have the opportunity to apply knowledge, they develop a more thorough understanding of the material addressed in class lectures and readings. The opportunity to apply knowledge—"to put sociology to work"—also causes students to become more enthusiastic learners.

Social problems are personally relevant; they affect our day-to-day lives. Divorce, poverty, violence, underemployment, youth gangs, drug addiction, the threat of nuclear war, and environmental pollution are but a few of the many social problems that directly or indirectly touch us all. We believe that the subject matter of social problems is especially well-suited to a "hands on" learning approach that actively involves students in applying sociological insights to social problems. The selections in this text, which consist of essays accompanied by exercises, encourage critical and creative thinking about both the causes of and solutions to social problems.

The essays in this volume address a wide range of contemporary social problems that are compatible with the topics covered in most social problems courses. Users of this text may tailor it to fit their course objectives and topics. The exercises that accompany the essays encourage students to integrate, evaluate, and apply their sociological knowledge. Some exercises require students to collect data using a variety of methods, including interviewing, content analysis, and researching public records. Detailed instructions are provided to ensure that the exercises can be completed independently by the student outside of the classroom and with minimal supervision.

The exercises are designed on perforated tear-out pages, which will minimize the burden on instructors as well as facilitate their use in the classroom. The exercises can be used to stimulate class discussion as students bring their exercises together and compare what they have discovered with their classmates. The results from some exercises can easily be pooled and used as basis for small-group or class discussion.

ACKNOWLEDGMENTS

Many people contributed to the development of this book. First, we would like to acknowledge the authors of the individual selections. Their range of scholarship, teaching skills, and practical experience distinguish this book. We must also acknowledge the contributions our students have made to the development of this book; students tried out these assignments and made many valuable suggestions for their improvement.

We also wish to thank the following reviewers for their helpful comments: Brenda Phillips, Texas Women's University; William M. Cross, Illinois College; Richard D. Reddy, State University of New York at Fredonia; Julia Glover Hall, Drexel University; and Bill Kornblum, City University of New York Graduate Center.

The staff of the Department of Sociology and Anthropology at the University of Texas at Arlington—Kathy Rowe, Roberta Shuffitt, Jane Nicole, and LaDorna Goff—also deserve our gratitude and thanks for their hard work in assisting in the preparation of this manuscript.

Finally, we wish to thank prospectively those users of this text who will contact us with feedback and suggestions for making this text even better in the future. We can be reached at (817) 272-2661 or by EMAIL:
DUNNDANA@UTARLG.UTA.EDU
WALLERD@UTARLG.UTA.EDU

Dana Dunn
David V. Waller

ANALYZING SOCIAL PROBLEMS: ISSUES AND APPROACHES

Social problems have been a focus of the sociological enterprise in the United States for more than a century. During the late nineteenth century, the United States was undergoing fundamental, fast-paced social change, which gave rise to a multitude of social problems. Industrialization in the Northeast created a steady stream of migration as rural dwellers were drawn to increased economic opportunities in the burgeoning industrial cities. Waves of immigrants from other nations also poured into the country, attracted by the prospect of a better life. The conditions that greeted these newcomers to the cities were quite different from what they had anticipated—crowded, crime-riddled slums, rampant poverty, factory "sweatshops" with long workdays and hazardous work conditions, and an often hostile social climate resulting from cultural clashes and economic competition among the diverse new residents of the cities. The relatively new discipline of sociology, with its scientific approach to studying human society, was ideally suited to analyzing the pressing social problems of the day.

Was the substance and nature of social problems 100 years ago similar to that of social problems today? Yes, and no. Some social problems are enduring ones. Many of the social problems you will encounter in this text—poverty, crime, unemployment, racial/ethnic and gender inequality—are longstanding ones. In numerous respects they are similar in nature to the problems of the past. For example, there are many today who come to the United States from other nations in search of a better life, only to find themselves victimized by poverty because of cultural and language barriers, and inadequate job skills. So-called illegal aliens cross the border between the United States and Mexico to encounter life circumstances not so very different from those who immigrated to this country a century ago.

The social problems you will read about in this text did not arise in a vacuum; rather, they emerged in an historical and cultural context. For example, many present-day patterns of racial/ethnic and gender discrimination are the legacy of the social structural and cultural circumstances of the past. It is no coincidence that employed women and black men today earn significantly less than their white male peers. These earning differences are due, in part, to past discrimination against women and blacks which continues, over the generations, to limit their opportunities. Linkages of this sort between social problems of the past and present are commonplace.

Some contemporary social problems are different from past problems. Often, past measures to remedy social problems simply gave rise to new and substantively different problems. For example, the same industrialized economy in the United States that created millions of new jobs and an improved standard of living for diverse segments of the population also created widespread environmental pollution—one of the most serious social problems facing the public today. Since the 1960s the state has attempted to create incentives for corporate America and most private citizens to become environmentally conscious. However, such consciousness-raising has largely come only after the state adopted regulations requiring the compliance of corporations and individuals. Not surprisingly, the huge expansion of court cases challenging such regulatory efforts in itself has contributed to the problems people have with the justice system in the United States. Because emerging social problems are rooted in past social arrangements, it is important to examine them in historical perspective, an approach taken by many of the essays in this text.

It is useful to study many social problems not only in historical but also in cross-cultural perspective, for several reasons. First, actions taken to address social problems in one society can have an impact on social arrangements and problems in another. When U.S.-based corporations export low-wage, low-skill, and hazardous jobs to developing societies, they are in effect addressing domestic problems (economic stagnation, pollution, unsafe work environments) by transferring them to another country. Cross-cultural analysis of social problems is also important because many of the problems we face today are global as they impact many, if not all, human societies. The issues addressed in Part IV of this text fall into this category. Comparative study of these social problems helps us to better understand the nature of these shared, global problems and informs the quest for remedies.

A TOOL KIT FOR THE ANALYSIS OF SOCIAL PROBLEMS

The sociological "tool kit" for analyzing social problems includes both research methods and theory. Sociologists employ these tools to scientifically study social problems, an approach that is very distinct from common-sense and media approaches to social problems. Research methods are techniques for systematically collecting and analyzing information. They include data-gathering techniques such as surveys, observation, and experiments, as well as statistical techniques which enable us to identify and interpret patterns in the data collected. Sociological theories are systematic explanations of social relationships and arrangements which can be tested using the research methods just described. Using these tools, the sociologist is able to "go beneath the surface" and explore social problems systematically and in-depth, moving well beyond often inaccurate and incomplete common-sense understanding.

The importance of sociological theory and methods for better understanding social problems can best be illustrated by contrasting the sociological assessment of social problems with that of other approaches. Consider the so-called problem of declining educational achievement addressed in Chapter 4. A widely held view today is that there is an achievement crisis in the public schools—that the schools are no longer providing essential, basic knowledge. The fact that U.S. students do not compare all that favorably to students from many other countries on standardized achievement tests is taken by the public as evidence of a serious problem in the schools. The media often fuels the concern by sensationalizing the topic with headlines like: "An 'F' in World Competition: A Major Test Shows U.S. Students Don't Measure Up" (*Newsweek,* February 17, 1992).

A sociological analysis of patterns of educational achievement must be sensitive to cultural, social structural, and historical arrangements in society. As a result, the sociological perspective causes us to draw different conclusions about student scores on standardized tests. Sociologists interpret the lower test scores of U.S. students as a result of the broad outreach of education in this country. Nations with significantly higher average student scores on standardized tests do not provide education to all; rather, they restrict access to education to more privileged segments of the population. Such students are culturally advantaged and more likely to do well in school.

In fact, in recent years the United States has broadened considerably the population base taking college placement exams such that it now reaches well beyond the more privileged groups in society. A sociological interpretation of declining educational achievement then might actually be taken as a positive sign that we have successfully expanded educational outreach to diverse segments of the population. This is not to suggest, however, that the educational institution is free of problems.

Micro- and Macro-Levels of Analysis. Sociologists can employ theory and method for better understanding social problems on two distinct levels: the micro-level and the macro-level. A micro-level approach to social problems involves taking a close-up view of social relationships and social structure—zooming in on the details. Such an approach is like placing the social problem and the human actors affected by it under a microscope for close scrutiny. In contrast, the macro-level approach is a "big picture" approach. It might be compared to using a wide-angle lens to view social problems such that the context for the problem is included in the frame.

Both micro-level and macro-level approaches are necessary for a thorough understanding of social problems. For this reason, the essays and exercises included in this workbook incorporate both approaches. The two vantage points provide different insights into social problems. For example, when viewed from a micro-level perspective, the problem of changing gender roles would require an in-depth examination of the division of labor in individual households and the balance of power in husband-wife relationships. From a macro-level perspective, the focus might be on gendered arrangements in the work place (e.g., sex patterning in occupations and the gender gap in pay) and how they interact with family structure to disadvantage women. Or, from a micro-level perspective, the problem of poverty would be analyzed by asking how individual traits and characteristics of the poor contribute to their poverty, as well as how individuals are affected by poverty. Macro sociologists would study poverty by focusing on social structural and cultural arrangements and how they contribute to poverty. In addition, a macro-level analysis of poverty would address the impact of poverty on the larger social system and the social institutions that comprise it.

Theoretical Perspectives and Social Problems. In addition to the micro/macro distinction, sociological theories can be categorized according to theoretical perspective. Theoretical perspectives are simply categories of theory that provide broad starting assumptions about society, social issues, and problems. One might think of theoretical perspectives as different "flavors" of theory. Just as different types of ice cream can be classified as chocolate, vanilla, or fruit-based, sociological theory can be categorized as functionalist, conflict, or interactionist. The functionalist and conflict sociology perspectives are more often macro-level perspectives, while the interactionist perspective is micro-level.

The *functionalist perspective* assumes that societies

are systems of interdependent parts; thus, they address social problems in terms of their effect on the system. Functionalists envision the social system as a relatively stable system and, in fact, social problems are often seen as sporadic disruptions of the otherwise stable social system. For this reason functionalist theories typically view social problems as bad or "dysfunctional" not only for the individuals affected by them but also for entire social systems. Interestingly, functionalists sometimes explain the persistence of enduring social problems by arguing that they actually play a role in maintaining the stability of the social system. Such problems may negatively impact individuals or parts of the social system such as the family, the economy, or the government, but they are viewed as contributing something positive to the larger system. For example, a functionalist analysis of poverty recognizes the negative impact of poverty for individuals, but it stresses several important functions for the larger social system which include motivating most people to work hard (so as to avoid poverty) and ensuring that there is always a supply of desperate persons willing to perform necessary, yet unpleasant and hazardous jobs.

The *conflict perspective* may also view society as a social system, yet it differs from the functionalist perspective in that the focus is on conflict or tension as the primary linkage between parts of the system. From the conflict perspective, the social problem of poverty results from competition for scarce and valued resources (e.g., money, power, prestige). Those in poverty are the less effective competitors. The conflict perspective does not view the poor as losers in the competition due to individual failings, but rather as a result of their disadvantaged position in the social system. In other words, conflict theorists take a macro-level point of view and argue that cultural and structural features of societies create privileges for some and disadvantages for others. Conflict theorists view the social problem of poverty as resulting from advantaged groups in society acting in their own interest and amassing a disproportionate share of scarce and valued resources. Thus, social problems like pollution—which are negative for the larger society—can be seen as resulting from the actions of advantaged groups pursuing their own economic interests (short-term interests, at any rate). Enduring social problems can be explained from this perspective by noting that the actions that give rise to them are beneficial for advantaged groups in the system. Pollution, for example, could easily become an enduring social problem because the costs to members of the advantaged group of eliminating it are seen as too high.

The third major theoretical perspective in sociology, *interactionism,* takes a distinctly different approach to social problems. Interactionists argue that social problems are subjective; that they are constructed through social interaction. Theories in this category address why some behaviors come to be labeled as problematic and others do not. For example, the labeling theory of social deviance explains why certain types of crime, while less costly and threatening to the public, are viewed as more problematic than other types of crime that may be rare or have less significant impact on individuals. The fact that the public is far more concerned about property crimes such as theft than the white-collar crime of embezzlement provides a further example. From the point of view of the interactionist perspective then, social problems are defined by the public's reaction to them.

Each of these three primary theoretical perspectives in sociology is useful for the study of social problems, their persistence, and the solutions to them, albeit in quite different ways. The selections in this workbook reflect the theoretical diversity of sociology; some selections even employ multiple perspectives to address the problem under study. As you proceed through the volume, attempt to identify the primary theoretical perspective utilized by the author of each selection. Challenge yourself even further by "playing devil's advocate" and approaching the problem from a different perspective.

USING *ANALYZING SOCIAL PROBLEMS:* APPLYING SOCIOLOGICAL KNOWLEDGE

This book contains a series of essays and exercises addressing contemporary social problems written by academicians and other professionals who are experts on the problems they address. The selections in this text are organized into four parts that pertain to the broad problem areas of Troubled Social Institutions, Inequalities, Social Deviance, and Global Social Problems. The social problems addressed in the essays and the exercises in these parts do not, of course, constitute an exhaustive list; they do, however, represent a sample of many commonly agreed-upon enduring problems and emerging ones.

The exercises following each essay require you to systematically apply the knowledge you acquire from reading the essay, as well as what you have learned from other class sources (e.g., lecture, films, books). Specifically, the exercises encourage you to begin thinking like a sociologist by applying concepts and theories to social problems. The subject matter of social problems is especially well suited to a "hands on" learning approach that requires critical and creative thinking because the issues being addressed are personally relevant to you. Issues like the education crisis, the rising cost of health care, underemployment, teen pregnancy, changing gender roles, environmental pollution, and nuclear war directly or indirectly affect us all.

The exercises vary in format. Some call for outside research using library, media, and other resources; others can be completed without reference to outside materials. Several of the exercises require you to collect data through a variety of methods included in the sociological tool kit (e.g., content analyses, interviewing, and existing public records). You will not be expected to employ these methods rigorously or in a sophisticated manner. A simplified version of the techniques regularly employed by trained sociologists is all that is required to complete the exercises. The amount of time required for completion varies from approximately one to three hours. Because the exercises are designed to keep the length of written answers to a minimum, much of the time you spend on this workbook will involve preparing your answers: reflecting critically on what you have read, gathering information, and organizing your ideas.

As you proceed through your course and this workbook, you will learn that sociology does not provide "self-contained" conclusions about pressing social problems. For this reason, there are many possible "correct answers" to most of the questions in the exercises. Similarly, insights from sociology offer many possible avenues for responding to social problems in the real world. These insights will be discussed in a brief concluding chapter addressing public policy formation and social activism.

PART I

TROUBLED SOCIAL INSTITUTIONS

The selections in this part focus on problems confronting five key social institutions: the family, the economy, education, medicine, and the criminal justice system. The first selection, by Janet Salzman Chafetz, examines family and work-related problems that occur as women attempt to juggle demanding family and employment responsibilities. Problems in the family are also addressed in two other selections. The Linda Rouse essay explores why the family, considered by most to be a safe haven and emotional refuge for its members, can actually become a very violent institution. The many social problems associated with teen pregnancy are reviewed in the selection by Monica A. Longmore.

Problems in educational institutions are examined in the Dorothea Weir selection. She describes the current concern over declining educational achievement and as-sesses both the severity of the "education crisis" and its causes. The Robert A. Hanneman selection explores the need for reform in the medical institution, especially in terms of access to affordable medical care. Problems in the medical institution resulting from the strains of a rapidly growing elderly segment of the population are the focus of the Jan W. Weaver and Stanley R. Ingman selection. The essay by Ramona Ford illustrates how the process of social change can give rise to new social problems and highlights how the restructuring of the global economy creates problems for the American work force. The Carol Y. Thompson selection examines the criminal justice system and suggests that the functioning of this institution is biased in favor of economically advantaged, nonminority individuals.

1

I Need a (Traditional) Wife! Employment-Family Conflicts

Janet Saltzman Chafetz

Labor-force roles require substantial time and energy commitments five days a week. Homes and families, especially when they include young children, also require substantial time and energy seven days a week. When a person combines a commitment to a spouse and children with a full-time occupation, the potential for conflict and strain is very real. This is especially true in a nation such as the United States, which defines family problems as private matters to be worked out by the individuals involved, and therefore offers few public resources to mitigate employment-family conflicts.

First I will look at strains and conflicts created within the family when both parents are employed, or when there is only one parent present and he or she is employed. Secondly, I will examine how being married, and especially being a parent, can cause problems on the job. In both cases, because of traditional gender expectations associated specifically with the wife/mother roles, the strains and problems women confront by combining family and employment are far greater than those experienced by men. Finally, I will discuss some public, employer, and private mechanisms that can help reduce some of the conflicts and strains discussed.

FAMILY STRAINS

Only a generation ago, married women and mothers in all but the poorest families rarely participated in the labor force, and when they did, it was usually on a temporary basis. Their full-time job was to take care of the home and its occupants, meeting their physical, social, and psychological needs. Beginning in the 1950s, and rapidly escalating by the 1970s, first wives and mothers with older children, and subsequently even married mothers of preschool-aged youngsters, flooded the labor market. In addition, divorce rates were rising and the number of single, employed mothers increased also. By 1990, 58 percent of all married women in the United States were employed, and approximately 60 percent of all mothers with preschool-aged children were as well. In fact, the U.S. Departments of Labor and Commerce report that 52 percent of mothers with children under age two were employed (Lindsey, 1994). A rapid increase in the number of married women and mothers of young children, regardless of marital status, participating in the labor force is a trend characterizing all highly industrialized nations during the last 20 to 30 years.

When homemaking is a full-time job, women usually work far more than the traditional 40 hour, five day workweek. Some estimates are as high as 70 to 80 hours spread over seven days. Moreover, when married women and single mothers enter the labor force, they do not relinquish responsibility for their gender-traditional domestic and child-rearing work. Repeated research in the United States and many other industrial nations clearly demonstrates that, on average, the husbands of full-time employed wives do very little more domestic work than the husbands of full-time homemakers. Moreover, employed wives average two to three times the number of hours of domestic/child-rearing work as their husbands (South and Spitze, 1994; Reskin and Padavic, 1994). When women divorce, their domestic workload actually decreases somewhat, suggesting that husbands create more work than they perform. Arlie Hochschild (1989) coined the term "second shift" to describe the extra workload of employed married women who return home from the office, shop, factory, hospital, or school each evening and weekend to several hours of mostly unshared cooking, cleaning, laundry, and child-care work.

However, research also consistently demonstrates that employed wives and mothers do substantially less domestic work than full-time homemakers. Some purchase domestic and child-care services by hiring others to do the work (e.g., maids and nannies), by eating out more often and buying take-out meals, by sending clothes out to be laundered, and by placing preschool children in day care (Bergmann, 1986). However, most families are not able to purchase many of these services, beyond the necessary one of providing care for young children, which takes a substantial bite out of all but the highest paychecks. Domestic chores, such as looking after younger siblings, cooking, or laundry, are often delegated to older children. Sometimes the mothers of employed women are available and willing to help out also. The primary way that employed women reduce the heavy drain on their time and energy that the second shift entails is to reduce their standards of domestic work (Reskin and Padavic, 1994). Meals are less elaborate, and laundry, ironing, cleaning, and dusting are simply done less often. When women are full-time homemakers, they may enhance their self-esteem by setting exceptionally high standards of domestic work (e.g., ironing bed linens, laundering daily, sewing clothes for the family) which can be easily reduced upon employment.

It is likely that in many families, tired employed mothers end up devoting less time and attention to their children than do full-time homemakers. While married fathers appear to be increasing their involvement in child care more than in other forms of domestic work, children in dual-earner and employed single-parent families probably average less parental attention than those whose mothers are not participating in the labor force. However, there is no evidence that this is harmful to the children (unless the attention deprivation is extreme). In fact, such children have been found to be more independent than the children of full-time homemakers, a trait normally highly valued in U.S. society. Moreover, the daughters of employed women have, on average, higher career aspirations than other girls, and their sons as well as their daughters tend to hold more gender equalitarian norms (Wilkie, 1988).

Regardless of the strains produced by the second shift, research has indicated that employed married women generally enjoy better mental health than full-time homemakers. A busy life that includes diverse roles, the opportunity to interact with other adults on a daily basis, a paycheck of one's own, and other intrinsic rewards from work roles apparently more than compensates psychologically for whatever strains may result from a very long workday and week. The problem remains, however, that relative to their husbands, employed married women confront a serious deficit of leisure.

As long as men escape full participation in the second shift, their wives (and all too often today former wives) will continue to confront strain from a too-heavy workload. The reason why men do not become more involved in domestic work is currently subject to debate among sociologists. Some contend that both women and men choose a gender-traditional division of household labor as a means of expressing and reaffirming their own and their partner's gendered self-concepts (Berk, 1985). Others argue that husbands continue to exercise more power within the family than their wives and can thus en-

force their preference to do very little second shift work (Chafetz, 1990). Regardless of the reason(s), the facts are clear and undisputed, and it is likely that the inequity of the situation is contributing to the high divorce rates characteristic of the United States and other industrial nations (Sanchez, 1994). Nonetheless, because mothers overwhelmingly gain custody of their children upon divorce, the second shift problem in not solved for women by divorce.

EMPLOYMENT CONFLICTS

Over a century ago, the industrial revolution created a sharp separation between the places where people perform work for pay, and those where they perform work that maintains and reproduces the family. As paid work moved out of households, men followed. Married women remained in a separate sphere at home, and engaged in unpaid domestic and child-rearing work. Given that most women married and divorce rates were low, most paid employment came to be defined as men's work. Jobs of all kinds were structured on the assumption that workers could and would concentrate their full attention on their work, able to do so because they had someone else to worry about maintaining their homes, their wardrobes, feeding them, and taking care of their children. That is, employers assumed that workers had wives. The husband/father roles became defined as virtually synonymous with "breadwinner" (and little else). By and large, this set of assumptions has not changed. Paid work for all but a few is conducted away from the home, precluding the simultaneous care of children, who are not welcomed at work sites for anything beyond a quick visit. Specific workdays and hours are relatively inflexible for most workers, and often overlap almost completely the times when pediatricians see sick children, teachers confer with parents, or any number of other domestic errands must be run. In the last 20 to 30 years, supermarkets and most retail stores began to stay open nights and/or weekends to accommodate employed people, but most service-providing organizations still do not.

Not only do employed women not have wives to take care of their needs and those of their children, many are wives (or at least mothers) with familial and domestic responsibilities. Some men, whose wives are employed, may not be able to count on them to provide domestic/child-care services, or they may wish to participate more fully than men traditionally have in the care of their children. A small number are also single, custodial parents. Such men will confront the same types of problems and conflicts as employed wives and mothers. Moreover, given traditional gender expectations, women may be somewhat "forgiven" by employers for allowing family-related needs to interfere with their job, because employers are likely to stereotypically assume that family is more important than job for women. However, it is a rare employer who will be equally understanding of a man who wishes to exercise the same option, rather assuming that men have wives who should be responsible for such matters.

Employer demands on workers vary by occupation. Therefore, the extent and kinds of problems people confront in the work place, contingent upon their familial statuses, vary somewhat by occupation. Looking first at professional, managerial, and other high-level white-collar occupations, employers of such personnel are often quite "greedy" in the time and energy they demand. They may expect "committed" employees to regularly work more than 40 hours per week at the office, to take work home, to entertain nights and weekends for business purposes, to travel extensively, to accept geographic transfers, and so on. Clearly, these kinds of expectations directly conflict with family responsibilities. If both spouses work in occupations with such demands, family-related strains are virtually unavoidable, short of one or both refusing to comply with expectations beyond a routine workweek. For single, custodial parents such expectations may be all but impossible to fulfill, given child-care considerations. If, as is the case more often for women than men, family commitment is regarded as at least equally valued as career commitment, employees may be loath to conform to the requests or demands of greedy employers. Partners in a dual-career family confront especially serious conflicts when one is offered a better job or a promotion entailing a geographic transfer, when the other may not be able to find a job in the new location that is equal to or better than the one she or he already has. A small number of couples, both of whom have demanding careers, live in cities separated by hundreds, even thousands of miles and see each other only on (some) weekends and vacations. This practice, referred to as a "commuter marriage," clearly extracts a toll on family life, especially if there are children still in the home, as evidenced by high divorce rates for such couples. Refusal to become involved in extra work, to accept a geographic transfer, or to convert their personal life into an extension of their jobs may lead employers to define such employees as insufficiently committed to their work, with the result that the employees fail to gain promotions and raises they would otherwise merit.

A few years ago the term "mommy track" was bandied about in the popular media. This term referred to a suggestion that employers should explicitly develop a slow track designed specifically for professional and managerial women who wanted to devote time and attention to their families yet still maintain their careers. Expectations on the job would be reduced, but the women were to expect fewer and slower raises and promotions, if any. The suggestion was met with cries of "sexism" by feminists and most managerial and professional women. These women felt that such a plan simply reinforces the idea that family responsibility is women's work, not work to be shared equally by both fathers and mothers. While the term was quickly abandoned, a slow track for actively parenting employees still exists in numerous places of employment. In fact, research shows that fathers who take

parental leave earn less income, even when prebirth income is controlled (Haas, 1990).

Although they may pay the price of being defined as uncommitted, many salaried white-collar workers have sufficient autonomy and flexibility in their jobs to allow them to take some time off during the day for family matters. Hourly wage workers, especially those who punch a time clock, may find it much more difficult to get medical attention for a sick child or run an important personal or family errand during normal work hours. If they do get time off for these purposes, their pay is typically docked for that time, which is a serious problem given their generally low wages. Employers of such workers usually do not expect more than a 40-hour workweek, although during times of especially heavy demand for their product or service, employers may pressure workers to work overtime hours, for which they are paid higher hourly wages. Salaried employees, by contrast, are usually not docked pay for taking a few hours off from their job, nor are they paid extra when they work more than a 40-hour week.

Some occupations are characterized by being heavily female in composition (e.g., primary and secondary schoolteaching, nursing and many allied health professions, secretarial and clerical work). Employers of these kinds of personnel often expect workers to need time off for family matters (Coser and Rokoff, 1982). Such occupations usually pay less than those occupations that require comparable levels of education and skill but are not female dominated. In choosing such work, women may sacrifice some income in return for more freedom to fulfill domestic obligations. For instance, for generations public schools have had a unique system of substitutes who were on call to come in to work on very short notice. This system reflects an assumption that, given an overwhelmingly female labor force, absentee rates for family emergencies will be high (Coser and Rokoff, 1982). The growth in recent years of businesses that provide temporary secretarial and clerical workers to employers may reflect this same set of expectations, as many more such workers are married and mothers now than in the past, when these jobs were filled mostly by young, single women before marriage. For schoolteachers, there is the added incentive that their hours and months of employment match those of their school-aged children, thereby solving child-care problems and reducing employment-family conflicts.

Regardless of type of employment, substantial domestic and familial obligations when added to a 40-hour workweek, make it extremely difficult for people to pursue additional training or education during their nonemployment hours. In foregoing additional training or education, workers also forego the promotions and raises that might accompany it.

Finally, in any type of job, domestic or familial crises may negatively impact the quality of work performed by employed persons. Workers can scarcely be expected to forget family problems upon entering the door of their work place. If a crisis is prolonged (e.g., a seriously ill child) or recurs frequently (e.g., a child who regularly gets into trouble at school requiring a parent-teacher conference each time), serious problems can result with employers who may not be overly sympathetic to frequent requests for time off or excuses for inadequate performance. Raises, promotions, even job security may be jeopardized.

REDUCING EMPLOYMENT-FAMILY CONFLICT

Conflicts between employment and family work obligations can be reduced without necessarily returning to the traditional system in which most workers have wives who do not work outside the home. Millions of dual-earner couples attempt to work out their own techniques for doing so every day, with varying levels of success and equity between the spouses. More importantly, some employers have developed practices that reduce such conflicts, and some agencies of government have established policies that do so as well.

At the level of individual families, I have already mentioned several strategies for reducing work overload and the resultant strain: (1) reducing the standards of domestic work; (2) purchasing domestic and child-care services; (3) having other family members (e.g., husbands, children, parents) perform more domestic work; (4) refusing to comply with the demands or requests of greedy employers (with a cost to one's career success, probably most often the woman's); and (5) choosing an occupation (e.g., schoolteaching) that allows more time for the family (with a cost to one's income, usually the woman's). Couples can add time to their day by shortening the time required to commute between home and employment. They may move closer to one (or both) partner's job site, or one (or occasionally both) can seek employment specifically based on proximity to home. In the latter case, it may entail foregoing a better job to take one more conveniently located, and again, this is a more likely choice for women than men. Employment-family conflicts can also be reduced by assuming a part-time job. The overwhelming majority of part-time workers are married women, both in the United States and in other industrial nations. They not only earn less but usually receive no fringe benefits.

As should be clear, most strategies developed by dual-earner couples to reduce employment-family conflicts inequitably reduce the wife's income and/or career mobility prospects. Employed wives and mothers therefore tend to be doubly disadvantaged: by assuming the bulk of the second shift, and by making most of whatever employment-related sacrifices the couple deems necessary. Both of these inequities could be abolished if we, as a nation, began to take women's employment commitments as seriously as men's, and to take men's domestic and familial responsibilities as seriously as women's. Either one without the other will not suffice.

Many employers have instituted policies in recent years that help reduce family-employment conflicts.

Many of these policies have not been developed explicitly for this purpose, however. Flex-time allows workers to choose to begin and end the workday earlier (or later) than "normal" (e.g., 7:00 A.M. to 4:00 P.M. rather than 8 to 5). By working slightly different hours, one parent can be available at each end of the children's school day. This type of policy was initially designed to reduce rush-hour traffic congestion in urban areas. Many employers need several shifts of workers because of their extended hours of operation (e.g. factories, hospitals, some types of retail stores such as 24-hour drugstores and supermarkets). By working different shifts (one the day shift, another a swing or night shift) spouses can arrange to have someone home at all times to look after young children and be available for both domestic work and family emergencies. Such couples may have very little time together, however, probably to the detriment of marital satisfaction and stability. A few employers (e.g., J. C. Penney and some governmental agencies) have recently begun to cut office expenses by having part of their work force "telecommute." Connected to their employer by computer, fax, and telephone, they conduct their paid work in their own homes and are therefore available for family emergencies and the care of somewhat older children who do not require constant supervision. Some other large employers have also developed day-care facilities attached to or in the vicinity of the work site (e.g., many universities), which allow parents to see their children at lunch, to spend their commuting time with their children, and to be close by if their children become sick or injured. Finally, employers increasingly grant workers "personal" or "family leave" time for family crises and emergencies, not just sick leave for themselves. However, such leave is often unpaid.

Government efforts to cope with employment-family conflicts have been sparse in this nation. Until 1993, when the U.S. government mandated that all but very small employers must grant parental leave upon the birth or adoption of a child, we were one of the only industrial nations to lack a guaranteed maternity leave policy. Before that, some employers granted it, some did not. Even now, although employers must reserve a person's job (or equivalent one) who is on parental leave, they do not have to pay the employee while on leave. In many European nations, either the employer or the government pays for one new parent to take a leave of absence. Whether paid or not, when offered parental leave most new parents who take advantage of the offer are women. Whether they personally prefer not to, or because of cultural constraints that define it as inappropriate, few men do so, even in Sweden, which, among all Western nations, has had the longest history of such leaves and the strongest governmental encouragement of men to use them. Some local school districts have begun to offer preschool for 3- to 5-year-old children and extended day or after-school programs to elementary school-aged children, which help to alleviate child-care problems for employed parents.

What else could be done to reduce employment-family conflicts and strains? In some European nations (e.g., Sweden and Germany), workers are beginning to demand a six-hour workday, which would provide more time for the family and/or less reason for women to accept part-time jobs. Greedy employers could rethink their criteria for assessing the commitment level of their employees. Work hours in many types of jobs could be made more flexible, and much more desk work could be conducted at home, reducing workers' hours at a central work site. Family-related service providers, such as pediatricians and dentists, could shift their work hours to begin and end several hours later (e.g., noon to 8:00 P.M.) a couple of days each week, thereby accommodating parents who work "normal" hours without too much sacrifice of their own familial responsibilities. Teachers could be required—and paid—to be available for parental conferences for a couple of hours per week either on Saturday or one evening. Pediatric medical and dental clinics could be housed in public schools, minimizing the burden on parents to get such attention for their children. With little medical cost, special rooms could be set aside in schools for moderately ill children (e.g., those with the flu or German measles) who, instead of staying home, could be cared for by school-based nurses. Parents could pay fees for school-based medical services, preschools, and extended-day programs according to their means, thus not overburdening taxpayers, while insuring decent care to all children. Beyond aiding employed parents, other long-term social benefits could result from such programs, such as enhanced productivity for employers, employment stability for parents, better health care for poor children, a reduction in the number of latch-key children, and perhaps even less juvenile crime. Taken together, the various employer and governmental policies and practices discussed here, if widely adopted, would not magically eliminate all employment-family conflicts, but they would reduce the total amount considerably. Unfortunately, it is unlikely that many of the policies and programs discussed above will be adopted on a wide scale in the United States in the foreseeable future, either by employers or by governmental units. Global economic competition is encouraging employers to increase productivity with fewer employees, thereby pressuring workers to work longer hours than was true several years ago. In short, to compete, employers believe they must become increasingly greedy. Nor are they likely to institute employee benefits that increase their short-term costs, even if they result in long-term benefits to worker morale and productivity. At all levels—local, state and national—governmental units in the United States have been cutting budgets and personnel, in response to citizen demands to reduce taxes and the national deficit. In recent years, there has been an increasing mood of political conservatism which de-emphasizes governmental solutions to most social problems (except crime control) and re-emphasizes private ones. As a nation, we have become increasingly suspicious of the capacity of governmental agencies to develop programs that enhance our collective well-being. In short, the prevailing national mood is in the direction of emphasizing family solutions to the kinds of employment-family conflicts discussed here, and it should be clear by now that such solutions are often inadequate and usually inequitable to women.

CONCLUSION

Domestic and familial obligations *are* work, and hard work at that. The tasks required of those who run a household and raise children are time, attention, and energy-consuming. Full-time jobs also consume substantial time, attention, and energy—some more so than others. Conflicts arise in the family largely because domestic work is not shared equitably by women and men. On the job, conflicts arise because family needs often do not neatly confine themselves to nonwork hours, because some employers are greedy of their employees' time and energy, and because family-generated stresses and problems cannot easily be forgotten while on the job.

In recent years some employers have begun to develop policies that, whether designed for these purposes or not, ease employment-family conflicts somewhat. In this nation, unlike many others, the government has contributed little to helping to solve such conflicts and strains. For the vast majority of single employed parents and dual-earner couples, strains and problems inevitably arise from the fundamental fact that employment in industrial societies is largely and inflexibly based on a "standard" workday and located outside the home. For most couples and single parents, the solution cannot be found by women opting out of the labor force, both because their income is essential to meet family needs and because many do not want to quit work. Moreover, our economy today is highly dependent upon the labor of millions of women who are also wives and/or mothers. In the absence of governmental policies and widespread employer practices designed to ease employment-family conflicts, spouses and parents are left largely on their own to devise solutions. Some, especially among those with a high income and/or reasonably flexible employment conditions, are able to so with relative ease. Many, however, end up paying a high personal price on the job, within the family, or both. Moreover, women are apt to pay a much higher price in both contexts than men. Employed single parents and dual-earner couples can be forgiven if they conclude: I need a (traditional) wife!

REFERENCES

Bergmann, Barbara
1986   *The Economic Emergence of Women.* New York: Basic Books.

Berk, Sarah Fenstermaker
1985   *The Gender Factory.* New York: Plenum.

Chafetz, Janet Saltzman
1990   *Gender Equity: An Integrated Theory of Stability and Change.* Newbury Park, CA: Sage.

COSER, ROSE LAUB and GERALD ROKOFF
1982   "Women in the Occupational World: Social Disruption and Conflict," in R. Kahn-Hut, A. Kaplan Daniels and R. Colvard, eds., *Women and Work*. New York: Oxford University Press.

HAAS, LINDA
1990   "Gender Equality and Social Policy," *Journal of Family Issues,* 11(4): 401–423.

HOCHSCHILD, ARLIE
1989   *The Second Shift.* New York: Viking Press.

LINDSEY, LINDA
1994   *Gender Roles: A Sociological Perspective.* Upper Saddle River, NJ: Prentice Hall.

RESKIN, BARBARA and IRENE PADAVIC
1994   *Women and Men at Work.* Thousand Oaks, CA: Pine Forge Press.

SANCHEZ, LAURA
1994   "A Panel Study of the Association Between the Gender Division of Housework and Marital Dissolution," Paper presented at the Annual Meeting of the American Sociological Association, Los Angeles.

SOUTH, SCOTT and GLENNA SPITZE
1994   "Housework in Marital and Nonmarital Households," *American Sociological Review* 59: 327–347.

WILKIE, JANE RIBLETT
1988   "Marriage, Family Life and Women's Employment," in A. H. Stromberg and S. Harkess, eds., *Women Working: Theories and Facts in Perspective*. Mountain View, CA: Mayfield, pp. 149–166.

EXERCISE 1

Name _____   Date _____

ID # _____   Class Time _____

I. Interview two married women who have at least one child at home under the age of 16 and a full-time job. One woman should have a managerial or professional career, the other a nonprofessional job (e.g., sales clerk or cashier, clerical, secretarial or data entry job, factory worker, waitress). OR separately interview both the husband and wife in one two-income family with at least one child at home under the age of 16. Structure your interviews so that you can complete the tables below, and answer the questions that follow based on what each respondent tells you. Plan to spend about a half hour to 45 minutes on each interview.

   A. Complete the following table.

	Respondent 1	Respondent 2
Occupation		
Spouse's occupation		
Duration at present job		
Age		
Children's ages		
Years married		
Level of education		
Spouse's education		

   B. How is the second shift work accomplished in their household(s)? Which family members do what kinds of tasks? What domestic/child-care services, if any, have they purchased and how often? How are decisions made as to who does what? Complete the following tables.

Respondent 1 (or married couple)

Individual Task	Who performs the task	Authority to decide	Hours spent weekly Wife	Hours spent weekly Husband	What proportion of the task do you purchase?
Child care					
Cleaning					
Cooking					
Errands					
Grocery shopping					
Laundry					
Yard work					
Other (specify)					

Respondent 2

Individual Task	Who performs the task	Authority to decide	Hours spent weekly		What proportion of the task do you purchase?
			Wife	Husband	
Child care					
Cleaning					
Cooking					
Errands					
Grocery shopping					
Laundry					
Yard work					
Other (specify)					

C. How do the people you interviewed feel about:

    1. the way domestic and child-rearing work is done in their family?

    2. the amount of such work they do compared to their spouse?

    3. the impact (negative or positive) of the wife/mother's employment on their family?

D. Did any of the people you interviewed:

    1. think their family responsibilities have affected them on the job? Explain.

    2. think they suffered on the job (e.g., not received the raises or promotions they might have otherwise) because of family-related reasons? Explain.

    3. think their employer was helpful when they needed time off for family reasons? Explain.

    4. change jobs or occupations, or refuse a geographical transfer or promotion because of family-related reasons? Explain.

Name _____   Date _____

ID # _____   Class Time _____

E. **1.** Summarize the differences and similarities in the extent and type of employment-family conflicts you see when comparing your respondents.

2. Why do you think any differences you note exist?

F. You are asked to write a memo to a joint government-employer task force charged with devising policies for minimizing the problem of family and work conflicts. What specific recommendations would you make based on what you learned from your interviews? List at least *three* specific recommendations in the space provided below.

1.

2.

3.

2

Domestic Violence: Hitting Us Where We Live

Linda P. Rouse

The family is widely considered a fundamental building block of society and an enduring source of personal fulfillment. It has been characterized as an island of affect in a sea of impersonal relations, a "haven in a heartless world" (Lasch, 1979). The home and family are idealized as a peaceful refuge from the world outside. The domestic arena of household affairs and duties is seen as a stabilizing force, safekeeping social values and contributing to individual and collective well-being.

The family is the social institution in American society that is expected to satisfy basic physiological, psychological, and social needs of children and adults. The many functions of the family include: (1) ensuring physical survival during the long dependency period of the human child, offering physical safety and economic support; (2) providing children with favorable conditions for personality development, meeting their psychological needs for love, approval and emotional security; and (3) socializing the young, fitting the child into society by modeling and teaching adaptive social behaviors. For adults, the family provides companionship, a sense of belonging, emotional support, financial assistance, and sexual gratification between consenting adults in a socially recognized relationship.

Yet the family has also been described as a cradle of violence (Steinmetz and Straus, 1973) and the marriage license as a hitting license (Straus, 1976) in recognition of the extent of domestic violence that is now regularly featured in the mass media and has been convincingly documented by social science researchers. Introductory sociology and social problems textbooks routinely present statistics on the incidence of various types of domestic violence—child abuse, spousal assault, homicide, elder abuse, sibling violence, marital rape, incest, and dating violence.

The precise incidence of domestic violence is debated because the figures reported depend on the definitions of abuse employed and the methods used to gather information on occurrence of particular events (Koss, 1993; McCurdy and Daro, 1994; Sadler, 1995). For example, if we count only the most severe cases of physical abuse of children that come to the attention of police and social service agencies, we miss more frequently occurring, less severe incidents. If child abuse encompasses neglect, as legislative definitions do in many states, the net is cast wider. How accurately can we detect all possible instances of children's failure to thrive due to deliberate acts of omission or commission by family members? Accepting the argument that infant mortality and malnutrition among poor children in a society with the national wealth of the United States is, in itself, child abuse adds millions to our estimated incidence. Sexual abuse of children in the home is hidden due to fear, guilt, and shame. Emotional abuse, which is difficult to define but assumed to be widespread, is typically not prosecuted, thus is rarely reported. Rape is known to be highly under-reported, particularly acquaintance or date rape, with most cases not coming to the attention of the police, and marital rape still has no legal standing in many states so, officially, there is no crime to report.

Generally speaking, abuse includes all "wrongful" treatment—behaviors that threaten the physical or emotional well-being of family members—while violence refers specifically to use of physical force. Even the most conservative existing estimates demonstrate clearly that domestic violence is not a rare occurrence in isolated instances of dysfunctional families and cannot be explained satisfactorily by reference to individual pathology. The family is a social setting in which, much more often than we like to acknowledge, adults and children are physically assaulted, sexually molested, and emotionally abused by other family members.

WHY VIOLENCE AT HOME OF ALL PLACES?

One approach in trying to explain the pervasiveness of domestic violence is to examine structural and interactional features of the family itself (Gelles and Straus, 1979). The distinctive characteristics of the family as a social institution set the stage for abusive relationships, making violence possible and even likely. Consider the following:

1. *Privacy.* Families in contemporary U.S. society operate outside public view. Since family life occurs in private, family violence is hidden "behind closed doors." Moreover, norms of noninterference protect the privacy of the family; outsiders are reluctant to interfere in what is regarded as essentially a private matter.

2. *Involuntary Membership.* Children do not choose their given family; marriage vows emphasize lasting commitment, and there are practical obstacles to divorce. Despite adverse conditions it may be particularly difficult or impossible for women and children to quit the family.

3. *Power Differentials.* These are built into family structure. Children are subject to parental authority, and final say in marital matters is traditionally vested in the male head of household. Individuals bring to family life ideas about their perceived rights to control other members' behaviors. The family reproduces in miniature both the "battle of the sexes" and the "generation gap."

4. *High Expectations.* Family sociologists note that unrealistic expectations and impossible ideals set for marriage and child rearing contribute to our high divorce rate and create disappointment and anger over failure of spouses and children to live up to our expectations.

5. *Role Diffuseness.* The range of interests and activities engaged in with family members means a wider arena for conflict. What we expect of family members is broader, more varied, and less well defined than, for example, in work relationships.

6. *Intensity of Involvement.* Our greater emotional investment in family relationships makes the stakes higher, the impact of failure keener, and motivation to fix (or punish) other family members more determined. Vulnerability heightens the sense of threat to self and degree of felt injury over offenses.

7. *Impinging Activities.* In the family, one person's choices potentially constrain the others' activities and opportunities. Individual freedom of action is limited. Inevitable conflicts of interest create continual need for compromise and adjustment.

8. *Time Spent Together.* Spending time together may exacerbate the above problems. Small irritations are enlarged by repeated exposure. Domestic violence typically occurs when family members are together for extended periods during evenings and weekends.

9. *Change.* Passage through the family life cycle generates change-related stress. Children move through various developmental stages; marriages are altered over time with outside circumstances and personal growth. Even welcome events such as a desired

pregnancy create unanticipated difficulties and require many adjustments.

10. *Discontinuity.* Work roles and family roles are not always complimentary. We are expected to leave the outside world behind each day when we return to the home, but this transition can be difficult. The demands and strains of the work place often spill over into the domestic sphere. Women today, as well as men, are struggling to balance the demands of work and family.

The family as a social institution does not operate in isolation from the larger society of which it is a part. Changes in community and society have an impact on family roles and relationships. For example, changes in the work place that lead to depressed wages, economic uncertainty, unemployment, or underemployment affect family finances and family interaction (Voydanoff, 1991). Families are not immune to the stresses of the outside world. Social disorganization and the variety of social problems that beset society reverberate in the home.

Moreover, most individuals in our society receive no formal training for coping with such stresses. Marital communication and parenting skills are assumed to occur naturally. Anyone who can have a child is basically accepted as qualified to parent until proven unfit. Such cultural beliefs overlook the personal and social resources needed to perform important and demanding family roles, resources which many individuals lack.

In addition, our society has a historical legacy of normative approval of violence within the family, illustrated by parents' legitimated use of force to discipline children and the notion that husbands expect obedience and may chastise their wives, using force if necessary. The "rule of thumb" in English common law specified that beatings should be confined to a stick no bigger in width than his thumb. Research shows that we are less likely to interfere or report an observed assault if we believe the persons involved are a couple. In such instances the behavior becomes "just a domestic quarrel," that is, a family affair and none of our business. Even today spanking is quite commonplace and husband-wife violence is frequent enough to suggest continuing socialization into acceptance of physical force in the family. Further evidence that society has been slow to address family violence is provided by historical cases such as the frequently recounted story of Mary Ellen, an abused child in New York City. Social workers trying to help Mary Ellen had to invoke the authority of the A.S.P.C.A., arguing that a child is also an animal, because no existing legislation protected children from cruelty in the home (Utech, 1994).

THEORETICAL PERSPECTIVES APPLIED TO DOMESTIC VIOLENCE

General theoretical perspectives on human society and social behavior add to our understanding of why violence occurs in the family. Gelles and Straus (1979) suggest that a variety of theories may apply to family violence. Social-psychological theories focus on individual experience in social context; at this micro-level of analysis, we obtain a close-up view of family violence, as with a photographic zoom lens. Structural and sociocultural theories focus on the history, structure, and culture of societies at large. The wide angle lens of the macro-level of analysis gives us a panoramic view of the bigger picture in which family violence is situated.

Social psychological theories include concepts such as frustration-aggression, social learning, symbolic interactionism, and social exchange. The frustration-aggression explanation hypothesizes that when an individual's goals are blocked, states of frustration and anger are experienced that lead to aggressive behavior. Aggression has been termed *instrumental* when it is used to deliberately attempt to control outcomes and *expressive* when it serves primarily to vent feelings. Many frustrating events occur within the family, and outside frustrations may be carried over into and expressed within the family. After a bad day at the office, family members become handy scapegoats for our anger. The frustration-aggression hypothesis, however, does not explain why some frustrated individuals react with aggressive behavior while others do not.

According to social learning theory, we learn about specific aggressive behaviors, the events that "provoke" them, and the circumstances in which their expression is tolerated or approved through explicit teaching, through observation and imitation, and by the consequences of engaging in such acts. When we are spanked, for example, we see that some uses of physical force are accepted in the family. We may learn that yelling or hitting are expected reactions when we are under stress and fail to observe models of alternate coping strategies. Witnessing others engage in aggressive behavior without negative consequences increases the likelihood we will ourselves behave aggressively (Bandura, 1973). To the extent that our own violent acts are rewarded, we are more likely to repeat them.

The conceptual framework of symbolic interactionism urges a closer examination of the meanings that violent acts have for participants in the domestic setting. "Definitions of the situation," brought into family relationships from past experience and continually renegotiated in ongoing family interaction, shape our actions. Consider statements made by family members such as, "Why do you make me hit you?" (parent to child after spanking); "I love you so much it hurts" (man choking his wife); "I'm sorry I have to do this but it's for your own good" (adult withholding food until elderly parent signs over power of attorney). These ways of interpreting domestic events are offered to "account for" violent acts. To understand domestic violence, we look at how social meanings are created, maintained, and modified in the family, and at their consequences.

Social exchange theory presupposes that family relationships involve exchanges of rewards and costs. Individuals are motivated to maximize or obtain rewards and to avoid or minimize costs. Reciprocally rewarding exchanges are expected, and participants feel angry when their outcomes are not satisfactory. Entering, leaving, or staying in a particular relationship depends not only on its "profitability" but on perceived alternatives. One reason women and children are targets of violence in the home is that misconduct toward them is not sufficiently costly to the perpetrator and is actually rewarded by compliance. Battered wives may stay in abusive marriages as long as there are still rewards despite the costs and especially if they see no viable options.

Sociocultural and structural theories address the implications of social stratification, patriarchy, and a violent culture. If use of physical force in the family is learned, what are the particular values, norms, and beliefs favorable to violence that exist in society as a whole? Evidence cited to illustrate infatuation with violence in the United States includes the prevalence of handguns (which contribute to lethal outcomes of domestic violence) and the steady stream of television and movie portrayals of violence which are promoted and accepted as entertainment.

Social stratification also contributes to family violence. We might expect to find domestic assault more common among (though not limited to) families of lower socioeconomic status, who are exposed to greater material deprivation, frustration, stress, and powerlessness. If use of physical force in interpersonal relationships is the resource of last resort, it should be resorted to more often among those in society lacking other resources—income, education, and occupational prestige—that enhance social status.

From the perspective of the larger social system, we may ask what purpose is served by violence in the family. Who is in a position to employ force and whose interests are thereby advanced? Theories of patriarchy (male dominance) note that men are granted and women are denied social resources as a class. Unequal power and dependence is not simply a result of individual differences but is generated and maintained by socially structured opportunities and constraints. This structure, moreover, is bolstered by an ideology of male dominance and entitlement that extends to the home. Gender role changes in U.S. society as a whole may be perceived as a threat to male privilege, prompting domestic violence by men as a means of reasserting control.

Theories expand our insight into factors contributing to domestic violence and suggest a variety of intervention strategies. Solutions lie partly in the direction of individual change (e.g., redefining the situation, learning nonviolent coping strategies); partly in the direction of larger-scale social change (e.g., in legislation, economic conditions, criminal justice, and social service responses). Micro and macro theories, focused on different levels of analysis, suggest different targets of intervention. Because complex multiple causes operate to shape human experience, a number of different approaches need to be combined in efforts to reduce or eliminate the various forms of domestic violence.

Before such actions will be taken, however, existing conditions must be recognized as a social problem. Social problems arise when individuals and/or groups take notice of objectionable circumstances and successfully bring them to public attention. The discovery of domestic violence in the United States, for example, began with child battering, later encompassed spousal assault and child sexual abuse, and, more recently, elder abuse. Domestic violence is a social problem today because certain behaviors have been identified and publicly defined as undesirable and unacceptable. Many previously tolerated domestic acts are now widely regarded as abusive. Values are the shared standards by which we judge existing conditions; the "shoulds" and "should nots" of society. To abuse family members is to treat them wrongly or improperly; to violate moral standards for how they should be treated. Further, collective action is taken because of a shared belief that something can and ought to be done about the condition. Private troubles are thus transformed into a social problem when society acknowledges and responds to particular social conditions.

THE CASE OF WIFE BEATING AS A SOCIAL PROBLEM

Violence in intimate relationships between men and women is not new, but recognition of the behavior as a social problem is recent. Prior to the 1970s, little notice was given to occurrence of violence and abuse in the context of marriage. Then the battered women's movement made the American public aware of the problem of "wife beating" (Schecter, 1982). Advocates favored conceptualizing the problem in terms of women's sexual, physical, and psychological victimization in American society. Domestic violence was viewed as a logical extension of political and social inequality in a sexist society. Feminist theories of patriarchy connect the physically assaultive behavior of battering men with male-female relationships in our society as a whole; men use violence to maintain control in the home. By 1980 research was growing on women as victims of violent abusive relationships, with some attention also given to the battering man.

Women are more likely than men to become victims of "battering"—intentional, repeated, severe physical abuse. Though researchers find use of physical force by women as well as by men in marital and dating relationships, its meaning and consequences differ. Typically, men do not regard female use of force such as slapping, pushing, or sexual pressuring as "menacing." While many husbands see their wife's aggressive behavior as relatively ineffective or nonthreatening, wives take their husband's use of violence seriously (Pagelow, 1984) and are, overall, more likely to be injured by men's use of physical force.

Despite the tendency of perpetrators to minimize the seriousness of domestic violence, spousal assault is a crime. An explanatory framework borrowed from crimi-

nology suggests that battering occurs when there is a convergence of:

MOTIVATED OFFENDER $+$ SUITABLE TARGET $+$ LACK OF EFFECTIVE GUARDIANSHIP

If a man is predisposed by socialization and personal inclination toward violence, and a wife is vulnerable because she is there in a devalued social position in a social system that does not protect her, he is able to enact physical violence in the home with impunity (no punishment), and she is forced to accommodate herself to his wishes (thus, he is actually rewarded).

As a result of the battered women's movement of the 1970s and the proliferation of research and publicity on wife beating, there is much greater awareness of this problem today. There is organized resistance to the idea that women are suitable targets and ongoing effort to create effective interventions, such as shelters for battered women and their children. Another approach is to change the criminal justice response to ensure arrest and conviction, thus increasing the costs to perpetrators of domestic violence.

Counseling programs have also been developed for the offender. Battering men come from a wide cross-section of occupations and display varying personal styles but are commonly described as men "fighting for control" (Gondolf, 1985). Assailants acknowledge attempting to control or dominate the female partner, perceiving her independence as threatening, and using any means needed to persuade or coerce her. Counseling for battering men typically rests on assumptions from social learning theory. If violence is a learned reaction to stress, alternatives can be learned (but the abuser is responsible for taking the steps necessary to change his behavior). Recognizing the larger social context of patriarchy, efforts are also made to redefine "masculinity" in terms of self-control not dominance.

Effective guardianship (i.e., social interventions that protect individuals from abuse by family members) is particularly important because any use of physical force, whether slapping, shoving, or throwing things, can have serious consequences and because the level of violence in the family tends to escalate over time. Unchecked, violence begets more violence. Patterns of interpersonal abuse that characterize assaultive marriages often begin to emerge earlier, in the dating stage of relationships.

DATING VIOLENCE

Studies of courtship violence beginning with Makepeace (1981) extended concern about wife battering to the dating and courtship period. The growing literature on physical abuse during courtship has included many studies of college students. Use of physical force among dating couples ranges from threats of violence through actual pushing, grabbing, slapping, punching, striking with an object, to, less frequent but more deadly, use of a weapon. Efforts to dominate a dating partner include closely monitoring activities, discouraging friends, continual belittling, and emotional manipulation as well as threats or use of overt force. Incidence estimates across different studies run from 19 percent of students sampled reporting "at least one direct personal experience as victim or aggressor" to as high as 36 percent engaged in "pushing, grabbing or shoving." Rouse, Breen and Howell (1988) found that 165 (28.2 percent) of the 585 college students they surveyed reported having been "pushed, grabbed or shoved," and 102 (17.4 percent) reported having been "struck, slapped or punched" in a dating relationship.

Dating violence has also been related to earlier family experience. Bernard and Bernard (1983) noted that for both men and women about three fourths of those who had observed or experienced abuse in their family of origin used the same form in their dating relationships: "Thus the female college student who was punched by her father is not only more likely to be abusive, but is also likely to punch her boyfriend. Her male counterpart who watched his mother throw things at her husband is not only more likely to be abusive but is quite likely to throw things at his girlfriend" (Bernard and Bernard, 1983).

Violence enters dating as well as marriage to the extent that participants are subject to the same types of interactional stresses and sociocultural influences. Comparisons of dating, cohabiting, and marital relationships help to clarify similarities and differences against the background of theoretical explanations for domestic violence. Structurally, marriage has complex and potentially contradictory effects. Greater emotional involvement in marriage might increase violence, but marriage also reduces role ambiguity and offers social supports typically not given to cohabiting couples. Dating behaviors reflect earlier socialization experiences and establish patterns that carry over into marital interaction. In dating, which is viewed as a rehearsal for marital roles, individuals draw upon what they learned growing up and on socially scripted expectations for romantic relationships. Dating provides a training ground for marital violence but also an opportunity to improve interaction skills and to terminate poor relationships before violence is "licensed" by marriage.

CONCLUSION

The family serves as a cornerstone of individual and collective well-being, but families must also adapt to changes in society and weather internal conflicts. Unique features of the family as a social institution contribute to the likelihood of abuse among family members. Despite variation in reported incidence due to the ways different types of family violence are defined and measured, we now know that domestic violence is not rare.

Domestic violence today is a social problem as a result of systematic efforts to inform the public about the nature, scope, and consequences of this social condition. The battered women's movement, for example, focused attention on wife beating and sexual abuse. Substantial use of physical force and sexual pressure has been found in dating as well as marital relationships, continuing early training in domestic violence. For children raised in abusive homes, witnessing husband-wife violence and/or being subjected to child abuse influences later beliefs, attitudes, and behaviors.

Different theoretical perspectives applied to domestic violence shape our understanding of causes and strategies for change. Macro-level remedies include addressing violence in American society at large, challenging patriarchy, providing jobs for the poor, increasing funding for child protective services, and arresting perpetrators of spousal assault. Micro-level approaches suggest educational and counseling interventions to resocialize family members (e.g., breaking the cycle of intergenerational transmission by redefining the situation, clarifying how early experiences influence propensity for violence, identifying poor coping mechanisms, modeling nonabusive problem solving, and improving interpersonal skills).

Domestic violence is prevented and treated by addressing a variety of causes: ultimately, by changing the attitudes, values, and actions that foster violence in individuals and society. Responses to domestic violence today emphasize the importance of no longer viewing this as a private matter. No longer condoning, excusing, or ignoring domestic violence lifts the silence that implies consent and brings us closer to a social context within which the positive functions of the family may be more nearly achieved.

REFERENCES

BANDURA, ALBERT
1973   *Aggression: A Social Learning Analysis.* Englewood Cliffs, NJ: Prentice Hall.

BERNARD, M. L. and J. L. BERNARD
1983   "Violent Intimacy: The Family as a Model for Love Relationships," *Family Relations* 32: 283–286.

GELLES, RICHARD J. and MURRAY A. STRAUS
1979   "Determinants of Violence in the Family: Toward a Theoretical Integration," in W. R. Burr, R. Hill, F. Ivan Nye and I. L. Reiss, eds., *Contemporary Theories About the Family,* Vol. I. New York: Free Press.

GONDOLF, EDWARD W.
1985   *Men Who Batter: An Integrated Approach for Stopping Wife Abuse.* Holmes Beach, FL: Learning Publications.

KOSS, MARY P.
1993   "Detecting the Scope of Rape: A Review of Prevalence Research Methods," *Journal of Interpersonal Violence* 8 (2): 198–222.

LASCH, CHRISTOPHER
1979   *Haven in a Heartless World: The Family Besieged.* New York: Basic Books.

MCCURDY, KAREN and DEBORAH DARO
1994   "Child Maltreatment: A National Survey of Reports and Fatalities," *Journal of Interpersonal Violence* 9 (1): 75–94.

MAKEPEACE, JAMES M.
1981   "Courtship Violence Among College Students," *Family Relations* 30: 97–102.

PAGELOW, MILDRED
1984   *Family Violence*. New York: Praeger.

ROUSE, LINDA P., RICHARD BREEN and MARILYN HOWELL
1988   "Abuse in Intimate Relationships: A Comparison of Married and Dating College Students," *Journal of Interpersonal Violence* 3: 414–429.

SADLER, A. E., ed.
1995   *Current Controversies: Family Violence*. San Diego, CA: Green Haven Press.

SCHECTER, SUSAN
1982   *Women and Male Violence: The Visions and Struggles of the Battered Women's Movement*. Boston, MA: South End Press.

STEINMETZ, SUZANNE K. and MURRAY A. STRAUS
1973   "Family as Cradle of Violence," *Society* 10 (September–October): 50–56.

STRAUS, MURRAY A.
1976   "Sexual Inequality, Cultural Norms and Wife-beating," *Victimology* 1 (1): 54–76.

UTECH, MYRON R.
1994   *Violence, Abuse and Neglect: The American Home*. Dix Hills, NY: General Hall.

VOYDANOFF, PATRICIA
1991   "Economic Stress and Family Relations," in C. F. Booth, ed., *Contemporary Families: Looking Forward, Looking Back*. Minneapolis, MN: National Council on Family Relations.

EXERCISE 2

Name _____   Date _____

ID # _____   Class Time _____

I. Answer each of the following questions in the spaces provided.

    A. Define the terms "domestic violence" and "abuse."

    B. List four types of domestic violence/abuse.

        1.

        2.

        3.

        4.

    C. Domestic violence is (check one):

        _____ accurately reported

        _____ over-reported

        _____ under-reported

    D. Briefly, defend your answer to part C above.

II. Many features of the family contribute to the likelihood of abuse:
privacy
involuntary membership
power differentials
high expectations
role diffuseness
intensity of involvement
impinging activities
time together
change
discontinuity

For each statement or example below, fill in the feature that best applies.

_____ **A.** Two teen-age brothers get into a fight because they both want to borrow the one family car.

_____ **B.** Children are a reflection of our ability as parents; we desperately want them to be "perfect angels."

_____ **C.** Sometimes we don't interfere when we see children pushed or slapped in public because we know that once a parent gets the child home the parent might do worse.

_____ **D.** Family members with more resources or authority are able to get their own way more often, with or without using violence.

_____ **E.** In the novel *The Burning Bed* a wife kills her abusive husband because she believes this is the only way she and her children can escape from his battering.

_____ **F.** Because family members interact in so many different ways across various types of activities, it is impossible to define in advance exactly how we should behave in all situations.

III. Each of the theoretical perspectives listed below have been used by researchers and professionals who work with cases of domestic violence.

    A. First, indicate whether each theoretical perspective is a micro or macro approach by circling the appropriate level of analysis.

        1. Frustration-aggression   micro   macro
        2. Patriarchy   micro   macro
        3. Symbolic interactionism   micro   macro
        4. Social exchange   micro   macro
        5. Culture of violence   micro   macro
        6. Social stratification   micro   macro
        7. Social learning   micro   macro

    B. Match each of the following comments about domestic violence with one of the theoretical perspectives listed in A above:

_____ **1.** American society glorifies violence.

_____ **2.** Child abuse is explained as a result of an individual parent's failure to achieve desired outcomes.

_____ **3.** Hitting a boyfriend or girlfriend in a jealous rage is interpreted as an expression of caring: "She (he) would not act this way if she (he) did not love me so much."

_____ **4.** Men feel a sense of social entitlement to impose their decisions in the family, with use of physical force if necessary.

_____ **5.** Spouse abuse is transmitted intergenerationally as children who have observed a parent's assaultive behavior act in similar fashion in their own relationships.

_____ **6.** Arrest, as compared to a reprimand or no action, is the most effective police response to domestic violence calls in reducing further incidents.

_____ **7.** As compared to middle-class families, lower-class families are more likely to use physical punishment to discipline their children.

    C. Imagine that you or an acquaintance have recently experienced physical or sexual violence in a marital or dating relationship. Using your local telephone directory, locate and list the name and number of a person or agency to call.

        Name: _____ Number: (   )

    D. Describe briefly what kind of assistance is likely to be provided.

3

Social Concern
About Teen-Age Pregnancy

Monica A. Longmore

U.S. teen-agers have one of the highest pregnancy rates among Westernized countries—twice as high as England and three times as high as Sweden. More than 1.2 million American teen-agers become pregnant each year. In other words, approximately one of every eight teen-age women between the ages of 15 and 19 becomes pregnant (Hatcher and Trussell, 1994). This rate has remained stable over the last 15 years. Almost two thirds of all teen-age mothers prefer to keep their babies rather than have an abortion or give up their babies for adoption. Often teen-age mothers struggle to finish high school and raise their children.

In recent years, teen-age pregnancy has been the focus of much social concern and public debate. Teen-age pregnancy has become less socially acceptable as it has become more socially visible (Furstenberg, 1991). Public debates center on several issues. First, Americans are concerned about the costs in terms of federally funded social services, which cost over $30 billion a year. Many people have come to believe that rather than assisting teen-age mothers, social service programs are ineffective, too costly, and do not discourage teen pregnancy.

Second, there is concern that teen-age pregnancies result in a moratorium on the mothers' emotional and intellectual growth (e.g., Gecas and Seff, 1990; Paik, 1992). In other words, it is thought that the teen-age mother suffers in the long run. For example, on average, only 5 percent of teen mothers get college degrees, compared with 47 percent of those who have children at age 25 or older. Chilman (1983), reviewing more than eight major investigations of the consequences of teen-age motherhood, reports that mothers often must put off school until later in life. Although not the only factor, teen-age pregnancy is one factor in many young women's decisions to drop out of high school. Keep in mind, however, that teen-age mothers typically performed poorly in school before pregnancy occurs (Brindis, 1993). Moreover, half or more of the teen-age mothers who drop out of school do complete high school later in life.

With respect to family size and marriage prospects, teen-age mothers often have larger families, especially if the teen-ager marries. In fact, the majority of unmarried teen-age mothers marry within a few years of giving birth to their first child. However, sociological studies indicate that early first marriage is associated with a greater likelihood of divorce. Additionally, teen-age mothers who do marry after the birth of their first child are less likely to return to school. Yet, teen-age motherhood per se does not necessarily lead to a long life of welfare dependence. In studies that control for race and original socioeconomic status, a woman's later occupational status, the number of hours she works, and wages are not affected directly by teen-age motherhood. Single teen-age mothers are only slightly more likely than married teen-age mothers or nonmothers with comparable social class and racial backgrounds to receive public assistance. However, women who were teen-age mothers are more likely to receive public assistance later in life when compared with the general population.

Much of the public debate regarding teen pregnancy focuses on concern for the children of teen-age mothers. Although the majority of teen-age mothers appear to be competent and nurturing, compared to older mothers, teen-age mothers are observed to be lower on verbal interaction with their babies.

About one third of the daughters of teen mothers will go on to become teen mothers themselves—perpetuating what is usually a cycle of severe poverty and hardship. Following Chilman's (1983) review of studies on the consequences of teen-age mothers for children, there are health, cognitive, personal, behavioral, and educational development outcomes. Assuming high-quality prenatal and later health care, teen-age motherhood does not negatively affect the physical health of the child. Controlling for poverty, racism, and family headship (single or two parent), children of teen-age mothers do not report significantly lower cognitive scores. With respect to academic achievement, findings tend to be mixed, with some studies reporting no significant differences in educational achievement and other studies reporting slight differences due to differences in cognitive development. Interestingly, sons appear to be more adversely affected than daughters with respect to academic achievement and cognitive development. A statistically significant number of children, especially sons, were reported as having behavioral problems. And a larger proportion of children of teen-age mothers were rated as slow in overall development. There is a greater tendency for the child of a teenage mother to experience divorce, single-parent households, and remarriages.

DEFINING TEEN-AGE PREGNANCY AS A SOCIAL PROBLEM

The issue of teen-age pregnancy and potential solutions are complex and not easily solved. Prior to the mid-1970s, few people talked about teen pregnancy. Unwed pregnancy was viewed as a serious social malady; but for the most part, society was unconcerned if an 18- or 19-year-old got married and had children (Luker, 1991). How did teen-age motherhood become a social problem? How was this social problem constructed?

Beginning in the mid-1970s, along with an increase in divorce rates, premarital pregnancy rates, premarital sex, and a lowering of first age of coitus, teen pregnancy began to be defined as a social problem. Social issues come to be viewed as social problems when the public views the issues as morally wrong, occurring frequently, and yet amenable to change (Stafford and Warr, 1985). Surprisingly, in spite of the concern for this new social problem, teen-age pregnancy rates did not increase as much as most Americans believe. Luker (1991) reports that from the early 1900s until the end of World War II, birth rates among teen-agers were relatively stable at approximately 50 to 60 births per thousand women. After World War II, teen-age birth rates, similar to the birth rates for all American women, increased significantly. The birth rate among teen-agers doubled in the baby boom years (1944–1960) to a peak of about 97 births per thousand teen-age women in 1957. Subsequent to the baby boom era, teen birth rates declined, and by 1975 the teen-age birth rate had declined to the rate that existed prior to World War II (Luker, 1991).

What has been increasing dramatically is the percentage of teen-age births that are premarital births. In 1970 babies born to unwed mothers represented about a third of all babies born to teen-age mothers (Luker, 1991). In other words, the majority of these mothers married. By 1980 premarital births were about half of all births to teenagers, and by 1986 almost two thirds of all births to teenagers were premarital births. These changes also vary by race. According to Luker (1991), the premarital birth rate rose from 6 to 24.8 per thousand unmarried teen-age white women, while for unmarried nonwhite teen-agers

the birth rate rose from 77.6 to 98.3 per thousand between 1955 and 1988. In other words, while the premarital birth rate has been quite high among nonwhite teen-agers, the rate, in recent years, has more than quadrupled for white teen-agers.

TEEN PREGNANCY: DEMOGRAPHIC AND SOCIAL PSYCHOLOGICAL APPROACHES

Why are teen-agers having babies before marriage? The answers to this question are not simple. Two approaches to discussing this issue include the demographic approach and the social psychological approach.

Demographers point out that increasingly women are postponing marriage but they are not postponing premarital sex (e.g., McLanahan and Sandefur, 1994; East, Felice and Morgan, 1993). Most important for this argument, the growth of premarital births has not occurred only among teen-agers. This increase has been even more rapid among older women. In 1970 teen-agers made up almost half of all premarital births in the United States. Births to teen-agers now account for less than one third of all premarital births. Conversely, premarital births represent a much larger percentage of births for teens than for older women. This demographic analysis, while informative, tells us little about the lives of the teen-agers who become mothers.

The social psychological approach argues that when alternatives to pregnancy and childbirth exist, young women tend to delay pregnancy and childbirth. Although 37 percent of all teen-age women are from poor and low-income families, 83 percent of teen-agers giving birth are from such families. Nearly one third of the fathers of babies born to girls who are younger than 15 years are 21 years or older (Landry and Forrest, 1995). An important social psychological factor influencing teen-age pregnancy is the teen-ager's perceptions of her options in life (e.g., Paik, 1992; East, Felice and Morgan, 1993). According to Anderson (1991), "[o]ne of the most important factors working against teen pregnancy is teenagers' belief that they have something to lose by presently becoming a parent: many believe that they have something to gain." Many teen-age mothers were not doing well at school before becoming pregnant. For these girls, the willingness to risk pregnancy and, once pregnant, the decision not to have an abortion or to have the baby adopted, may be influenced by their perceptions that they have no other options than to be a mother.

ARE THERE SOLUTIONS?

Although there is a consensus that teen-age pregnancy is a problem for society, for the mother, and for the development of the child, this consensus has not led to clear public policies that have succeeded in diminishing the problem (Rhode, 1993; Brindis, 1993). Commentators and public policy makers often argue that teen-age pregnancy can easily be dealt with by abstinence, contraception use, and abortion.

Regarding abstinence, although we do not need to necessarily assume that the proportion of sexually active teen-agers will remain constant, there is evidence to indicate that the incidence of sexual activity among the teen-age population is high, and the inception of coitus occurs at an earlier age for females now than 20 years ago. These changes place a greater percentage of teen-agers at risk of becoming pregnant. Studies indicate that white females are beginning to have sex at an earlier age, which may be one reason their rate of premarital pregnancy has quadrupled over the last decade.

Many commentators also note that there are obstacles to contraceptive use. While it is true that the most teen-agers know about contraception, whether they have sufficient knowledge of and easy access to contraceptives is quite another matter. For example, in a study reported by Hatcher and Trussell (1994), 38 percent of the teen-agers using oral contraceptives became pregnant a second time within 15 months of their first birth. Others suggest that better abortion services for pregnant teen-agers who choose not to give birth and support programs for those who choose to put their children up for adoption are needed.

Choices among policy solutions are influenced by our values. However, if teen-age premarital pregnancy and childbearing are to decline from the relatively high levels over the past 20 years, progress will have to come in one or more of the above policy directions. Current trends toward reductions in family planning budgets, access to abortions, and AFDC at both state and federal levels do not bode well for future rates of teen pregnancy.

REFERENCES

ANDERSON, ELIJAH
1991   "Neighborhood Effects on Teenage Pregnancy," in C. Jencks and P. E. Peterson, eds., *The Urban Underclass*. Washington, DC: Brookings Institution.

BRINDIS, CLAIRE
1993   "Antecedents and Consequences: The Need for Diverse Strategies in Adolescent Pregnancy Prevention," in Annette Lawson and Deborah L. Rhode, eds., *The Politics of Pregnancy*. New Haven, CT: Yale University Press.

CHILMAN, CATHERINE
1983   *Adolescent Sexuality in a Changing American Society*. New York: John Wiley.

EAST, PATRICIA L., MARIANNE E. FELICE and MARIA C. MORGAN
1993   "Sisters' and Girlfriends' Sexual and Childbearing Behavior: Effects on Early Adolescent Girls' Sexual Outcomes," *Journal of Marriage and the Family* 55 (November): 953–963.

FURSTENBERG, FRANK JR.
1991   "As the Pendulum Swings: Teenage Childbearing and Social Concern," *Family Relations* 40: 127–138.

GECAS, VIKTOR and MONICA A. SEFF
1990   "Families and Adolescents: A Review of the 1990s," *Journal of Marriage and the Family* 52 (November): 941–958.

HATCHER, ROBERT A. and JAMES TRUSSELL
1994   "Contraceptive Implants and Teenage Pregnancy," *The New England Journal of Medicine* 331 (18): 1229–1230.

LANDRY, DAVID J. and JACQUELINE BARROCH FORREST
1995   "How Old Are U.S. Fathers?" *Family Planning Perspectives* 27: 159–161.

LUKER, KRISTIN
1991   "Dubious Conceptions: The Controversy Over Teen Pregnancy," *The American Prospect* 5 (Spring): 73–83.

McLANAHAN, SARA and GARY SANDEFUR
1994   *Growing Up with a Single Parent: What Hurts, What Helps*. Cambridge, MA: Harvard University Press.

PAIK, SOOK I.
1992   "Self-Concept of Pregnant Teenagers," *Journal of Health and Social Policy* 3 (3): 93–111.

RHODE, DEBORAH L.
1993   "Adolescent Pregnancy and Public Policy," in Annette Lawson and Deborah L. Rhode, eds., *The Politics of Pregnancy*. New Haven, CT: Yale University Press.

STAFFORD, MARK C. and MARK WARR
1985   "Public Perceptions of Social Problems: Some Propositions and a Test," *The Journal of Applied Behavioral Science* 21 (3): 307–316.

EXERCISE 3

Name _____   Date _____

ID # _____   Class Time _____

I. The well-being of children of teen mothers is affected in many ways and by many things.

    A. List at least three specific ways in which a teen mother's *age* may affect the well-being of her children.

        1.

        2.

        3.

    B. What other factors can affect the well-being of the children of teen mothers? List at least three specific factors and briefly describe their likely impact on the child's well-being.

        1.

        2.

        3.

II. The governor of your state has announced the formation of a special task force composed of representatives of local government, industry, community leaders, and citizens to recommend alternative strategies for dealing with the needs of teen parents and their children and for minimizing teen pregnancy in years to come. You and many others have accepted the governor's request to serve on the task force.

    A. Summarize the likely concerns of each of the following task force members regarding the consequences of teen pregnancy. Respond in a short sentence or two for each.

        1. A high school principal

        2. A hospital administrator

        3. The county's largest private-sector employer

        4. An anti-abortion organization leader

        5. You (your own view)

B. Given the range of opinions about the consequences of teen pregnancy and the role of government in helping to alleviate the problem, what specific recommendations to the governor might the task force members develop about the role government should play in reducing the number of teens who become pregnant? List three specific recommendations and a justification for each in the spaces provided below. Formulate realistic recommendations and discuss obstacles to their implementation.

    1. Recommendation:

       Justification:

       Obstacles to implementation:

    2. Recommendation:

       Justification:

       Obstacles to implementation:

    3. Recommendation:

       Justification:

       Obstacles to implementation:

III. Examine age at first birth and patterns of teen pregnancy for three generations of your family.

    A. Describe the patterns of parental age and childbirth in your own family. Record the appropriate data for each part of the table that applies to you.

	Present age	Age at first birth	Number of children
Your child			
You			
Your mother			
Your mother's mother			
Your father's mother			

    B. Does your family exhibit any similarities with respect to the patterns of teen pregnancy discussed in this essay? Describe specifically how the patterns in your family are similar or dissimilar to those described in the essay.

4

The Achievement Crisis and School Reform: From "Basics" to "Excellence"

Dorothea Weir

Over the past three decades, critics of American public education have claimed that the declining performance of American students on standardized tests is evidence of ineffective schools, eroding academic standards, and a need for educational reform. In the long-running debate over test scores, the press, the general public, and elected officials have almost completely accepted the premise that student achievement is declining nationally. At the same time, many experts inside the educational community do not believe that achievement data support the argument that students learn less today than they did in the recent past. This article focuses on several aspects of the ongoing controversy over declining achievement. How have test scores changed during recent years, and what factors have been considered to contribute to the changes? How have educators, policy makers, and the general public interpreted the evidence of test scores? What reforms in the public education system have resulted?

Declining test scores first drew widespread public attention in 1966, when the Educational Testing Service (ETS) reported that average scores on the Scholastic Aptitude Test (SAT), the country's most widely used college admissions test, had dropped for three years in a row. From the early 1950s, when SAT scores were first published, to the early 1960s, average scores had been fairly stable, fluctuating between 472 and 479 on the verbal portion of the exam, and from 490 to 502 on the math portion. The initial drops from 1963 to 1966 were not large, but scores continued to fall each year and the size of the declines grew. By 1976, the verbal score had dropped about 45 points and the math score about 35 points from the levels of the 1950s.

News of the falling scores set off a national wave of concern and criticism. Sidney P. Marland, former Commissioner of Education under President Nixon and head of the College Entrance Examination Board, organized a panel (known as the Wirtz Commission) to investigate the situation. The panel's report, issued in 1977, declared that "[n]o topic related to the programs of the College Boards has received more public attention in recent years than the unexplained decline in scores earned by students on the Scholastic Aptitude Test." The National Institute of Education convened a special conference on the falling test scores. The Department of Health, Education, and Welfare was already investigating declining reading skills. The American Educational Research Association and the National Council on Measurement in Education hastily organized conferences and seminars to examine trends in test score data.

Experts could not agree about the meaning of the score decline. The College Board maintained that the SAT was an academic ability test designed to predict a student's preparedness and aptitude for college-level work, and was never intended to assess the performance of the nation's schools. Indeed, according to the College Board, one of the greatest virtues of the SAT was that it was "curriculum-free" and provided a good measure of student aptitude no matter what course of study had been followed in high school. The Wirtz Commission report (1977) pointed out that SAT guidelines "warn[ed] sharply against misuse [of SAT scores] as measures of the broader effectiveness of elementary and secondary education in general." Analysis of results of other nationally administered tests, such as the reading and writing tests given by the National Assessment of Educational Progress (NAEP), showed mixed results rather than overall declines. Even more confusing, the Preliminary Scholastic Aptitude Test (PSAT), taken by high school juniors, showed score declines similar to the SAT only *after* 1973, and achievement tests administered in conjunction with the SAT by the College Board showed declines in four subjects and gains in six. Even for the SAT, the picture was mixed, with some groups, particularly African Americans, showing average score *increases* over the period during which overall scores declined. How could these conflicting findings be resolved?

Professionals in the field of educational measurement looked for answers within the tests and the testing process. One explanation frequently advanced was that the SAT score drops resulted largely from a change in the composition of the student group taking the test. More students were staying in school longer, and these included a large number of low-income students who tended to score lower on standardized tests. Between 1940 and the late 1960s, the proportion of 17-year-olds who graduated from high school grew from about 50 percent to about 75 percent. The proportion of students who went on to college also increased considerably, from 16 percent in 1940 to about 45 percent in 1968, as more jobs that once required only a high school diploma began to demand a college education. Also, the SAT itself was used more widely than in earlier decades. Before World War II, only a few private, selective colleges required applicants to take the SAT. However, as more and more students applied for college admission, many less selective public colleges and universities began to use the SAT as part of their screening process. The number of students who took the SAT each year grew from about 80,000 in 1950 to over 1 million in the middle 1960s. The Wirtz Commission found that between two thirds and three fourths of the drop in scores from 1963 to the early 1970s could be attributed simply to changes in the composition of the group taking the test.

While experts within the educational community disagreed over the significance of the score declines, the popular press and the public quickly accepted the drop in test scores as firm evidence of deficient academic standards in American schools. Declining student achievement was discussed in the national news media as potentially the most serious problem facing American education. In 1975, *Newsweek* ran a cover story on what it dubbed the "literacy crisis" in America, declaring that "the U.S. educational system is spawning a generation of semi-literates." The Wirtz Commission itself broadened the controversy beyond the issue of test score declines, finding: "(1) that less thoughtful and critical reading is now being demanded and done, and (2) that careful writing has apparently about gone out of style" (1977).

Other problems besides falling test scores contributed to growing dissatisfaction with public education. As the "baby boom" generation passed out of high school, fewer students were enrolled in the public schools, but expenditures for education continued to rise at a rate exceeding that of the consumer price index. At the same time, the country experienced simultaneous inflation and recession, the "stagflation" of the late 1970s. Employers complained that high school graduates could not perform adequately on the job because of their inability to read, write, and calculate, and that some could not even complete a job application form. Colleges and universities reported increases in the number of entering first-year students needing remedial reading and writing courses. In a few highly publicized lawsuits, students and parents accused school districts of "educational malpractice" because the districts had awarded high school diplomas to graduates they had failed to teach to read or write (Ravitch, 1983). Furthermore, while educational equity had been widely advanced in the 1960s as the answer to persistent problems of social inequality, attempts to reduce educational disadvantages of poor and minority children had not substantially reduced inequality throughout the society. Head Start, Title I of the Elementary and Secondary Education Act of 1965, the Emergency School Assistance Act, and a multitude of other programs had provided unprecedented amounts of federal aid to states and to local districts, with few immediately obvious results. Expectations for the social impact of educational change had been unrealistically high, given the multitude of factors that contribute to poverty. Increases in federal and state funding were never great enough to offset differences between rich and poor districts in available dollars per student. Nevertheless, many among the general public saw rising federal expenditures and growing local property taxes as "throwing money at schools" to little effect. In an atmosphere of public discontent with the educational system, the highly publicized SAT declines compounded the perception that educational quality had deteriorated.

The presumed decline in educational standards was attributed to conditions outside as well as inside the schools. The parents of the baby-boom generation were blamed for embracing permissive child-rearing practices advocated by experts such as Dr. Benjamin Spock, thereby producing an overindulged generation without the self-discipline or motivation to work hard in school. Family patterns were changing. Many observers believed that rising divorce rates and a corresponding growth in the number of single-parent families were resulting in more disruption in the lives of students and less supervision at home. The percentage of married women who had school-aged children and worked outside the home was increasing rapidly, up from 28 percent in 1950 to 49 percent in 1970 and to 62 percent by 1980. Many observers considered television to be especially pernicious, reducing students' attention span and encouraging passivity. A commonly quoted estimate was that, by the age of 18, a child would have spent 11,000 hours in school and 17,000 hours watching television.

Critics of the schools were ready to find fault with current educational practices. A common target was the "open education movement" of the 1960s and early 1970s. Books such as Jonathan Kozol's (1967) *Death at an Early Age* and Herbert Kohl's (1967) *36 Children* indicted the schools for "destroying the souls of children" (Ravitch, 1983, p. 237). Charles Silberman's (1971) *Crisis in the Classroom* described public schools as "grim joyless places" and denounced their "preoccupation with order and control, their slavish adherence to the timetable and lesson plan, the obsession with routine qua routine, the absence of noise and movement, the joylessness and repression. . . ." Silberman and others advocated a model of education that was flexible in its subject matter, responsive to students' interests, and based on experiential rather than textbook learning. They envisioned the teacher as a facilitator who provided the child with opportunities to learn (Ravitch, 1983). While the open education movement caught fire among professional educators, and especially among younger teachers, many outside the schools saw open education as too permissive, leading to lax academic standards and lack of discipline. Some placed the blame for falling test scores on increased numbers of electives and the watering down of content in required courses, pointing to schools that offered science-fiction and radio-TV-film classes as substitutes for traditional literature courses, or awarded course credit for subjects such as Family Living. Other critics blamed the "dumbing down" of curriculum, asserting that newer textbooks and materials used simpler language and addressed less difficult concepts than the texts of a generation ago. Some claimed that teachers had become less competent and knowledgeable as more lucrative occupations opened up to college-educated women, and called for higher salaries or stricter professional standards to improve teacher quality.

It was not surprising that the public response to declining test scores and perceived lowering of educational standards came in the form of the "back-to-basics" movement. This movement originated not among professional educators (many of whom still strongly supported the ideals of open education), but among business leaders, state legislators, and the general public. Supporters of the basics movement had two primary concerns. First, they were alarmed that high schools were graduating students who could not read and write, issuing diplomas that were essentially meaningless. Second, they did not trust teachers and school administrators, many of whom they saw as part of the problem, to make necessary reforms, so they were looking for a way to hold schools more accountable to the general public. Supporters of the basics movement called for a return to the teaching of traditional subjects such as reading, writing, and arithmetic in the elementary schools, and English, science, math, and history in the high schools. Along with reinstatement of a conventional curriculum, they advocated older methods of instruction involving drill and practice, recitation, homework, and frequent testing. "No frills" was a catchword of the basics movement, meaning decreased numbers of electives, elimination of "social service" courses such as drug education, and an increase in hours spent in required courses. The basics movement sought to alter the culture of the schools far beyond restoring traditional curriculum and instruction. Many back-to-basics advocates also endorsed restoring strict dress codes or requiring school uniforms, increasing emphasis on patriotism, and imposing sterner discipline.

Minimal competency testing was an important part of the basics movement. Beginning in the middle 1970s, many states introduced minimal competency tests (MCTs), also known as "basic skills" tests, as an attempt at holding schools accountable for student achievement. MCTs were intended to show whether students had ac-

quired specific skills required of them by certain grade levels. They tested students' proficiency against minimum achievement standards in basic subject areas such as reading, mathematics, and science. The most common use of these tests was to qualify (or disqualify) students for high school graduation. Many states also used them at lower grade levels, most commonly to identify students for remedial programs and less frequently to make decisions about promotion to the next grade. By 1980, 29 states had implemented MCT programs, and eventually about two thirds of the states introduced competency testing, although a few subsequently abandoned their programs.

Thus, at a time when many educators were questioning the uses of testing, public support for expanded testing grew. In 1984, a national survey reported that 65 percent of Americans favored a standardized test as a prerequisite for obtaining a high school diploma, while only 29 percent were opposed. Some supporters of MCTs believed that requiring all students to attain a minimum standard would focus the attention of educators on the needs of low-achieving students who had been ignored in many school systems, and force schools to provide greater help for underachievers. Similarly, it was thought that ending "social promotion" (the practice of promoting students with their age group regardless of academic performance) by requiring all students to pass a test to be promoted to the next higher grade would motivate students to work harder in school instead of merely sliding by. Many outside the educational system also believed that the only way to improve the quality of public education was to impose an external set of standards as a yardstick against which school performance could be measured. Those who supported the back-to-basics movement were particularly eager to use rising test scores to demonstrate that their reforms were indeed working. Some saw MCTs as providing a kind of state guarantee of the value of a high school diploma, validating the proficiency of its owner.

The basics movement soon came under attack, however. Opponents of state minimal competency testing charged that teachers were "teaching to the test" and substituting drill and practice using multiple-choice worksheets for more academically challenging activities. They argued that because only basic skills were tested, schools were reducing instruction to the lowest common denominator. This lowered the standards for many students, especially high-ability students. High achievement and a challenging curriculum for all students had become less important than making sure that all students could meet the low minimum standards. At the same time, those students who had difficulty reaching the minimum standards and failed the tests were in danger of becoming discouraged and dropping out (Zancanella, 1994).

Further, the tests themselves incurred strong criticism. In some cases, MCTs were hastily assembled by state education agency employees who did not always have extensive training or experience in developing tests. Also, it was not clear that state tests measured what was being taught in the schools, or that teachers and students were adequately informed about what subject matter the tests covered. Legal challenges to MCTs arose in several states, most commonly from students who had been denied high school diplomas because they failed a state test. In *Debra P. v. Turlington* (1981), the court ruled that Florida's MCT requirement for high school graduation violated individual students' rights to due process, stating: "We believe that the state administered a test that was, at least on the record before us, fundamentally unfair in that it may have covered matters not taught in the schools of the state."

Despite the spread of minimal competency testing and increased emphasis on basic subjects, national SAT scores did not improve but continued to drop year by year throughout the late 1970s. In 1981, President Reagan's Secretary of Education, Terrell H. Bell, responding to "the widespread public perception that something is seriously remiss in our educational system," created the National Commission on Excellence in Education (NCEE). In its 1983 report, *A Nation at Risk,* the NCEE declared that "a rising tide of mediocrity" threatened American schools, and that weaknesses in public education endangered the country's predominance in business, science, and technology. Once again, the arguments of the NCEE for education reform were supported by the evidence of standardized test scores: "The College Board's Scholastic Aptitude Tests . . . demonstrate a virtually unbroken decline from 1963 to 1980. Average verbal scores fell over 50 points and average mathematics scores dropped nearly 40 points."

In other ways, though, the newly declared crisis in education was significantly different from the crisis of the mid-1970s. While reflecting some key issues of the basics movement, such as concern over functional illiteracy among high school graduates and the need for remedial education and training in the work place, *A Nation at Risk* gave greater emphasis to the problems of scientific and technological illiteracy, increasing demand for workers with advanced skills, and a lack of "higher order intellectual skills" among high school students. It also voiced criticisms of the basics movement, signaling a new turn in the argument over educational standards. It decried the swing from college preparatory to "general track" courses in high school, high enrollment in remedial English and mathematics courses, and low numbers of students taking courses such as French, geography, and calculus—subjects notably *not* tested by MCT programs. It called for ". . . a public commitment to excellence and educational reform," asserting that "we should expect schools to have genuinely high standards rather than minimum ones" and explicitly stated that " '[m]inimum competency' examinations . . . fall short of what is needed, as the 'minimum' tends to become the 'maximum,' thus lowering standards for all."

"Excellence" became the catchword of the school reform movement of the 1980s. The Education Commission of the States, a group of state governors with a strong interest in educational issues, published its report, *Action for Excellence: A Comprehensive Plan to Improve Our Nation's Schools,* in 1983. The National Science Board (1983) warned that "[o]ur children could be stragglers in a world of technology. . . . America must not become an industrial dinosaur . . . the 'basics' of the 21st century . . . include communication, and higher problem-solving skills, and scientific and technological literacy." Redefinition of the "basics," a call for a more stringent academic curriculum with greater emphasis on math, science, and technology, and the need to teach students higher-order thinking skills were echoed in numerous reports of educational boards and commissions at federal, state, and local levels.

How to achieve excellence was less readily agreed upon. The NCEE, among others, argued that more, not less, testing was needed. *A Nation at Risk* advocated a nationwide system of state and local standardized tests but not a federally imposed set of tests. *America 2000* (1991), a set of reform proposals developed by the U.S. Department of Education under President Bush and Secretary of Education Lamar Alexander, went further and outlined a national system of assessments, to be called the American Achievement Tests, and a national curriculum. Although neither of these proposals has yet been acted upon, many states have expanded their accountability systems. For example, in 1994, Texas schools went from state-mandated competency testing in three grades (fourth, eighth, and tenth) to testing in all grades from third through tenth. Subject-matter tests in science and social studies were added to existing tests in reading, writing, and mathematics. Statewide final examinations were also introduced in high school courses such as algebra and biology.

Advocates of this view contend that administrators, teachers, and students will reach higher standards if they are required to, with rewards for those who succeed and penalties (including loss of jobs for teachers and administrators and loss of accreditation for schools and districts) for those who do not. Those who favor accountability achieved through high-stakes testing also argue that it is an efficient way to achieve curricular reform. If teachers teach to the test, then what the test covers is what students will learn. Essentially, those who write the tests may be writing the subject-matter curriculum for an entire state.

This argument has not escaped opponents of the current testing programs. Among these are many who are interested in reforming curriculum and instruction, who believe that students learn best through discovery and direct experience. They hold that their efforts to introduce more "hands-on," experienced-based activities into the school day are frustrated by testing programs that rely on paper-and-pencil, multiple-choice tests, and thus compel teachers to concentrate on those kinds of activities. Current testing programs, they say, emphasize and measure test-taking skills and memorization of isolated facts rather than true knowledge and learning. A movement has grown, primarily among teachers and teacher educators, for the use of performance assessments (Wiggins, 1989), sometimes called "authentic assessments" or "portfolio assessments." Performance assessments are tests that "require students to create answers or products that demonstrate what they know or can do" (Office of Technology Assessment, 1992), such as writing an essay, conducting a science lab experiment, or playing a piece of music on the piano. Performance assessment is not new. It was the usual way of assessing student performance before multiple-choice testing was introduced. Its supporters point out that it is the most common method used in business and the military (OTA, 1992). An increasing number of states are now including performance assessments as part of their statewide testing programs. The most commonly used types of performance assessment are writing samples (used in 31 states) and short-answer test items, but at least two states, Kentucky and New Mexico, are evaluating portfolios of student work as part of their statewide testing programs. Primary concerns are defining appropriate performance tasks for various subject areas; consistency of evaluators' judgments from one combination of evaluator, student, and school to the next; and the relative efficiency and cost-effectiveness of using these assessment methods on a large scale (Taylor, 1994).

Those who support a return to local control of schools hold a third point of view. They are opposed to expansion of state-level control over schools and want local school boards, administrators, teachers, and parents to have a greater say in what is taught and tested. State legislators appear to be ambivalent over this issue, possibly because they are reluctant to release local districts from state control, yet concerned about the costs that states incur in implementing large-scale testing programs. For example, Senate Bill 1, introduced in the Texas legislature in 1995, called for "home rule" school district charters to be issued to selected districts. Under Senate Bill 1, home rule districts would be required to comply with the state testing system, but districts and even single campuses would have greater leeway in applying for waivers releasing them from state mandates. The same bill also proposed that Texas eliminate its high school exit MCT by the 1997–1998 school year and replace it with a series of end-of-course examinations for required courses.

Throughout the history of public education, reformers have frequently challenged the methods and practices of the schools. What made the calls for change in the 1970s and 1980s so successful and widely listened to? In part, their claims were based on empirical evidence few critics could refute: Student scores on standardized tests were in decline. Furthermore, the impetus for reform came, not from those who were closely associated with the educational system and familiar with its workings, but from legislators and the general public. Today's reformers seek to change the system not from inside, but through "remote control," by imposing requirements that would force administrators and teachers to carry out necessary changes within the schools to raise student achievement.

Somewhat ironically, the means to assess the relative merits of efforts to reform the performance of the public schools will be the performance of students on achievement tests. Thus, it should come as no surprise if controversies over assessment continue to dominate the debate over school reform for years to come.

REFERENCES

College Entrance Examination Board (Wirtz Commission)
1977   *On Further Examination: Report of the Advisory Panel on the Scholastic Aptitude Test Score Decline.* Princeton, NJ: College Entrance Examination Board.

Debra P. v. Turlington
1981   644 F.2d 397 (5th Cir.).

Education Commission of the States
1983   *Action for Excellence: A Comprehensive Plan to Improve Our Nation's Schools.* Denver, CO: Education Commission of the States

Kohl, Herbert
1967   *36 Children.* New York: New American Library.

Kozol, Jonathan
1967   *Death at an Early Age: The Destruction of the Hearts and Minds of Negro Children in the Boston Public Schools.* New York: Houghton Mifflin.

National Commission on Excellence in Education
1983   *A Nation at Risk: The Imperative for Educational Reform.* Washington, DC: U.S. Government Printing Office.

National Science Board Commission on Precollege Education in Mathematics, Science, and Technology
1983   *Educating Americans for the Twenty-First Century.* Washington, DC: National Science Foundation.

Ravitch, Dianne
1983   *The Troubled Crusade: American Education 1945–1980.* New York: Basic Books.

Sheils, Merrill
1975   "Why Johnny Can't Write," *Newsweek* 86, no. 23: 58–65.

Silberman, Charles E.
1971   *Crisis in the Classroom: The Remaking of American Education.* New York: Random House.

Taylor, Cathrine
1994   "Assessment for Measurement or Standards: The Peril and Promise of Large-Scale Assessment Reform," *American Educational Research Journal* 31, no. 2 (Summer): 231–262.

U. S. Congress, Office of Technology Assessment
1992   *Testing in American Schools: Asking the Right Questions.* Washington, DC: U.S. Government Printing Office.

U.S. Department of Education
1991   *America 2000: An Education Strategy.* Washington, DC: U.S. Department of Education.

Wiggins, George
1989   "Teaching to the (Authentic) Test," *Educational Leadership* 47, no. 7 (April): 41–47.

Zancanella, Don
1994   "The Influence of State-Mandated Testing on Teachers of Literature," *Educational Evaluation and Policy Analysis* 14, no. 3 (Fall): 283–295.

EXERCISE 4

Name _____   Date _____

ID # _____   Class Time _____

I. This exercise concerns the portrayal of public education in the mass media. Find and read at least two recent articles about student achievement or test scores in a local newspaper or in a national news magazine. Answer the following questions about the articles you select and attach a copy of them to the exercise you turn in.

Hint #1: When searching for articles, look for words like "accountability," "quality," "excellence," and "standards," which are usually associated with evaluations of education today.

Hint #2: As a general rule, it is best to staple attachments to work you turn in.

    A. Briefly summarize the conclusions of each article.

        1. Article 1:

        2. Article 2:

    B. Regardless of whether the articles are concerned with high or improving scores or poor or declining test scores, do the articles or anyone interviewed in them question the testing process itself? If so, highlight or underline the text in the article concerned with such questions and summarize these discussions in the spaces provided below.

        1. Article 1:

        2. Article 2:

    C. To what or whom are the test scores discussed in the articles attributed (e.g., schools, teachers, administrators, students, families, broader societal influences)? Explain below.

        1. Article 1:

        2. Article 2:

II. This exercise asks you to interview a teacher or an administrator (e.g., assistant principal) in a public school. Visit any elementary, middle, or high school accessible to you. (Note that while most schools welcome visitors, you should call the principal's office in advance to inform the school of the purpose of your visit, to ask permission to enter school grounds, and to find a teacher or an administrator willing to be interviewed.) If you are unable to visit a school, try to arrange a telephone interview. Your goal is to develop a sense of the emphasis placed on testing in the schools and the classroom.

    A. Some possible questions to ask administrators:

        1. May I see (and possibly have) a copy of the school district's published testing schedule?
        2. May I see any quantitative indexes which rank the school you are studying relative to other schools?
        3. How does your school weigh the importance of standardized testing?

    B. Some possible questions to ask teachers:

        1. How strongly is testing emphasized?
        2. Should greater emphasis be placed on testing?
        3. How much classroom time is spent in preparation for testing?
        4. How many days during the year are spent in testing for students at each grade level?

    C. Write down any additional significant questions you asked during the interviews.

    D. Summarize the responses of the person you interviewed.

        1. Identify his or her rank, title, and years of service.

        2. Write the interview results here.

5

Your Money or Your Life: Access to Medical Care as a Social Problem

Robert A. Hanneman

During 1994, the President of the United States proposed that Congress pass legislation that would result in all Americans being covered by medical insurance. Supporters of "universal coverage" argued that access to medical care is a basic social right, but that the high cost of medical care, in effect, denied this right to citizens who did not have medical insurance. Even opponents of the President's proposal agreed that the American medical care system was an "institution in trouble" and that reform was needed. But there were sharp disagreements about how to reform the medical care system. Opponents of the President's proposals raised objections to government intervention into medical care and worried that the cost of providing universal coverage would be too great and would result in higher taxes and federal deficits. Many different proposals were considered, but none were adopted.

Why is it that something as uninteresting as medical insurance has come to be regarded as a national social problem to be debated in Congress? Is the American medical care system really in trouble? If there are serious problems, what are their causes? What can we do about reforming medical care, and why are there such strong disagreements about what we should do about it?

Public debates about social problems are often complex, emotional, and filled with contradictory truths, half-truths, and outright lies from interested parties. Social scientists need to take a "step back" from the debates and try to see social problems in a broader perspective. The social scientist must seek to understand why social institutions, like medicine, perform the way they do. That is, before we can examine possible solutions, we must try to understand the causes of the problem. To gain a broader perspective on contemporary social problems, it is helpful to make comparisons. What are the problems with American medicine, and what are the trends? Are the problems of American medical care unique, or are they similar to those in other similar societies?

THE STATE OF AMERICAN MEDICINE: EFFECTIVENESS

In part, the problems of contemporary American medical care are the result of its own past success. Over the last 100 years, advances in medicine have been part of the cause of dramatic declines in mortality and disease in the United States and elsewhere. As medical care has become more effective, people have come to believe in it and to expect continuing progress. But, making rapid progress in overcoming health problems is becoming more difficult. In a sense, the "easy" medical problems have already been solved, leaving the difficult ones. We have learned to prevent death and disability from many diseases that used to be major killers. Most of the technologies for dealing with these "old" problems (e.g., smallpox, cholera, polio, tuberculosis) are relatively simple and inexpensive. But, as we have conquered these health problems, we have changed the nature of the health care problems in our population. Medical knowledge, along with other factors, has dramatically reduced the number of people who die very young and has all but eliminated death from many major infectious diseases. As a result, people live much longer now than they did a century ago, and have very different medical problems. Far more of our efforts today go toward the treatment of conditions for which we have only "halfway" technologies. That is, some treatments prolong life and reduce suffering, but do not cure such major killers as heart disease, cancer, pulmonary disease, and other "age-related" conditions.

The health of the American population is excellent by world standards but unexceptional compared to the other advanced nations. Americans do not live quite as long, on average, as people in many European countries (though Americans who do live to be age 65 can expect to live as long as those who do in most European nations).

39

FIGURE 5.1: Life Expectancy at Birth, 1993

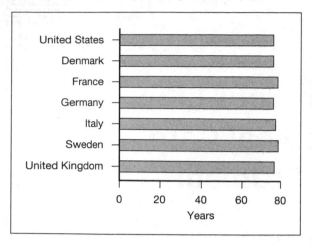

SOURCE: *Statistical Abstract of the United States, 1993.*

FIGURE 5.3: Medical Expenditures as a Percentage of GDP, 1993

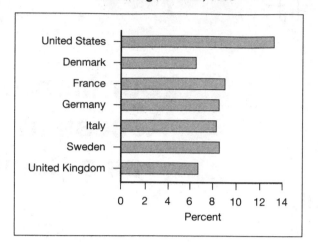

SOURCE: *Statistical Abstract of the United States, 1993.*

Infant mortality is believed to be a sensitive measure of societal health, because it reflects the health and medical care of both mothers and infants. Infant mortality rates (deaths of persons in the first year of life after a live birth) are higher in the United States than in many European nations. Some comparisons are shown in Figures 5.1 and 5.2.

Because of past successes in improving societal health in both the United States and the other wealthy nations, the rate of improvement in life expectancy and infant mortality have slowed markedly in recent decades. And, in all of the wealthy nations, the average age of the population has been increasing rapidly. As a result, improving population health overall is becoming more difficult, and this trend can be expected to continue into the next millennium.

THE STATE OF AMERICAN MEDICINE: COST

One of the major reasons that medical insurance and access to medical care has become a social problem in the United States is financial; many people are questioning if we, as a society, can afford to continue to provide medical care in the same way as our medical problems change and our population ages. Again, to get perspective on the situation, it is useful to make some comparisons. In Figure 5.3, we can see that the United States spends significantly more of its wealth on medical care than many (actually, all) of the European nations; in Figure 5.4, we can see that the share of our national wealth (measured by gross domestic product, or GDP) devoted to medical care has been increasing quite rapidly in recent decades.

The basic reasons for the increasing cost of medical

FIGURE 5.2: Infant Mortality Rates, 1993

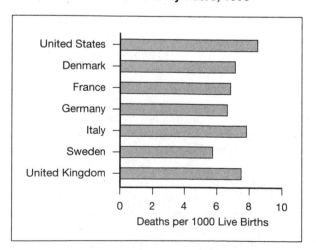

SOURCE: *Statistical Abstract of the United States, 1993.*

FIGURE 5.4: U.S. Medical Expenditures as a Percentage of GDP, 1960–1992

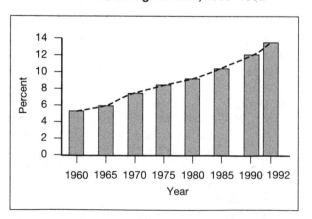

SOURCE: *Statistical Abstract of the United States, 1993.*

care are the same in the United States as in the European nations. Easy medical problems have been solved, leaving difficult medical problems. Medical technology and knowledge have become more sophisticated and more expensive to develop and apply. The populations are aging and confronting more long-term diseases for which we do not have cures. People believe in the efficacy of medical treatment and, due to our remarkable growth in societal wealth (at least until the middle 1970s), have been able to afford to pay more and more for it.

THE STATE OF AMERICAN MEDICINE: SOCIAL ORGANIZATION AND SOCIAL EFFICIENCY

The trends we have seen above suggest that Americans are spending more and more money for slower and slower improvements in population health. This situation of declining social efficiency confronts all of the wealthy nations. But, one thing stands out in the comparisons we have made. The health of Americans is not as good as that of our European counterparts, and we are paying considerably more for medical care. The problems of medical technology and aging of the population are very much the same between Europe and the United States. So, why is the United States so different? To understand why different societies facing the same types of problems produce different performances, we need to look at social organization. That is, we need to look for differences in how societies organize themselves to go about solving similar problems.

One possible answer to the question of the lower social efficiency of American medicine could be that Americans simply spend too much on medical care. They go to the doctor too often for problems that don't absolutely require medical treatment, and they go to the hospital for problems that don't really need hospitalization. If this were true, then the reason for the higher relative cost of medical care in the United States would be "excess demand" leading to higher levels of consumption of medical services in the United States than elsewhere. But, this does not seem to be the answer. Among the seven nations we have been comparing, the United States has the fewest hospital beds and physicians per capita (though the differences among the nations are not very large). So the answer does not seem to be that Americans consume too much medical care.

The more likely answer is that the United States somehow does a poorer job than its European counterparts in making socially efficient choices about which people are to receive what kinds of care. Efficiency in medical care service delivery comes from delivering the services that do the most good in terms of population health per dollar spent. Where possible, this means delivering basic services that prevent or cure life-threatening and disabling conditions inexpensively to the people most at risk for health problems.

This is where the question of medical insurance arises, because who pays the bill determines what services are available to which people. In Figure 5.5, we can see that the United States is very different from European countries in who pays for medical care. In Figure 5.6, we can see how the situation in the United States has been changing rapidly.

It may surprise most people living in the United States to learn that over 40 percent of the bill for medical care is paid by government—mostly through Medicare (primarily medical insurance for older or chronically disabled Americans) and Medicaid (primarily medical insurance for people with low incomes). But, compared to the European countries, private out-of-pocket payments and private insurance are higher in the United States. In most other wealthy nations, about three quarters of the costs of medical care are paid by government—almost twice as much as in the United States. In 1960, over half of the medical expenditures in the United States came directly from individuals and families. By 1990, only 21.7 percent of the bill was paid directly, and almost 80 percent was paid by insurance, either governmental or private. To understand who gets what medical care in the United States, and why the United States appears to make socially inefficient choices in medical care, we need to understand medical insurance.

PAYING THE BILL AND MAKING CHOICES: "SHE OR HE WHO PAYS THE PIPER, CALLS THE TUNE"

In 1992, we spent an average of $3,094 on medical care for each man, woman, and child in the United States. For a family of four, this amounts to about $12,000; more than one-half the official poverty line. The average cost of spending a day in the hospital that same year approached

FIGURE 5.5: Shares of Medical Expenditure, 1991

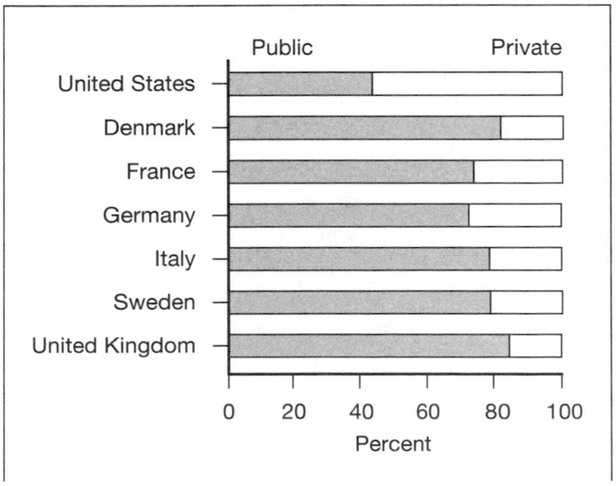

SOURCE: *Statistical Abstract of the United States, 1993.*

FIGURE 5.6: U.S. Medical Expenditure by Source

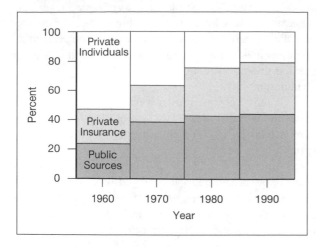

SOURCE: *Statistical Abstract of the United States, 1993.*

$1,000 (U.S. Bureau of the Census, 1993). Without adequate medical insurance, a major accident, illness, or chronic disability is a financial disaster that can place a severe strain on any family. Of course, these figures are only averages. Most young people and people who did not have insurance or high incomes spent less; many people who were older, had the misfortunes of chronic disability, severe accidents or illnesses, and who had good medical insurance spent a great deal more.

Medicare insurance pays much of the bill for older and chronically disabled Americans, who are major consumers of medical care. Medicaid pays much of the bill for persons and families receiving welfare. Persons who do not fall in these categories rely on private medical insurance (usually provided through an employer) and on payments out of pocket. As our population ages and the technology of medicine continues to increase, the costs of Medicare have increased and can be expected to continue to do so. Throughout the 1980s the proportion of families living in poverty (and particularly families with young children) in the United States increased, increasing the costs of Medicaid.

For those "in the middle" who rely on private insurance, the 1980s and early 1990s have been a difficult time. Large employers have cut back on middle management and permanent employees—in part to avoid the high cost of providing medical insurance. Small employers, particularly in the rapidly growing service industries, provide either limited or no medical benefits. As a result, the proportion of Americans who have no medical insurance (public or private) has been rising rapidly. In 1987, about 31 million Americans (12.9 percent of the population) had no insurance; by 1993, nearly 40 million persons (15.3 percent) had no coverage (U.S. Bureau of the Census, 1993). These Americans at risk of catastrophic medical costs are more likely to be younger working families with children. Those at risk are also disproportionately composed of the less-well-educated and ethnic minorities who are less likely to have permanent and stable employment that provides medical insurance coverage. These patterns of allocation of medical coverage have consequences for the social efficiency of medical care delivery: getting the largest amount of the kinds of care that preserve life to the people who need it most.

Good medical insurance for older Americans means that they are able to make effective demand on the delivery system. However, the medical conditions of older persons are more likely to be chronic, and difficult and expensive to treat. While effective treatment of age-related conditions may have very important effects on the quality of life, it does not result in dramatic improvements in the length of life. Therefore, these high and rapidly growing expenditures for medical treatment of the aged are reducing the social efficiency of American medicine. But the aged are a growing and politically powerful group, and reform of Medicare will be difficult. Changing the prevailing pattern of treatment for the aged, such as rationing health care, is also a difficult moral issue that raises fundamental questions about our social values.

Government medical insurance for those in poverty clearly does provide services where it is most efficiently consumed: to younger persons, and particularly women and children who are at greater risk for medical problems because of their poverty. However, medical treatment of persons in poverty is severely limited, and it cannot solve the problems of poor education, poor nutrition, and dangerous living conditions. In contrast to the aged, the poor are a politically weak group. Efforts to balance budgets and reduce the size of the government have slowed the growth of Medicaid expenditures, and even further cuts in Medicaid are a possibility in the coming years. But reducing medical aid for the poor may be socially inefficient; the poor are mostly young (almost 30 percent of all children are raised in poverty) and expenditures on the young and poor can improve the overall health of the population at relatively low cost.

Ironically, our best medical insurance coverage (plans provided by private employers) assures that the best and most services are available to those who need them least: persons who have reasonably well-paying jobs, have relatively secure incomes, are well educated and middle aged, and who have lower levels of severe medical problems. Those who fall in the middle—who do not have good jobs but are not officially in poverty—have limited access to either governmental or private insurance. As a result, they consume less medical care than they need. The burden of this inadequate care falls on relatively younger persons and children, where good care can cure effectively and cheaply, and prevent long-term disability. Absence of any medical insurance for this growing group of Americans is also socially inefficient in that failure to provide preventive care will result in even greater and more costly demands on the Medicare system over time.

LOOKING FOR ANSWERS

Are American medical care institutions "in crisis"? The answer depends on your perspective. American medicine is among the most technologically advanced in the world and offers remarkable choice and resources to those who can afford it. Yet the trends we have discovered and the comparisons we have made are quite disturbing: American medicine is much more expensive than European systems, and produces little difference in overall societal health. We have seen that the main reason for this is that our medical institutions do a relatively poor job of allocating the most beneficial kinds of care to the people who most need them. The total cost of the system is increasing rapidly with technology and the aging of the population; these increasing costs are leaving more and more middle- and working-class Americans without effective access to medical treatment.

Policy makers in the medical industry and government are searching for answers, and many changes are already occurring that are fundamentally transforming medical institutions in the United States. Government-sponsored medical insurance for the aged and disabled has been one of the most rapid areas of growth in medical expenditure. Attempts are being made to control these cost increases in a number of ways. Insurance premiums charged to covered persons have been increased, and there are proposals to make the benefits received by the insured subject to income taxation. The goal of this plan is to place a greater cost burden on those among the aged and disabled who have high enough incomes to pay more. Government-sponsored medical care and medical insurance for the poor has also been an area of rapid growth in expenditure (Hollingsworth, Hage, and Hanneman, 1990). Here too, efforts are being made to control costs—primarily by limiting the availability of services and making it more difficult to qualify to receive coverage. Private employers are also acting to hold down costs indirectly by providing limited or no medical benefits for temporary and part-time workers, and by excluding from coverage "preexisting" medical conditions (i.e., medical problems that existed when an employee changes jobs).

Both government and industry have moved toward *managed care* and *health maintenance organizations* (HMOs) as a way of organizing medical coverage. These types of plans make specific contracts about what insurance will pay for specific services, and they place restrictions and conditions on certain expensive types of treatments. HMO plans pay the medical care providers specific amounts per person per year, rather than the actual costs of treatments delivered. As a result, the organizations that deliver medical treatments have strong financial incentives to emphasize preventive and basic medical services, and to de-emphasize expensive specialty care.

These changes in who pays the bill and how they do it are rapidly changing the way that medical care is organized in the United States. Hospital-based high-technology care based on the use of specialist physicians is becoming a smaller part of our medical care delivery system. Hospitals are increasingly becoming parts of large "chains" managed by medical care corporations. Fewer and fewer physicians operate in private practice, and more and more are basically employees of HMOs and medical corporations. As a result, American consumers of medical care often find that they have fewer choices about their medical treatment and physician. Maintaining access to medical insurance can also be a deciding factor when people compare employment opportunities.

Whether the changes that are already occurring will solve the "crisis" in American medical care institutions is far from certain. What is certain is that changes will continue to occur. You have an important role to play in the direction that these changes take through your choices as a consumer of medical care and as a politically active citizen. The choices that you make are important, because it is "your money or your life."

REFERENCES

HOLLINGSWORTH, J. ROGERS, JERALD HAGE, and ROBERT A. HANNEMAN
1990 *State Intervention in Medical Care: Consequences for Britain, France, Sweden, and the United States, 1890–1970.* Ithaca, NY: Cornell University Press.

U.S. BUREAU OF THE CENSUS
1993 *Statistical Abstract of the United States: 1993.* Washington, DC: U.S. Government Printing Office.

EXERCISE 5

Name _____   Date _____

ID # _____   Class Time _____

I. The essay makes a number of factual claims about how American medicine is changing. A researcher should always check the facts before arriving at a conclusion. Your task is to go to the library and check a few facts. The essay claims that American medical care is becoming less based on hospitals and specialists, and that there is less emphasis on medical research than there was a decade ago. Locate information in the *Statistical Abstract of the United States* for a recent year to see if these claims are true. Summarize what you find in the spaces provided below.

    A. According to the *Statistical Abstract of the United States,* how has the proportion of American physicians who provide general practice or family practice in office-based practice been changing? Attach a photocopy of the table you used to reach a conclusion.

    B. Is the number of hospitals in the United States increasing or decreasing? Are expenditures for medical research as a share of all medical expenditures increasing or decreasing? Attach photocopies of the tables you used to answer these questions.

    C. The essay makes claims about the kinds of people who are most "at risk" for not having medical insurance. In the space below explain what kinds of people are least likely to have medical insurance. Attach photocopies of the tables in the *Statistical Abstract of the United States* you used to answer the question.

D. The essay claims that health maintenance organizations (HMOs) are growing rapidly as a way of providing managed care. In the space below explain whether this is true. Attach photocopies of the tables in the *Statistical Abstract of the United States* you used to answer the question.

E. What kinds of ethical dilemmas does the talk of efficiency raise? Discuss these briefly in the space provided below.

6

Aging and Health Care

Jan W. Weaver and Stanley R. Ingman

Americans are more concerned than ever before about the nation's health care system due to the shift in the age and health characteristics of the U.S. population. Since the beginning of the century, the older population has become a larger and more influential segment of American society. As a result of this shift, the current system is under strain, and Americans are questioning the availability and quality of future health care and social services.

SHIFTS IN THE U.S. POPULATION

Demographic Characteristics. The United States contains the second largest population of people age 65+ in the world, numbering 31.6 million individuals (U.S. Bureau of the Census, 1987). Since 1900, a shift in the proportion of older and younger individuals has occurred in the United States. At the beginning of the twentieth century, 4.1 percent of the total U.S. population was 65 and older and 40 percent of the population was comprised of people under age 18. By 1990, the elderly[1] comprised 12.6 percent of the total population, or one in eight Americans, while the percentage of young people[2] decreased to 28 percent (U.S. Bureau of the Census, 1992). Between 1990 and 2030, the 65+ population will double; the 85+ population, as the fastest growing age group, will triple in size (see Figure 6.1). Due to the aging of the "baby boomers" and people living longer, there will be proportionately more elderly than young people in the population by the year 2030.

Between 1946 and 1964, the United States experienced the highest birth rates in its history. The large number of people born during those years will be 65 years old between 2011 and 2029. The population not only will contain a greater proportion of older people but also will be comprised of more older people living longer. However, not all of the years a person lives will be active and independent ones. Figure 6.2 displays the proportion of the life

cycle during which a person might expect functional dependency.

In 1990, 14 percent of the 65+ population was comprised of minorities. Although nonwhite and Hispanic populations currently have a smaller proportion of elderly than the white population, the older minority population is expected to increase more rapidly in the twenty-first century than the older white population. Between 1990 and 2030, the older white population will grow by 92 percent, compared with a growth of 247 percent for the older black population and people of other races and 395 percent for older Hispanics. However, in 2030 the proportion of the white population that is elderly will remain higher than the proportion of the population that is elderly for blacks and Hispanics (see Figure 6.3). Although the diversity of the population has come to be recognized as a national strength, health care programs in the United States are characterized by unacceptable disparities linked to racial and ethnic groups (U.S. Department of Health and Human Services, 1990; see also U.S. Department of Health and Human Services, 1985).

One compelling disparity in health care for older people relates to socioeconomic status. In 1989, 11.4 percent of people over 65 were below the poverty level. The poverty rate of the oldest old (people who are 85+) was 18.4 percent in 1989—more than twice the 8.8 percent rate of the young old (ages 65–74) (U.S. Bureau of the Census, 1990). Women are substantially more likely to be poor than men; only 7.8 percent of men age 65+ are below the poverty level, compared with 14 percent of the women. Poverty rates are also higher for people not living in families. Change in marital status, particularly due to the death of a spouse, is an important reason contributing to differences in income among the elderly. More than half of the population age 65 to 74 is married, while nearly three quarters of those age 85+ are widowed (U.S. Bureau of the Census, 1990). The greater the accumulation of these factors (age, gender, race/ethnicity, and living

FIGURE 6.1: Percent of Persons Younger than 18 and Older than 65 in the Population: 1900 and 2030

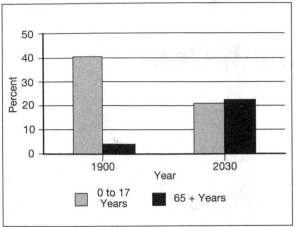

SOURCE: U.S. Department of Health and Human Services. (1991a). *Aging America: Trends and Projections.* DHHS Publication No. (FcoA) 91-28001. Washington, DC: USDHHS.

FIGURE 6.3: Percentage of Persons 65+ by Race and Hispanic Origin: 1989 and 2030

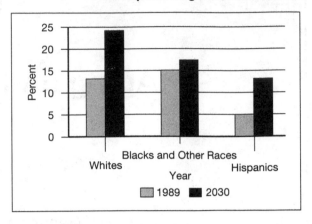

SOURCE: U.S. Department of Health and Human Services. (1991a). *Aging America: Trends and Projections.* DHHS Publication No. (FcoA) 91-28001. Washington, DC: USDHHS.

arrangements), the greater the risk of poverty. As shown in Figure 6.4, poverty rates are much higher among minority elderly than among white elderly, and higher among people who are not living in families. The highest poverty rates are among elderly black women living alone; three of every five have incomes below the poverty level.

Health Status. In addition to the change in the age of the U.S. population from young to old, the types of diseases people experience have also shifted during the twentieth century. Whereas acute conditions (i.e., diseases and illnesses that have a short duration) were prevalent at

the beginning of the century, chronic conditions resulting in long-term impairment or disability are now the predominant health problem for older individuals. The leading chronic conditions for the elderly in 1989 were arthritis, hypertension, hearing impairments, and heart disease (USDHHS, 1991a: 112). Since chronic conditions lead to disabilities and functional impairment, a sharp rise is expected in the number of frail elderly in need of institutional and community-based care in conjunction with the upcoming changes in the size and characteristics of the older population.

Disability associated with chronic conditions is

FIGURE 6.2: Years of Healthy Life as a Proportion of Life Expectancy in the U.S. Population (1980)

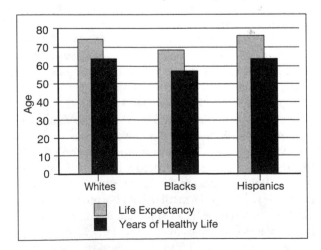

SOURCE: U.S. Department of Health and Human Services. (1990). *Healthy People 2000: National Health Promotion and Disease Prevention Objectives.* DHHS Publication No. (PHS) 91-50212. Washington, DC: U.S. Government Printing Office.

FIGURE 6.4: Percent of Elderly Below the Poverty Level, by Select Characteristics

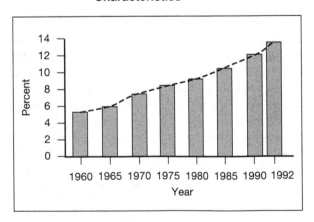

SOURCE: U.S. Bureau of the Census. (1990). Money income and poverty status in the United States: 1989. *Current Population Reports,* Series P-60, No. 168.

measured by determining limitations in major activities, activities of daily living, and instrumental activities of daily living. The role of perceived health is also an important factor since knowledge of underlying disease, recognition of physical disabilities, and awareness of functional limitation all negatively affect individuals' perceptions of their health status (Johnson and Wolinsky, 1994: 26–27). Since some individuals adapt better than others to chronic health problems and associated limitations, the relationship between disability and functional limitation is variable.

Older people are diverse in health and chronic conditions. The majority of elderly (71 percent) view their health as excellent or good (National Center for Health Statistics, 1990). People 65 and older tend to take better care of their health than the nonelderly. Although they exercise less, the elderly are not as likely as the nonelderly to smoke, be overweight, drink, or report that stress has adversely affected their health (USDHHS, 1991b).

The growth in the number of older persons with functional difficulties will have a dramatic impact on health care and social services in coming years. In 1988, 22.6 percent of people over 65 suffered a limitation in major activity. The 1987 National Medical Expenditure Survey (NMES) identified 19.5 percent of the noninstitutionalized population over the age of 65 that reported either ADL (activities of daily living) or IADL (independence in activities of daily living) limitations. The likelihood of suffering a chronic condition increases rapidly with advanced age. While 5.9 percent of all persons aged 65 to 69 experience difficulty with at least one ADL, 34.5 percent of those 85 and older have ADL limitations (Leon and Lair, 1990: 8). Gender differences are significant for all areas of functional status and increase with advancing age. Consistently higher proportions of women have ADL limitations in all age groups (Leon and Lair, 1990: 8). Fewer elderly who live with a spouse have ADL/IADL limitations when compared to those who live alone or with other relatives. Almost 8 percent of the elderly living with a spouse experience one or more ADL limitations, compared with 13.3 percent of those who lived alone and 15.6 percent of those who live with other relatives (Leon and Lair, 1990: 10).

SHIFTS IN POLICY AND PRACTICE

Care for the elderly in the United States has taken a slow start in comparison to other countries with comparable levels of socioeconomic development. Social Security was not established until 1935, and Medicare, Medicaid, and the Older Americans Act did not appear until the 1960s. In comparison to the limited social support, income, and services provided for the elderly in the United States, countries such as Sweden, Denmark, and Holland have a long history of providing high levels of income support, medical care, sheltered housing in a variety of forms, and social services designed to prevent social isolation for their older citizens (Gill and Ingman, 1994: 1).

Medicare and Medicaid. With the advent of Medicare in 1965, persons 65 and older experienced improved access to medical care and hospitalization. Medicare is a federal health insurance program for the aging that is divided into two basic components: Part A, hospital insurance, and Part B, supplemental medical insurance. Part A pays for hospital care and for restricted amounts of skilled nursing care and home health care. All individuals who are eligible for Social Security benefits are automatically eligible for Medicare, Part A. Part B, the supplemental medical insurance portion of Medicare, covers physician services, hospital outpatient services, additional home health care, diagnostic laboratory and X-ray services, and a variety of miscellaneous services. All individuals who are eligible for Part A are also eligible for Part B by paying a monthly premium.

A number of disadvantages associated with the costs and benefits of the Medicare system persist. Several important health expenses are either excluded or given limited support by Medicare. Social services and most community-based care services (e.g., adult day care and respite care) are not covered, and the eligibility requirements on home care strictly limits its accessibility. Prescription drugs are also excluded, requiring many elderly persons to pay substantially for their medications. Additional excluded services include eyeglasses, hearing aids, dentures, and routine dental care (Lammers, 1983).

In addition to limited coverage, the cost of Medicare, for both the government and the consumer, has not been contained. Medicare costs continue to escalate, and the share of the gross domestic product (GDP) allocated to health care continues to rise. In 1990, 12.2 percent of the GDP ($666 billion) was spent on health care, with the elderly population averaging more than three times the annual medical expenditures of persons less than age 65 (USDHHS, 1991b). Although approximately 70 percent of those on Medicare also have supplemental private insurance policies, the elderly spent $67 billion out-of-pocket for health care in 1991 (Rubin and Koelln, 1993).

Hospital discharge practices thrust elderly persons back into the community sicker and poorer than they were previously. The Prospective Payment System (PPS), implemented in 1984, has resulted in earlier hospital discharge and sub-acute care by nursing homes and community care agencies. Long-term and community-based care systems are burdened with an increasing demand for services and an increase in the number of elderly requiring care (Estes and Swan, 1993).

The Medicaid program, enacted by Congress in 1965, represented a major expansion in federal contributions to the states for the provision of health care to needy persons of all ages. Individuals whose income and assets are below a designated level established by the federal government are eligible for Medicaid. They are also eligible for Supplemental Security Income (SSI), a means-tested cash assistance program, and for in-kind programs such as food stamps and subsidized housing (Browne and Olson, 1983). Under Medicaid, the states are responsible for providing numerous services, including inpatient services, outpatient hospital services, physician care, X-ray and laboratory services, nursing home care, and optional services (Lammers, 1983: 149). Consequently, access to long-term and community-based care has improved, but individuals must either already meet poverty level criteria or "spend down" their resources in order to qualify.

Older Americans Act. The Older Americans Act (OAA) of 1965 and its Comprehensive Service Amendments of 1973 and 1978 represent an attempt to establish a system of coordinated social services for elderly citizens (Browne and Olson, 1983). The act created the Administration on Aging (AoA), which serves as a national focal point for the needs and concerns of the older population. The AoA's functions include the dissemination of information and technical assistance, and the distribution of grants to states and organizations for more effective utilization of available resources on behalf of the elderly. The OAA involves the aging network[3] which includes the AoA, state aging commissions, and area agencies on aging.

Aging activities within each state are presented in the state's annual aging plan. The plan includes a series of commitments for the aging network within the state to respond to the needs of older citizens. The state unit on aging serves as a management linkage between the AoA and the area agencies and assists in prioritizing and coordinating the state aging plan. The state unit is also responsible for facilitating the flow of fiscal and program resources to the area agencies (Browne and Olson, 1983: 211).

Alternative Care Trends. The future direction of aging policy is being influenced not only by shifts in the size and demographic characteristics of the elderly population but also by the nation's economic status. Existing programs have improved the living conditions and health status of older Americans through retirement income security, health care, and social services. However, considerations of cost, rather than concern for improving quality of life, will most likely influence future policy choices (Browne and Olson, 1983; Estes and Swan, 1993; Gill and Ingman, 1994). Public support for aging programs is being debated around such issues as the sustainability of the Social Security system and the economic consequences of government funding for various services. Future policy decisions will most likely reduce or eliminate benefits of existing programs and emphasize the need to direct limited resources to older persons with demonstrable needs (Browne and Olson, 1983). Service providers and policy makers, meantime, will need to continue to develop improvements in the efficiency and organizational methods of providing care. Strategies will include coordinating the delivery of care and applying cost-sharing formulas for individuals who can afford to pay.

INNOVATIVE PRACTICE MODELS

A number of programs and systems have developed in the United States that serve as models for quality elder care provisions. These programs are designed to promote health and/or prevent disease or impairment at lower costs. The quality of life for frail older adults is related to what has been called a "trinity" of factors: housing, income, and good health (Billings, 1982: 4). Studies indicate that "the quality of life for elderly people who remain in the community and receive care is better than for those who enter long-term care facilities" (Billings, 1982).

Housing is a key factor in the quality of life for older people since "it provides a secure and meaningful old age or magnifies the disability and isolation that too often accompany advanced years" (Redfoot and Gaberlavage, 1991: 35). Chronic health problems or disabilities are often exacerbated by substandard housing conditions and inadequate services combined with limited income (Billings, 1982: 4). A number of housing options are available for older people in the United States, including public housing, rent supplements, mortgage assistance, and special programs such as Community Development Block Grants for neighborhood preservation.

Older people sometimes require support services[4] within a continuum of care to remain in their homes and communities. Public housing is available in a number of forms, including single dwelling units and multiple-unit structures that provide independent living, assisted living, or congregate living opportunities. Case management or care coordination is often used to determine the support services necessary to assist the person. Case management involves two basic ideas: (1) multidisciplinary involvement and a holistic approach toward meeting the client's needs, and (2) a capacity for obtaining the entire range of services that might be needed by persons with multiple problems (Lammers, 1983).

The On Lok program in San Francisco, Connecticut Community Care, Inc., and the Community Systems Development Project in Oklahoma provide three examples among many of innovative programs in the United States that have made significant advances toward cost effectively meeting the needs of the older population.

On Lok. On Lok Senior Health Services[5] was formed in 1971 in response to community concern for the frail elderly of San Francisco's Chinatown, North Beach, and Polk Gulch neighborhoods. On Lok began as a daytime health center where seniors could receive health care, social services, and hot meals. In 1979, On Lok launched a Medicare-funded demonstration of the consolidated model of long-term care in which a multidisciplinary team formulates, coordinates, and provides all medical care and social services required by its participants. Since 1983, On Lok has had Medicare and Medicaid funding that allows complete care provisions to participants who are eligible for nursing home care. Services include day health care, primary medical care, transportation, meals, recreational therapy, social services, physical and occupational therapy, and in-home services. In addition, acute hospital and nursing home care, laboratory services, pharmacy, specialized services (e.g., optometry, audiology, dentistry, podiatry, and psychiatry), and medical specialty services (e.g., cardiology, radiology, neurology, etc.) are provided under contract.

Connecticut Community Care, Inc. Connecticut Community Care, Inc.[6] evolved from the Triage demonstration project of the 1970s that was designed to test the concept of a cost-effective, single-entry system for the provision of community-based health and social services for the elderly. Project Triage was formed in Connecticut in 1974 to assist its clients in gaining a range of homemaker, nutrition, and chore services through a single agency, thus avoiding multiple agencies and rigid federal requirements (Quinn, 1979). Triage and other demonstration projects experimented with different case management models (e.g., broker, service management, and managed-care models) as a means of developing plans of care and delivery of services. The lessons learned from the Triage demonstration resulted in an upgraded long-term care delivery system that has shown evidence of increased life-quality benefits for the persons receiving care (Quinn, 1993).

Community Systems Development Project of Oklahoma. The Community Systems Development Project,[7] a health reform initiative of the state of Oklahoma, began its development in 1990. The project was implemented as a community coalition by the Aging Services Division of the Department of Human Services and the Long-Term Care Authority of Tulsa, formed in 1988 as the only public authority in the nation created specifically to address long-term care. The objectives of the project include the development of a model long-term care system, which, when integrated with acute care, will provide comprehensive health care. State, county, and municipal governments are involved with local community representatives in Tulsa to develop a long-term care system similar to those in Germany, Sweden, and Switzerland. The project is expected to take eight to ten years to complete. Accomplishments thus far include the establishment of a community coalition comprised of consumers, service providers, advocates, and funders; the development of the project's strategic plan; and the implementation of a Home and Community Based Services (HCBS) Medicaid waiver in Tulsa. The project will incorporate federal waivers and demonstration projects to test managed care, continuous quality improvement, and local administration of services. Although the project is being developed in Tulsa, the goal is to develop a statewide system of quality, cost-effective long-term care services (Karns, 1992).

CONCLUSION

Care for the elderly, particularly the frail elderly with long-term care needs, will continue on an arduous course as the size of the older population expands and the cost of providing health care and social services escalates in the twenty-first century. Creators of a long-term care system designed to meet the demands of the next century are faced with a health care industry focused on acute rather than chronic care and reimbursement that favors institutional rather than community-based care. As a result, services are fragmented, uncoordinated, and often nonexistent in many communities, and family budgets and emotions are seriously strained due to caregiving responsibilities.

The solutions for the next century must cost less, link services to assure that needs are being met, and maintain or enhance the quality of older persons' lives. Managed care, such as health maintenance organizations (HMOs) or preferred provider organizations (PPOs), is currently developing as a model for the delivery of long-term care in the twenty-first century. Managed care refers to an insurance plan that uses prospective financing to purchase services for clients based on a thorough needs assessment and an efficient plan of care. The model is designed to improve the individual's continuity and quality of care while simultaneously controlling costs. Yet several concerns arise about the managed care system. Overall costs could increase if community-based services are extended to more users, and the quality of care could diminish since the liability for excess costs is placed on the providers. Research and policy debate must continue to assure an affordable and accessible long-term care system that effectively meets the needs of the aging population.

NOTES

1. Throughout this chapter, the terms "elderly," "older individuals," "older population," and the like refer to persons 65 and older.

2. Young people are defined throughout this paper as individuals 18 and under.

3. The term "aging network" refers to the totality of agencies, organizations, interest groups, service providers, and management and professional staff that is broadly concerned with aging policy, services, and program development.

4. Examples of support services include a range of nutrition programs, homemaker and chore services, adult day care, and home health care.

5. On Lok Senior Health Services, 1441 Powell Street, San Francisco, California 94133, (415) 989–2578.

6. Connecticut Community Care, Inc., 43 Enterprise Drive, Bristol, Connecticut 06010, (203) 589–6226.

7. Community Systems Development Project, Oklahoma Department of Human Services, Aging Services Division, P.O. Box 25352, Oklahoma City, Oklahoma 73125–0352, (405) 521–2281.

REFERENCES

BILLINGS, GLORIA
1982   "Alternatives to Nursing Home Care," *Aging* (March–April): 2–11.

Browne, W. P. and L. K. Olson, eds.
1983 *Aging and Public Policy: The Politics of Growing Old in America*. Westport, CT: Greenwood Press.

Estes, C. L. and J. H. Swan
1993 *The Long Term Care Crisis: Elders Trapped in the No-Care Zone*. Newbury Park, CA: Sage.

Gill, D. G. and S. R. Ingman, eds.
1994 *Eldercare, Distributive Justice, and the Welfare State: Retrenchment or Expansion*. Albany, NY: State University of New York Press.

Johnson, R. J. and F. D. Wolinsky
1994 "Gender, Race, and Health: The Structure of Health Status Among Older Adults," *The Gerontologist* 34 (1): 24–35.

Karns, D. S.
1992 "Tulsa Shapes 'Best Practices' for Oklahoma LTC Reform," *Networks* (October 16). Washington, DC: National Council on the Aging.

Lammers, W. W.
1983 *Public Policy and the Aging*. Washington, DC: CQ Press.

Leon, J. and T. Lair
1990 *Functional Status of the Noninstitutionalized Elderly: Estimates of ADL and IADL Difficulties*. (DHHS Publication No. [PHS] 90–3462). National Medical Expenditure Survey Research Findings 4, Agency for Health Care Policy and Research. Rockville, MD: Public Health Service.

National Center for Health Statistics
1990 *Current Estimates from the National Health Interview Survey, 1989*. Vital and Health Statistics, Series 10, No. 176.

Quinn, J.
1979 *Triage, Inc.: An Alternative Approach to Care for the Elderly, 1974–1979*. Hartford, CT: Connecticut Department on Aging.

Quinn, J.
1993 *Successful Case Management in Long-Term Care*. New York: Springer.

Redfoot, D. and G. Gaberlavage
1991 "Housing for Older Americans: Sustaining the Dream," *Generations* (Summer–Fall): 35–38.

Rubin, R. M. and K. Koelln
1993 "Determinants of Household Out-of-Pocket Health Expenditures," *Social Science Quarterly* 74 (4).

U.S. Bureau of the Census
1987 *An Aging World*. International population reports, Series P-95, No. 78.

U.S. Bureau of the Census
1990 *Money Income and Poverty Status in the United States: 1989*. Current Population Reports, Series P-60, No. 168.

U.S. Bureau of the Census
1992 *Statistical Abstract of the United States: 1992*. Washington, DC: U.S. Government Printing Office.

U.S. Department of Health and Human Services
1985 *Report of the Secretary's Task Force on Black and Minority Health*. Washington, DC: USDHHS.

U.S. Department of Health and Human Services
1990 *Healthy People 2000: National Health Promotion and Disease Prevention Objectives*. DHHS Publication No. (PHS) 91–50212. Washington, DC: U.S. Government Printing Office.

U.S. Department of Health and Human Services
1991a *Aging America: Trends and Projections*. DHHS Publication No. (FcoA) 91–28001. Washington, DC: USDHHS.

U.S. Department of Health and Human Services
1991b *Health Insurance, Use of Health Services, and Health Care Expenditures*. National Medical Expenditure Survey, Research Findings, 12 (December): 2–18.

EXERCISE 6

Name _____   Date _____

ID # _____   Class Time _____

I. This exercise involves interviews with two elderly persons.

    A. Using the following questionnaire, interview the first elderly person to determine his or her health and social problems and needs. Indicate the answers below.

       1. How old are you?

       2. Who lives with you?

       3. Do you have any health problems? If so, what are they?

       4. Do you have difficulty performing any of the following activities without help?

____ Heavy housework	____ Go shopping
____ Light housework	____ Prepare meals
____ Walk	____ Take a bath

       5. Do you consider yourself to be in excellent, good, fair, or poor health?

       6. How is your hearing?

       7. Do you take any medications? If so, what are they for?

       8. Who do you call if you need help?

       9. Do you have any income in addition to your monthly social security check? Please explain.

     10. Do you have a Medicare supplemental insurance policy?

     11. Do you ever have trouble paying your medical expenses (e.g., hospital or doctor bills) that Medicare does not pay? How about paying for prescription medicines? Please explain.

     12. Are you a member of an HMO or a PPO? If so, do you find it helpful or does it cause problems? Please explain.

    B. Using the following questionnaire, interview a second elderly person to determine his or her health and social problems and needs.

       1. How old are you?

       2. Who lives with you?

       3. Do you have any health problems? If so, what are they?

       4. Do you have difficulty performing any of the following activities without help?

____ Heavy housework	____ Go shopping
____ Light housework	____ Prepare meals
____ Walk	____ Take a bath

5. Do you consider yourself to be in excellent, good, fair, or poor health?

6. How is your hearing?

7. Do you take any medications? If so, what are they for?

8. Who do you call if you need help?

9. Do you have any income in addition to your monthly social security check? Please explain.

10. Do you have a Medicare supplemental insurance policy?

11. Do you ever have trouble paying your medical expenses (e.g., hospital or doctor bills) that Medicare does not pay? How about paying for prescription medicines? Please explain.

12. Are you a member of an HMO or a PPO? If so, do you find it helpful or does it cause problems? Please explain.

II. Based on the interview data you collected, answer the following questions.

A. Briefly describe any health problems reported by the persons you interviewed.

B. Did you identify any social problems or needs? For example, do the people have adequate family support and income to assure their safety and well-being?

C. How do the people you interviewed perceive their health and socioeconomic status? Does their perceived health seem to coincide with your observations? Explain.

D. Do you think the people's health care and social service needs are being met? Are they receiving adequate medical care? Can you think of any social services that might benefit the people you interviewed? Explain.

E. Do the people you interviewed have supplemental Medicare coverage? If so, is it an HMO or a PPO? Do they seem to understand the HMO/PPO concept? Explain.

Name _____   Date _____

ID # _____   Class Time _____

III. Identify health care and social service organizations in your community that serve the elderly, and answer the following questions.

    A. List the names of the organizations below.

    B. Does your community have the following services available to assist older citizens? Check all that apply.

____ Home care	____ Home health care
____ Home-delivered meals	____ Errand services
____ Adult day care	____ In-home assistance with personal care
____ Senior companion program	____ Information and referral
____ Medical transportation	____ Curb to curb passenger-assisted transportation
____ Health promotion/education	
____ Other (describe):	

    C. Do you consider any services that are *not* available in your community necessary or unnecessary? Explain.

7

The Problems of U.S. Workers in a Restructuring Global Economy

Ramona Ford

In many ways, the position of the working class in the United States has improved since the early decades of this century. The changing role of the United States in the global economy, however, has brought new problems for U.S. workers. Those in the working class were once hopeful that they or their children would eventually join the middle class. Today they merely hope to avoid "losing ground." The declining position of U.S. workers is particularly notable compared to the position of workers in other industrialized countries. For example, income inequality in the United States today is the greatest among all industrial nations with the exception of Australia (U.N., 1994). Second, because we lack universal health care and extensive safety-net programs that are common among other industrial nations, health care indicators (e.g., longevity, infant and maternal mortality) reveal that our nation is one of the most unhealthy in the industrialized world. Our health problems are compounded by the lack of quality affordable day care, parental leave with pay, apprenticeships for youth, and child support programs, which are found in other industrial nations (Freeman, 1994). What is more, the threat of job loss and poverty accompanying the declining incomes in the middle and lower classes are affecting people's perceptions of the quality of life (Newman, 1993). Even some mainstream economists are beginning to project the possible negative long-run effects of a declining middle class and a growing group of unemployed and underemployed (Bernstein, 1994).

Technology has dramatically changed the organization of work since the early 1970s. The effects of this restructuring have not been evenly felt across social classes but have instead resulted in increased economic concentration. Today the top 1 percent of the U.S. population still owns approximately 37 percent of the nation's wealth—stocks, bonds, plant and equipment, etc. About two thirds of the nation's wealth is still controlled by the top 10 percent of the population. The overall U.S. economy is growing slowly, but real wages (i.e., the wage rate minus inflation) declined 20 percent over the last two decades (Batt and Appelbaum, 1993; Labor Research Association, 1993). The decline in real wages is also felt differently by different groups in the population. For example, real wages for young urban black workers declined by approximately 50 percent (Farrell, 1992). For the population as a whole, average family net worth (homes, cars, savings, investments) fell by 12 percent from the late 1980s through the early 1990s (Moody, 1994).

Except for recession years, job growth in the United States during the 1980s has been healthy with 18 million jobs created. A closer look at these new jobs reveals that most are lower-paying jobs in the service sector (Clark, 1994). Bluestone and Harrison (1987) found that 44 percent of the jobs created between 1979 and 1985 were at or below minimum wage, and only 10 percent paid above $29,000 (a modest family income for 1985). At the same time, millions of well-paid blue-collar jobs and middle management and professional white-collar jobs have been lost in the downsizing of corporate America and the restructuring of the American economy. In the 1980s, for example, there were 3 million jobs lost in the manufacturing sector alone. In a major survey of employers conducted by the American Management Association, more than half the jobs eliminated by the companies surveyed were salaried personnel (Henkoff, 1994). Moreover, the substantial increase in low-wage jobs during the last few years has resulted in an upward turn in the rate of poverty. The consequences of poverty are particularly felt by women, minorities, children, and the very old.

Another employment trend of increasing prominence in the United States involves the growth of the temporary or part-time work force. Sometimes known also as contingency or contract workers, such employees make up one quarter of the work force, and most of these 21 million jobs do not carry health insurance or retirement plans (Hammonds, 1994). Many of the jobs newly created in the 1980s and 1990s were temporary or part-time. For example, nearly 54 percent of newly created jobs in the economic recovery of the early 1990s were part-time positions (Judis, 1994). Moreover, 7 million workers (6 percent of the work force) are multiple job holders according to Department of Labor estimates, as increasing numbers of full-time job holders find it necessary to "moonlight" or work one or more additional part-time jobs in an effort to earn a livable wage (Uchitelle, 1994). The shift from full- to part-time employment in the economy is widespread. Not surprisingly, "temp" agencies now employ nearly 2 million people. Manpower, Inc., which supplies temporary workers, was in fact the country's largest private employer in 1992 with over 600,000 "employees" in the United States alone (Moody, 1994).

Unemployment is also a particular problem for the working class. In the first place, the average rate of unemployment was higher in the 1980s and 1990s than it was in the 1950s and 1960s. The official rate of unemployment as measured in the United States includes as unemployed only those people actively seeking employment within the last four weeks. Excluded from the official rolls of the unemployed are discouraged workers who have given up looking for work all together and those who want more work but are employed only an hour or so a week. The labor force participation rate (e.g., the proportion of the population aged 16 and over that is employed or seeking employment) has declined for men and increased for women—particularly women with infants and children under 18 years of age. An important difference in comparing unemployment in the United States and other industrial nations is that while the official unemployment is somewhat higher in Western European industrial nations, their unemployment compensation and training programs are stronger (Freeman, 1994).

VIEWS OF THE REAL WORLD

How should the conditions facing workers in the United States be interpreted? Broadly speaking, we may distinguish between conservative and liberal approaches to understanding the situation of workers.

The Conservative Approach. The politically conservative ideology generally does not recognize the plight of the worker as especially problematic. Increased unemployment over the past 20 or so years is, for example, the result of a temporary mismatch between technological advances and human capital (worker skills and attitudes). The views of economists Krugman and Lawrence (1994) provide an example of the conservative human-capital argument. They argue that workers have not increased their education, technical skills, and work incentives to keep up with modern technological needs. Social services designed to buffer workers in a bad economy, it is argued, only promote pathological families and disincentives to work (Murray, 1984). The real social problem, if there is one, is the many barriers to free trade in the U.S.

and global economy (such as regulation of industries, tariff barriers, trade unions, taxes on the wealthy, environmental and worker safety laws, etc.). Eliminate such barriers, it is argued, and the market will largely "solve" the unemployment problem in the United States because the unemployed would be motivated to seek job training and employment in firms that paid them attractive wages. In sum, only less interference in the "free market" coupled with fewer social services will solve the so-called "problems of the worker" in the United States.

Many economists have argued that allowing free trade and flow of capital at home and abroad will improve the wealth of nations and, eventually, their working citizens, as corporate profits and the gross national product (GNP) increase. Trade pacts, such as NAFTA (North American Free Trade Agreement), the Uruguay round of GATT (General Agreement of Tariffs and Trade), and the formation of the WTO (World Trade Organization) are necessary and beneficial because they work to reduce or eliminate tariffs and nontariff barriers to free trade. It should come as little surprise that many policy makers in Latin American countries who now advocate the privatization of government-owned industries are economists who were educated in major U.S. universities. In the United States, the dominant approach to economic growth is a version of supply-side economics. Supply-side economists argue that corporations and the wealthy are most able to provide the kinds of investment capital needed to create new jobs for the middle and working classes. Cutting their taxes and relaxing their social and environmental responsibilities will stimulate aggregate economic growth. Conservatives also maintain that labor union and collective bargaining create inefficiencies in markets and within individual firms by hindering their ability to compete effectively in world trade. Moreover, they advocate cutting government spending on most social services because the expenditures reduce investment in businesses and create disincentives to work.

These proved to be influential arguments under the Reagan administration. Tax codes were restructured to lessen the tax burden on corporations and high-income families. Starting with Reagan's destruction of PATCO, the air-traffic controllers union, union "busting" became widespread. Corporations could once again hire permanent replacement workers when workers went out on strike with impunity from the National Labor Relations Board (NLRB). Environmental laws went unenforced, and worker health and safety regulations were relaxed by underfunding the Environmental Protection Agency (EPA) and the Occupational Safety and Health Agency (OSHA) and through the appointment of probusiness agency heads. The minimum wage and social welfare programs, such as Aid to Families with Dependent Children (AFDC), failed to keep pace with inflation. The poverty line—the formula used to measure the "official" level of poverty in the United States—was not revised to fit the changing market basket. The resulting misrepresentation of the actual rate of poverty limited the eligibility of millions of people for various kinds of social services (Corbett, 1993). The first few years of the 1990s saw little change in policy and practice, even under less ideologically driven administrations.

The Liberal Approach. The liberal, or social democratic, view is that worsening conditions of workers *is* a problem. Economists such as Bernstein and Mishel (1994), Barnet and Cavanaugh (1994), Freeman (1994), MacEwan (1994), and Kuttner (1989, 1994) argue that the working class cannot wait for the benefits of economic growth to "trickle down." The changing structure of the economy, compounded by Reaganomics in practice, is quickly eroding the few political and economic gains working and middle classes have won in previous decades. Tax incentives for corporations that earn profits on foreign investments, the erosion of occupational safety and environmental law, and the decline of unions have only increased the economic and political power of those who own capital. The liberal solution is investment in human capital, such as universal health coverage, a greater supply of affordable housing and quality affordable day care, and more investment in education. They advocate dissipating economic power by backing small business startups and more employee ownership of corporations. Cooperation between the government and industry in consumer-oriented research and development and the sensible conversion of defense industries to consumer and industrial products would ameliorate many of the side effects of the end of the Cold War.

Liberals use European countries for models of successful business-labor-government partnerships that might be adapted effectively to the United States scene. Parliamentary forms of governance, for example, have allowed for many political parties backed by blue- and white-collar labor to compete openly in elections for political office. In addition, voting occurs on weekends rather than regular working days. Consequently, the electoral process is more open and voter participation rates are consistently higher than in the United States. Free air time is provided to all parties, reducing the role of wealthy special-interest groups in the political process. Most Western European industrial nations also have laws that require worker representatives be elected to serve on the boards of directors of large corporations. Consequently, workers have a meaningful voice in influencing company policies. Organized labor's stronger position in politics and in the corporation have resulted in better wages, benefits, and programs that have helped Western European workers acclimate more readily to the new global economy.

TAKING ACTION

In the United States, there is a pervasive belief that workers who do not work to increase their social position do not deserve to do so. Maybe that is why the general public accepts the enormous advantages favoring the elite. In addition, the mass media fail to provide a clear picture of the economic situation so that the public can shape a coherent opinion. Low voter turnout in elections at all levels of governance reflect the loss of confidence in the power of the ballot box and in the political system to work for the public good. Apathy, frustration, and the lack of knowledge and resources discourage most people from attempting to remedy the social problems facing the working and middle classes.

When grass-roots activism does occur, it is not always in the direction of social justice and progress for the entire society. Often it is exclusive and oriented toward what members perceive as beneficial to their own small group. Hate groups, growing more vocal and more willing to act on their hatred, often blame other unempowered groups, such as women, ethnic minorities, and immigrants, as the causes of economic problems. These hate groups are unaware of how truly marginal minority groups are in economic and political spheres. Minority status does not give a group control or even substantial influence in the system. Weak groups do not create employment opportunities, set interest rates, or dictate the level of the minimum wage. Perhaps by attacking other such marginal groups, they, in a sense, attack their own marginality and lack of influence.

Fortunately, all of the news is not bad. There are many efforts to bring about positive systemic change at the grass-roots, national, and international levels. The alternative press reports some of these activities. *Utne Reader* provides a digest of information from other alternative press sources; *Multinational Monitor* (a Ralph Nader organization) reports negative activities of corporations at home and abroad; *In These Times, Mother Jones, The Progressive, The Nation,* and the like do investigative reporting not found in the mass media; *Common Cause, Washington Monthly,* the *Washington Spectator* give critical analyses of U.S. political processes; and *Ms.* magazine covers issues affecting women here and in the Third World countries. Nongovernmental organizations (NGOs) are participating in both research and direct action that affect the quality of life of individuals and communities. Environmental groups such as Greenpeace and Worldwatch have their research publications. Oxfam and Food First analyze food production and distribution and also help feed the hungry at home and abroad. Amnesty International keeps tabs on political prisoners in the United States and elsewhere. Habitat for Humanity keeps readers abreast of where housing for the poor is being built by volunteers in rural and urban areas in the United States and other countries. Native American communities are beginning to organize to gain control over the use of their lands as sites for toxic waste. Metropolitan neighborhoods are organizing to rid their communities of hazardous waste sites, be they secondary lead-smelting operations in West Dallas, Texas; chemical plants in Institute, West Virginia; or petrochemical plants along the Mississippi River in Lousiana (Bullard, 1990).

Internationally, some NGOs are working to create or save jobs by setting up worker-owned companies and to improve worker rights in other companies. Ford Foundation's annual report provides a list of grass-roots revolving funds that it supports financially, such as the Grameen Bank in Bangladesh, which was the prototype for later microbusiness loan funds in the United States (Good Faith Fund in Arkansas, Lakota and Cherokee Funds, South Shore Bank in Chicago), Latin America (Accion), and elsewhere. *GEO Newsletter* (Grassroots Economic Organization), *Employee Ownership* (National Center for Employee Ownership), and *Co-op Quarterly* (Industrial Cooperative Association) report on worker ownership here and abroad. Workers, especially women, in many countries form cooperatives for producing and marketing their products and services. Occasionally, workers buy out their plants when threatened with shutdown. A large number of U.S. companies are now completely owned or majority-owned by employees (Krimerman and Lindenfeld, 1992). *AFL-CIO News, Labor Notes, Union Democracy,* and *Labor Research Reports* give a more rounded picture of labor union activities here and in other countries, both in promoting worker ownership and in supporting workers' rights to organize in the United States and in the Third World.

Many states in the United States have organizations such as the Industrial Areas Foundation, a hub for networking state grass-roots organizations. The Texas Industrial Areas Foundation, for example, offers services to over 300 grass-roots groups in Texas. The philosophy behind these organizations combines elements of liberation theology, social justice, community self-help, nonviolent community-based resistance, and liberation education (Rogers, 1990). The future of such efforts depends in large part on the ability to move workers and whole communities closer to the center of decision making that affects their future.

CONCLUSION

Long ago it was pointed out that "eternal vigilance is the price of liberty." Adopting that to the present, we might want to add that quality of life—which includes liberty and democracy in both the political and economic realms—must be understood and protected by citizens in a global economy. Given today's technology and the structure of global economic relations, the idea of local community is beginning to give way to the idea of a global community in which each of us is the other's neighbor. Citizens can work for a long-run view in which there is more social justice for the mass of humanity, or we can allow elites to profit in the short run at the expense of the bottom 80 percent of the population.

The new global economy will indeed be an enormously wealthy one, analysts admit, and many Americans will reap the rewards, but the vast majority of workers in the United States will not. In the 1930s worldwide depression, John Maynard Keynes pointed out the necessity of government planning and intervention to include and support the bottom sectors of capitalist economies, if capitalism were to be sustained. Over the years even conservative economists—including Adam Smith, Charles E. Lindblom, Karl Polanyi, Joseph Schumpeter, and Nobel laureate Wassily Leontief—have noted that the market is really good for creativity and innovation, but is not good for long-run social justice and distribution (Kuttner, 1989). The other industrial countries of Western Europe and even Japan (except for women workers) have done a better job of promoting income equality and providing social services and education to upgrade the quality of life for their citizens. In the United States the dominance of Social Darwinist ideology discourages collective action by out-of-power groups and long-term planning for prosperity of the entire society. The United States has downward middle-class mobility, rising crime rates, racism, and increased poverty for women and children. Surely this is enough reason to call people concerned about the direction of national policy to attention and active participation. Inequality of income and quality of life are the result of political and economic decisions, not laws of nature set in concrete.

REFERENCES

BARNET, RICHARD J. and JOHN CAVANAUGH
1994 "Think Global. Then Think Again," *Co-op America Quarterly* 35: 14–16. (Excerpt from *Global Dreams: Imperial Corporations and the New World Order.* New York: Simon & Schuster.)

BATT, ROSE and EILEEN APPELBAUM
1993 "Labor's New Agenda," *Dollars & Sense* 189: 6–7, 26.

BERNSTEIN, AARON
1994 "Inequality: How the Gap Between Rich and Poor Hurts the Economy," *Business Week* 3385: 78–83.

BERNSTEIN, JARED and LAWRENCE MISHEL
1994 *The State of Working America.* Washington, DC: Economic Policy Institute.

BLUESTONE, BARRY and BENNETT HARRISON
1987 "The Grim Truth about the Job 'Miracle': A Low Wage Explosion," *The New York Times,* Forum Section 15.

BULLARD, ROBERT D.
1990 *Dumping in Dixie: Race, Class, and Environmental Quality.* Boulder, CO: Westview Press.

CLARK, JOSH
1994 "No Good Jobs? Seven Economic Writers Offer Their Analyses of What's Wrong with the American Economy, Possible Remedies, and the Future of American Jobs," *Mother Jones* 19 (2): 34–38.

CORBETT, THOMAS
1993 "Child Poverty and Welfare Reform: Progress or Paralysis?" *Focus* 15 (1): 1–17.

FARRELL, CHRISTOPHER
1992 "Where Have All the Families Gone?" *Business Week* 3272.

FREEMAN, RICHARD B., ed.
1994 *Working Under Different Rules.* New York: Russell Sage Foundation.

HAMMONDS, KEITH H.
1994 "Rethinking Work," *Business Week* special issue: 74–87.

HENKOFF, R.
1994   "Getting Beyond Downsizing," *Fortune* (January).

JUDIS, JOHN B.
1994   "What's the Deal?" *Mother Jones* 19 (2): 22–32.

KRIMERMAN, LEN and FRANK LINDENFELD, eds.
1992   *When Workers Decide: Workplace Democracy Takes Root in North America.* Philadelphia: New Society Publishers.

KRUGMAN, PAUL R. and ROBERT Z. LAWRENCE
1994   "Trade, Jobs and Wages," *Scientific American* 270 (4): 44–49.

KUTTNER, ROBERT
1989   "Changing Occupational and Reward Structures," in D. Stanley Eitzen and Maxine Baca Zinn, eds., *The Reshaping of America: Social Consequences of the Changing Economy.* Englewood Cliffs, NJ: Prentice Hall, pp. 85–102.

KUTTNER, ROBERT
1994   "Where Have All the Good Jobs Gone?" *Business Week* 3387: 16

LABOR RESEARCH ASSOCIATION
1993   "Restoring Employee Rights Is Good for America," Video. New York: Labor Research Association.

MACEWAN, ARTHUR
1994   "Markets Unbound: The Heavy Price of Globalization," *Dollars and Sense* 195: 8–9, 35.

MOODY, KIM
1994   "When High Wage Jobs Are Gone, Who Will Buy What We Make?" *Labor Notes* 183: 8–9, 13.

MURRAY, CHARLES
1984   *Losing Ground: American Social Policy, 1950–1980.* New York: Basic Books.

NEWMAN, KATHERINE S.
1993   *Declining Fortunes: The Withering of the American Dream.* New York: Basic Books.

ROGERS, MARY BETH
1990   *Cold Anger: A Story of Faith and Power Politics.* Introduction by Bill Moyers. Denton, TX: University of North Texas Press.

UCHITELLE, LOUIS
1994   "Surveys Find Increase in Multiple Jobholders. *Austin (Texas) American-Statesman,* August 26, D1, p. 3.

UNITED NATIONS
1994   *Human Development Report: 1994.* New York: Oxford University Press.

EXERCISE 7

Name _____   Date _____

ID # _____   Class Time _____

I. Choose one of the following controversial issues: immigration, the North American Free Trade Agreement (NAFTA), the national minimum wage, toxic dumps in minority or poor neighborhoods, national health insurance, the Environmental Protection Agency (EPA) regulations concerning automobile emissions standards. Select *two* articles focused on the issue you selected, one from each of the following indexes of periodical literature or similar indexes: (1) the mass print media (e.g., from *Readers' Guide*), (2) the business press (e.g., from the *Business Periodicals Index)*, and (3) the alternative press (e.g., from the *Alternative Press Index*). (Your library may have these or similar indexes available in print, on-line, or on a CD-ROM disc.) Answer the following questions for each article in the spaces provided below.

   A. Provide a complete citation for each article you examined (author, title, journal volume and issue number, pages, and publication date).

      1. Article 1:

      2. Article 2:

   B. Was the article slanted toward a conservative, big-business approach, or toward a liberal, people-empowerment approach, or was it neutral?

      1. Article 1:

      2. Article 2:

   C. What basic arguments were put forth? What types of supporting evidence or data were used?

      1. Article 1:

      2. Article 2:

II. During the 1980s the U.S. government supported a conservative supply-side economic policy—tax breaks for corporations and the wealthy, cuts in government regulations, lax enforcement of environmental protections and worker safety, less labor protection under the National Labor Relations Board (NLRB), cuts in social service programs. The argument was that more investment would be made in plants and equipment, people would be forced off welfare into low-wage jobs, business would prosper, benefits would trickle down to workers and their communities. Using data from the *Statistical Abstract of the United States* or other reference sources, answer the following questions:

   A. What was the average annual growth rate of the U.S. GNP (gross national product) in constant dollars (adjusted for inflation) for the following years:

1. 1980–1984   _____
   2. 1985–1989   _____
   3. 1990–present   _____

B. What trends are discernible in corporate mergers and acquisitions in the 1980s and 1990s?

C. What was the net investment in plants and equipment in manufacturing during these years?

D. During this period, what happened to the average weekly earnings of workers in constant dollars? Cite your evidence.

E. What happened to the distribution of money income of families by fifths (i.e., the percentage of income received by the top 20 percent, 2nd, 3rd, 4th, and bottom 20 percent)?

F. Look at the above data and draw some tentative conclusions about where corporate profits were going and what was happening to the income of families at various economic levels.

8

Is the Criminal Justice System Biased?

Carol Y. Thompson

Questions about inequities in the criminal justice system over the last few decades have prompted researchers to study very closely the outcome of criminal justice policies and decisions for people of different ethnic, racial, and social-class backgrounds. The public's increasing fear of and concern about crime, coupled with research showing discriminatory treatment within the American criminal justice system, have fueled reform movements that have resulted in federal and state sentencing reform, probation and parole guideline reform, and a plethora of programs aimed at creating a tougher yet more equitable criminal justice system. Despite massive efforts to reform the system, scholars, politicians, the media, and the public today are still asking the question, "Is the criminal justice system giving out equal justice for all?"

THE NATURE OF BIAS IN THE CRIMINAL JUSTICE SYSTEM

To say that the criminal justice system is biased is to say that the system yields results that favor or disfavor one or more groups over others and, by extension, certain individuals over others. One form of bias is discrimination, a condition in which individuals within the system are treated differently. An example of discrimination would be a judge who as a matter of policy gives sentences of two years to women found guilty of aggravated assault but gives sentences of three years to men found guilty of the same crime. In this case the application of different sentencing standards based on the sex of the offender would discriminate against the male offenders. Another form of bias that might occur is disparity. Disparity occurs when the same standards are applied to all groups, but the application of those particular standards adversely or favorably affects some groups more than others. An example would be implementing a sentencing policy that allows offenders found guilty of major forms of larceny the

choice of spending one year in jail or paying a $5,000 fine. The policy is applied equally to all those found guilty of larceny; however, those who cannot afford to pay $5,000 must serve the jail term. This sentencing policy has a much greater impact on the poor because they not only have to spend a year incarcerated but also usually suffer additional financial losses in the form of lost wages and seizure of property due to unpaid bills. For some there are also social costs in the form of disrupted parent-child and spousal relationships. Those who are able to pay the fine avoid the additional financial and social costs.

This essay is concerned with examining whether African Americans or those of lower social-class standing are treated more harshly than others by the criminal justice system. To determine whether this is true, we must look at the way these groups are treated within the system and how the system's rules affect them.

CRIMINAL JUSTICE DATA SOURCES

Any examination of bias in the criminal justice system first requires an explanation of the types of data used by criminologists. The two major sources of official criminal justice data in the United States are the Uniform Crime Reports (UCR) and the National Crime Victimization Surveys (NCVS). The UCR data are derived from law enforcement agencies and include crime incidents reported to or obtained by the police. These data do not reflect crimes that go unreported or undetected. The NCVS data are collected by the Bureau of Justice Statistics in conjunction with the U.S. Bureau of the Census. The data are derived from a very complex national survey of a sample of households and provide information about crime incidents and the victims for both reported and unreported crimes, excluding homicide.

There are additional sources of data on offen and crime useful to criminologists studying the is bias. These data often come from individual states and special divisions within the criminal justice system and are compiled from official records acquired from a variety of sources, including courts, police departments, social service departments, and correctional agencies.

ARE ARRESTS BIASED?

UCR arrest statistics reveal disturbing racial patterns in arrest rates. Approximately, 34 percent of all people arrested are minority and 68 percent are white (U.S. Department of Justice, 1993: Table 4.11). Although white Americans represent the largest number of criminal arrests, in general minorities are arrested for crimes at higher rates than their representation in the population (Mann, 1993). Regarding arrests for violent crimes, for example, African Americans represent approximately 47 percent of the arrests even though they represent only 12 percent of the U.S. population. This pattern is also true for Hispanics, who comprise approximately 7 percent of the population but represent 14 percent of arrests for violent crime (Mann, 1993).

Interpretations of these data have been controversial. Some criminologists argue African Americans and Hispanics are overrepresented in the crime statistics simply because they commit disproportionate numbers of crimes. Others, however, argue that the high arrest rates are indicative of racially discriminatory practices employed by the criminal justice system. Specifically, it has been suggested that deployment patterns of police departments are racially biased because they focus on street crime rather than white-collar crime. The view is that if police were as concerned with "crimes in the suites" as they are with crime in the streets, the proportion of crimes committed by blacks and whites would be similar (Pepinsky and Jesilow, 1984). Others have suggested that these patterns are more a reflection of a class bias rather than race bias (Wilbanks, 1987). They argue that deployment practices target areas associated with high levels of unemployment and poverty. A well-known deployment strategy that targets poor areas of the city is the "drug crackdown." This strategy involves increases in the level of patrol and arrests in an attempt to disrupt the drug trade. Minority people are overrepresented in these impoverished areas, and therefore any crime they commit is more likely to be detected.

In her book *Power, Ideology and the War on Drugs,* Johns (1992) argues that the enforcement tactics used in the "war on drugs" definitely focus on poor and minority populations. In fact, she states, drug panics have been used historically to target minority populations and legitimate their oppression. Johns (1992) and Mann (1993) ⁱ that what is defined as criminal are the practices ˢ and the poor use to escape oppression, disˢ d frustration. Support for this position is ia and Turner's (1985) work which evaltrict guidelines-based sentencing poli-

cies. They found that the overrepresentation of blacks in particular in the crime and sentencing statistics is the result of policies instituted by the U.S. Congress, such as those which mandate stiffer penalties for drug offenses involving crack cocaine. The sentences associated with crack cocaine, a drug more common to blacks, are two times longer than sentences associated with powdered cocaine, a drug more common to whites. The conclusion to be drawn from the literature on apprehension strategies and arrest statistics is that poverty and race are very important factors in whether or not one will have contact with the criminal justice system. Research suggests that bias results from specific drug laws that target minority and poor citizens.

In his book *Malign Neglect,* Tonry (1995) identifies three major reasons why police target minority and poor neighborhoods. First, for a variety of reasons it is easier to make arrests in socially disorganized neighborhoods than in urban blue-collar and urban or suburban white-collar neighborhoods. More of the activities of life, including drug distribution and sales take place in streets and alleys in poor neighborhoods. In working- and middle-class neighborhoods the activities are likely to occur indoors. Second, it is easier for undercover narcotics officers to penetrate networks of friends and acquaintances in poor urban minority neighborhoods where strangers are more common. Third, it takes more work and time to make a single drug bust in middle-class neighborhood than in a poor neighborhood. Since officers and departments use the number of arrests made as a measure of productivity and effectiveness, it is more expedient and rewarding to the department to target poor neighborhoods (Tonry, 1995). Alfred Blumstein (1993) offered a similar explanation for disproportionate rates of minority arrests in his presidential address to the American Society of Criminology.

Bias in arrest decisions is another hotly debated topic among criminologists. The question is: "Do police take race, ethnicity, and/or class into consideration when deciding whether or not to arrest suspects?" The significant gap between the arrest probabilities for whites and minorities for almost all crimes might suggest to some that police officers do target minorities for arrest. It is clear that police have much discretion in carrying out their duties. This discretion allows the officer to decide whether to enforce, and the degree of effort necessary to enforce, particular laws. Often the police perception of community standards and attitudes influences the decision to arrest. Minority citizens may be stopped for questioning in areas of the city where they are not usually seen or for driving cars which seem beyond their means (Wilkins, 1985; and Mann, 1993). It can be argued that using a "status" such as race as a criterion for decision making results in bias against those who hold that status.

Researchers have found evidence that both supports and refutes the claim that police arrest decisions involve bias. For example, Smith and Visher (1981) in their study of police arrest decisions from 24 police departments found that race does play an important role in police discretion. Also, Dannefer and Schutt (1982) found that racial bias was often a factor in police decisions to arrest juveniles. Critics, however, argue that there is little evidence that police officers make biased decisions with respect to arrest of minorities. They argue that other factors such as the demeanor, attitude, and personal and social characteristics of the suspect are the most influential factors in police decisions to arrest (Wilbanks, 1987). Also, it has been suggested that the majority of police officers do not operate in an unfair and unjust manner and that gender and minority bias among police has decreased over time (Wilbanks, 1987; Senna and Siegel, 1993). Perhaps the best research on this subject attempts to tie together the two sides of this argument. Studies indicate that minority and class status are related to attitudinal, demeanor, social, and personal characteristics of suspects (Smith and Visher, 1981). This suggests that minority and poor citizens possess many of the attitudinal, social, and personal characteristics that increase the likelihood of arrest. Minority and poor citizens are less trusting of the police, show less respect, and in certain circumstances are more socially visible than white citizens. These characteristics make arrest more likely. This position asserts that police are not purposefully targeting minorities for arrest, but the arrest criteria they employ disproportionately single out offenders who are minority and/or poor.

However, some studies show that the targeting of minority citizens for arrest represents conscious overt prejudice on the part of some police officers (Sherman, 1980: 80; Campbell, 1980; Black and Reiss, 1970). In his study, Campbell (1980) found three fourths of the police studied expressed prejudice against blacks. Other studies show that lower-income minority citizens express hostile feelings toward the police, and that minority and lower-income citizens have less favorable attitudes toward police than whites and those with middle incomes (Scaglion and Condon, 1980). This hostility, at least in part, is due to extensive police surveillance and patrolling in minority and poor neighborhoods. Many minority and poor citizens who have not committed crimes have had direct contact with the police or have family or friends who have had such contact. Thus, minority citizens often demonstrate disrespect and antagonism toward police in part because of these negative contacts (Mann, 1993). As Sherman (1980) suggests, when considering the hostility between police officers and minorities, demeanor is a crucial factor in police-minority citizen encounters and does not negate the possibility that the demeanor may be a reaction to racial prejudice initially exhibited by an officer.

IS SENTENCING BIASED?

There is considerable research on sentencing and incarceration that can help us investigate the question of whether sentencing and imprisonment practices in this country are biased. First, it is necessary to note that the number of offenders incarcerated in our prisons and jails has more than doubled since 1980 (Senna and Siegel, 1993). Approximately 1,349,510 persons are incarcerated in American jails and prisons, or about 1 incarcerated for every 200 free Americans (U.S. Department of Justice, 1991). The growth in prison populations can be linked to changes in governmental policies and laws concerning drugs and violent crime. The federal government and many state governments have instituted mandatory and determinate sentencing laws and limits on early release via parole (Senna and Siegel, 1993). The changes in laws and policies have had a differential impact on minorities and whites in this country. It is difficult to make generalizations for some minority groups since most data on prisons and jails only includes counts for whites and blacks. Data from the last decade show a distinct trend in the racial composition of state and federal prisons. In general there has been a decrease in white and an increase in black percentages (U.S. Department of Justice, 1991, 1993). The same trend is found in the composition of jail populations: a steady increase in the black and a decrease in the white inmate population. Moreover, there are differences in the length of prison terms for whites and blacks. McDonald and Carlson (1993) found that on average black offenders sentenced to prison were given sentences that were 41 percent longer than whites. Michael Tonry (1995) states that most people are uneasy about the fact that black rates of incarceration are six to seven times higher than white rates. This uneasiness is warranted since blacks comprise about 13 percent of the U.S. population but represent about 50 percent of prison and jail populations.

Does this disproportionality in imprisonment represent bias in sentencing practices? To answer this question, researchers compare the sentences given to offenders who have committed similar crimes. The difference in actual sentence length, if a difference exists, may reflect bias. To determine whether "real" bias exists, researchers then try to account for the differences by considering offender-specific characteristics that are important to sentencing decisions (e.g., number of prior arrests, seriousness of crime, a weapon present). After offender-specific characteristics are considered, any remaining difference that cannot be accounted for by the researchers is likely to be the result of real bias.

There is considerable research available on sentencing bias. Alfred Blumstein (1982, 1988) has conducted two of the most comprehensive studies on racial disproportions in sentencing and imprisonment. He concludes that a large amount of racial disproportion in prison populations can be explained by differential rates of arrest but not by sentencing practices. This means that a black man who is arrested for a crime is no more likely to be sentenced to prison than a white man who is arrested for a crime. However, more blacks are arrested in the first place and then end up in prison as a result of that arrest. A similar conclusion was reached by the National Academy of Sciences Panel on Sentencing Research (Blumstein, Cohen, Martin, and Tonry, 1983). They concluded after reviewing the major studies on sentencing practices in the

United States that factors other than racial discrimination in sentencing account for the disproportionate representation of black males in U.S. prisons. Also, Klein, Petersilia and Turner (1990) found that race had no independent effect on the prediction of who went to prison or the length of prison sentences within specific categories of crimes. Thus, major research over the past decade has concluded that the disproportionate nature of black imprisonment is not the result of sentencing bias (Tonry, 1995). However, this does not mean that racial bias does not exist. It is simply not occurring in any significant way at the sentencing stage. The same rules are being applied to those who come into contact with the system.

If sentencing bias is not a real factor, what does account for the disproportionate numbers of blacks being imprisoned? The answer appears to be in the policies that govern what kinds of crimes get the attention of the criminal justice system and the penalties levied for those crimes. Two major changes in policy occurred at approximately the same time that changed dramatically the fate of minority and poor offenders in this country. The first was the sentencing reform movement which resulted in the Sentencing Reform Act of 1984 and the Federal Sentencing Guidelines adopted to decrease sentence disparity among offenders. The second change was the war on drugs policy of recent presidential administrations and the Anti-Drug Abuse Act of 1986.

Sentencing guidelines appeared, on the surface, to be an equitable way of dispensing justice. Such guidelines attempted to limit judicial discretion by making sure that offenders convicted of similar crimes served similar sentences. Also, many of the guideline programs gave mandatory sentences for some crimes such as murder, drug offenses, and for multiple convictions, thus rendering many offenders ineligible for probation and parole. The guideline movement gained momentum and soon many states and the federal prison system adopted guideline sentencing policies.

Since the institution of guidelines, few studies have found evidence of racial bias at the point of sentencing (Wilbanks, 1987). In Minnesota, one of the first states to adopt guidelines, researchers found that guidelines increased overall fairness in the sentencing system (Tonry, 1995). In simple terms, the use of guidelines seemed to decrease discrimination in the sentencing process. However, the news hasn't been all good. There are many vocal critics of this method of sentencing, and they suggest that guideline justice may prevent discrimination but it does not prevent racial disparity in the system. Petersilia and Turner (1985) evaluated federal sentencing guidelines and found that in fact some of the criteria used for determining sentence length resulted in racial differences. For example, some jurisdictions give enhanced sentences for prior offenses. Since blacks are more likely than whites to have prior arrest records (often for relatively minor offenses), they are more likely to receive long sentences. In another study, Meithe and Moore (1985) demonstrated that because of specific criteria utilized in sentencing decisions (e.g., prior convictions, weapon present, drug offenses), those of minority and lower economic status were more likely to be sentenced. They also found that black offenders were more likely to be charged with weapons violations, so they were more likely to receive prison terms. Some defense attorneys and researchers who have studied decision making by judges oppose the use of guidelines because they prevent judges from considering mitigating circumstances and individual differences such as mental competence, the exact nature of a previous conviction, and community/family support available to the offender (Griswold, 1988).

Guideline-oriented justice was implemented at about the same time that America launched an attack on drugs, and the drug war's effect on prison populations has been dramatic. In fact, most research suggests that it is the single most important cause of the prison population increases of the last two decades (Tonry, 1995). In 1979, 6.4 percent of state and 25 percent of federal inmates were imprisoned for drug-related crimes. However, by 1991 25 percent of state inmates and 56 percent of federal inmates had been convicted of drug-related crimes (Tonry, 1995). Arrest and sentencing data from every level of the criminal justice system show an increase in the incarceration rates for minorities as a result of the war on drugs.

The emphasis on prosecuting the drug use of minority and poor citizens can't be justified if one considers the usage rates of minority versus white citizens. For example, data on drug use show that black Americans are less likely to have used drugs than white Americans for all major drugs of abuse except heroine (NIDA, 1991). In 1990, 41 percent of drug arrestees were black, but only 10 percent of blacks reported that they had ever used cocaine (compared with 11.7 percent of whites), 1.7 percent reported ever using heroin (compared with .07 percent of whites), 31.7 percent reported ever using marijuana (compared with 34.2 percent of whites), and 3.0 percent reported hallucinogens (compared with 8.7 percent of whites) (NIDA, 1991). An increase in drug arrests is a principle reason that the proportion of blacks in prison has risen dramatically.

The combined effect of guideline justice and the war on drugs has been disastrous for the poor minority population, especially blacks. Even though the criminal justice system has overcome much of the discrimination that existed before sentencing reform, racial disparity still exists. That is, minorities, especially blacks, are still much more likely as a group to suffer disproportionately at the hands of the criminal justice system by having greater numbers of contacts with the agents of criminal justice and serving longer sentences when convicted.

CONCLUSION

When looking at the arrest and sentencing patterns of the past 20 years, three statements can be made concerning bias. First, at the arrest and sentencing stages of the criminal justice process, poor minorities are present in numbers greatly out of proportion with their presence in the U.S. population. Second, the proportion of minorities, especially African Americans, arrested and given stiff sentences has steadily increased. Third, the disproportionate numbers of minorities receiving prison sentences is not the result of overt racial discrimination within the system but the result of policies and guidelines that produce negative outcomes for poor and minority citizens. We can conclude then that the criminal justice system, while becoming less biased in one way, has become more biased in another. Although the criminal justice system has adopted policies that result in less overt discrimination within the system, it has adopted other policies that have produced alarmingly disparate results for poor minority citizens.

REFERENCES

BLACK, DONALD and ALBERT J. REISS
1970 "Police Control of Juveniles," *American Sociological Review* 35: 63–77.

BLUMSTEIN, ALFRED
1982 "On the Racial Disproportionality of United States' Prison Populations," *Journal of Criminal Law and Criminology* 73: 1259–1281.

BLUMSTEIN, ALFRED
1988 "Prison Populations: A System Out of Control?" in Michael Tonry and Norval Morris, eds., *Crime and Justice*, Vol. 10. Chicago: University of Chicago Press.

BLUMSTEIN, ALFRED
1993 "Making Rationality Relevant." The American Society of Criminology Presidential Address. *Criminology* 31, no. 1 (Feb.): 1–16.

BLUMSTEIN, ALFRED and JACQUELINE COHEN, SUSAN E. MARTIN, and MICHAEL TONRY, eds.
1983 *Research on Sentencing: The Search for Reform.* Report of the National Academy of Science Panel on Sentencing Research. Washington, DC: National Academy Press.

CAMPBELL, VALENCIA
1980 "Double Marginality of Black Policemen: A Reassessment," *Criminology* 20: 301–318.

DANNEFER, DALE and RUSSELL K. SCHUTT
1982 "Race and Juvenile Justice Processing in Court and Police Agencies," *American Journal of Sociology* 87: 1113–1132.

GRISWOLD, DAVID
1988 "Deviation from Sentencing Guidelines: The Issue of Unwarranted Disparity," *Journal of Criminal Justice* 16: 317–339.

JOHNS, CHRISTINA J.
1992 *Power, Ideology and the War on Drugs.* New York: Praeger.

KLEIN, STEPHEN, JOAN PETERSILIA and SUSAN TURNER
1990 "Race and Imprisonment Decisions in California," *Science* 247: 812–816.

McDONALD, DOUGLAS C. and KENNETH E. CARLSON
1993 *Sentencing in the Federal Courts: Does Race Matter?* Washington, DC: U.S. Department of Justice, Bureau of Justice Statistics.

MANN, CORAMAE RICHEY
1993 *Unequal Justice: A Question of Color.* Bloomington: Indiana University Press.

MEITHE, TERANCE and CHARLES MOORE
1985 "Socioeconomic Disparities under Determinate Sentencing Systems: A Comparison of Preguideline and Postguideline Practices in Minnesota," *Criminology* 23: 337–363.

NIDA (NATIONAL INSTITUTE ON DRUG ABUSE)
1991 *National Household Survey on Drug Abuse: Population Estimates 1990.* Washington, DC: U.S. Government Printing Office.

PEPINSKY, HAROLD E. and P. JESILOW
1984 *Myths That Cause Crime.* Cabin John, MD: Seven Locks Press.

PETERSILIA, JOAN and SUSAN TURNER
1985 *Guideline Based Justice: The Implications for Racial Minorities.* Santa Monica, CA: Rand Corporation.

SCAGLION, RICHARD and RICHARD CONDON
1980 "Determinants of Attitudes toward City Police," *Criminology* 17: 485–494.

SENNA, JOSEPH and LARRY J. SIEGEL
1993 *Introduction to Criminal Justice,* 6th ed. St. Paul: West Publishing.

SHERMAN, LAWRENCE W.
1980 "Causes of Police Behavior: The Current State of Quantitative Research," *Journal of Research in Crime and Delinquency* 17: 69–100.

SMITH, DOUGLAS and CHRISTY VISHER
1981 "Street-Level Justice: Situational Determinants of Police Arrest Decisions," *Social Problems* 29: 267–277.

TONRY, MICHAEL
1995 *Malign Neglect.* Oxford: Oxford University Press.

U.S. DEPARTMENT OF JUSTICE
1991 *Correctional Populations in the United States.* Washington DC: U.S. Department of Justice.

U.S. DEPARTMENT OF JUSTICE
1993 *Sourcebook of Criminal Justice Statistics 1992 and 1993.* Washington DC: U.S. Department of Justice.

WILBANKS, WILLIAM
1987 *The Myth of a Racist Criminal Justice System.* Monterey, CA: Brooks/Cole Publishing.

WILKINS, ROY
1985 "Stop and Frisk," in A. Neiderhoffer and A. S. Blumberg, eds., *The Ambivalent Force: Perspectives on the Police.* New York: Holt, Rinehart & Winston.

EXERCISE 8

Name _____   Date _____

ID # _____   Class Time _____

I. As discussed in the essay, people's attitudes concerning the criminal justice system vary by race. Give the following questionnaire concerning bias in the criminal justice system to at least five white students and five minority students. Record the student responses on the Survey Tabulation Forms. While your sample will not be representative of racial attitudes in general, the results can be used to develop a better sense of differences among students. After administering the survey, compare the findings for white and minority students by answering the questions provided in the last portion of this exercise.

Questionnaire Instructions. Do not write directly on the questionnaire. Instead, record the responses of each person surveyed on the tabulation forms following the questionnaire. Do not read aloud the part of the questions in parentheses.

To insure that each respondent understands that his or her answers to the questions will be kept confidential, read the following statement aloud to each respondent *before* you administer the questionnaire:

"This survey is designed to examine people's attitudes toward racial bias in the criminal justice system. Your responses will be held in strict confidence, and the data will be tabulated and analyzed in such a way as to ensure confidentiality. There are no right or wrong answers to the questions. Please choose the response that comes closest to your feelings concerning each question."

Student Questionnaire

A. *Equality of Courts:* Some people think the courts are doing a good job in treating all defendants the same. Others think that some defendants are treated more harshly than others. In your opinion, are the courts giving equal treatment to offenders of all races and ethnicities?

_____ No

_____ Yes

B. *Court Discrimination:* (Ask this question if the respondent answered "yes" in part A above. If the respondent answered "no" to part A, check never.) In your opinion, how often do courts discriminate against minority citizens because of their race or ethnicity?

_____ Never

_____ Almost never

_____ Sometimes

_____ Often

_____ Almost always

C. *Equality of Police:* Some people think the police are doing a good job in treating all citizens the same. Others think that some citizens are treated more harshly than others. In your opinion, do the police treat all citizens equally regardless of race?

_____ No

_____ Yes

D. *Police Discrimination:* (Ask this question if the respondent answered "yes" in part C above. If the respondent answered "no" to part C, check never.) In your opinion, how often do the police discriminate against minority citizens because of their race or ethnicity?

_____ Never

_____ Almost never

_____ Sometimes

_____ Often

_____ Almost always

E. *Criminal Justice System Biased:* All things considered, do you feel the criminal justice system is biased against minority citizens?

_____ No

_____ Yes

F. *Respondent's Race/Ethnicity:*

_____ African American

_____ Asian

_____ Hispanic

_____ White

_____ Other

Survey Tabulation Form

Use the following forms to record the survey responses from each of your respondents at the time of the interview.

Respondent 1:

A. Are courts giving equal treatment? _____ No _____ Yes

B. How Often Courts Discriminate:

_____ Never _____ Almost never _____ Sometimes _____ Often _____ Almost always

C. Do the police treat all citizens equally? _____ No _____ Yes

D. How Often Police Discriminate:

_____ Never _____ Almost never _____ Sometimes _____ Often _____ Almost always

E. Criminal Justice System Biased: _____ No _____ Yes

F. Race/Ethnicity: _____ African American _____ Asian _____ Hispanic _____ White _____ Other

Name _____   Date _____

ID # _____   Class Time _____

Respondent 2:

    A. Are courts giving equal treatment? ____ No ____ Yes

    B. How Often Courts Discriminate:

    ____ Never ____ Almost never ____ Sometimes ____ Often ____ Almost always

    C. Do the police treat all citizens equally? ____ No ____ Yes

    D. How Often Police Discriminate:

    ____ Never ____ Almost never ____ Sometimes ____ Often ____ Almost always

    E. Criminal Justice System Biased: ____ No ____ Yes

    F. Race/Ethnicity: ____ African American ____ Asian ____ Hispanic ____ White ____ Other

Respondent 3:

    A. Are courts giving equal treatment? ____ No ____ Yes

    B. How Often Courts Discriminate:

    ____ Never ____ Almost never ____ Sometimes ____ Often ____ Almost always

    C. Do the police treat all citizens equally? ____ No ____ Yes

    D. How Often Police Discriminate:

    ____ Never ____ Almost never ____ Sometimes ____ Often ____ Almost always

    E. Criminal Justice System Biased: ____ No ____ Yes

    F. Race/Ethnicity: ____ African American ____ Asian ____ Hispanic ____ White ____ Other

Respondent 4:

    A. Are courts giving equal treatment? ____ No ____ Yes

    B. How Often Courts Discriminate:

    ____ Never ____ Almost never ____ Sometimes ____ Often ____ Almost always

    C. Do the police treat all citizens equally? ____ No ____ Yes

    D. How Often Police Discriminate:

    ____ Never ____ Almost never ____ Sometimes ____ Often ____ Almost always

    E. Criminal Justice System Biased: ____ No ____ Yes

    F. Race/Ethnicity: ____ African American ____ Asian ____ Hispanic ____ White ____ Other

Respondent 5:

    A. Are courts giving equal treatment? ____ No ____ Yes

    B. How Often Courts Discriminate:

____ Never ____ Almost never ____ Sometimes ____ Often ____ Almost always

    C. Do the police treat all citizens equally? ____ No ____ Yes

    D. How Often Police Discriminate:

____ Never ____ Almost never ____ Sometimes ____ Often ____ Almost always

    E. Criminal Justice System Biased: ____ No ____ Yes

    F. Race/Ethnicity: ____ African American ____ Asian ____ Hispanic ____ White ____ Other

Respondent 6:

    A. Are courts giving equal treatment? ____ No ____ Yes

    B. How Often Courts Discriminate:

____ Never ____ Almost never ____ Sometimes ____ Often ____ Almost always

    C. Do the police treat all citizens equally? ____ No ____ Yes

    D. How Often Police Discriminate:

____ Never ____ Almost never ____ Sometimes ____ Often ____ Almost always

    E. Criminal Justice System Biased: ____ No ____ Yes

    F. Race/Ethnicity: ____ African American ____ Asian ____ Hispanic ____ White ____ Other

Respondent 7:

    A. Are courts giving equal treatment? ____ No ____ Yes

    B. How Often Courts Discriminate:

____ Never ____ Almost never ____ Sometimes ____ Often ____ Almost always

    C. Do the police treat all citizens equally? ____ No ____ Yes

    D. How Often Police Discriminate:

____ Never ____ Almost never ____ Sometimes ____ Often ____ Almost always

    E. Criminal Justice System Biased: ____ No ____ Yes

    Race/Ethnicity: ____ African American ____ Asian ____ Hispanic ____ White ____ Other

RIMINAL JUSTICE SYSTEM BIASED?

Name _____   Date _____

ID # _____   Class Time _____

Respondent 8:

    A. Are courts giving equal treatment? ____ No ____ Yes

    B. How Often Courts Discriminate:

    ____ Never ____ Almost never ____ Sometimes ____ Often ____ Almost always

    C. Do the police treat all citizens equally? ____ No ____ Yes

    D. How Often Police Discriminate:

    ____ Never ____ Almost never ____ Sometimes ____ Often ____ Almost always

    E. Criminal Justice System Biased: ____ No ____ Yes

    F. Race/Ethnicity: ____ African American ____ Asian ____ Hispanic ____ White ____ Other

Respondent 9:

    A. Are courts giving equal treatment? ____ No ____ Yes

    B. How Often Courts Discriminate:

    ____ Never ____ Almost never ____ Sometimes ____ Often ____ Almost always

    C. Do the police treat all citizens equally? ____ No ____ Yes

    D. How Often Police Discriminate:

    ____ Never ____ Almost never ____ Sometimes ____ Often ____ Almost always

    E. Criminal Justice System Biased: ____ No ____ Yes

    F. Race/Ethnicity: ____ African American ____ Asian ____ Hispanic ____ White ____ Other

Respondent 10:

    A. Are courts giving equal treatment? ____ No ____ Yes

    B. How Often Courts Discriminate:

    ____ Never ____ Almost never ____ Sometimes ____ Often ____ Almost always

    C. Do the police treat all citizens equally?: ____ No ____ Yes

    D. How Often Police Discriminate:

    ____ Never ____ Almost never ____ Sometimes ____ Often ____ Almost always

    E. Criminal Justice System Biased: ____ No ____ Yes

    F. Race/Ethnicity: ____ African American ____ Asian ____ Hispanic ____ White ____ Other

II. Assignment Questions

A. What percentage of your respondents feel that the courts do not offer equal treatment?

No _____ percent

Yes _____ percent

B. Do minority student and white student opinions differ concerning the equality of courts? (*Note:* For the purpose of analysis, if respondent's race or ethnic identity is African American, Asian, Hispanic, or Other, he or she is recorded as minority.) To answer this you must put the appropriate count for each type of response in the appropriate cell in the following table.

Equality of Courts	Nonwhite	White	Total
No	_____	_____	_____
Yes	_____	_____	_____
Total	5	5	10

C. Among your respondents, what is the most common response to the question about court discrimination? What is the most common response on the part of minority students? What is the most common response on the part of white students? Fill in the table below to answer these questions.

Court Discrimination	Total	Nonwhite	White
Never	_____	_____	_____
Almost never	_____	_____	_____
Sometimes	_____	_____	_____
Often	_____	_____	_____
Almost always	_____	_____	_____
	10	5	5

D. Do minority student and white student opinions differ concerning police and the equal treatment of citizens? If the opinions differ, how do they differ? Put the appropriate count in each cell in the table.

Police Equality	Nonwhite	White	Total
No	_____	_____	_____
Yes	_____	_____	_____
Total	5	5	10

E. Among your respondents, what is the most common response to the question about police discrimination? What is the most common response of minority respondents? What is the most common response of white respondents? Fill in the table below to answer these questions.

Police Discrimination	Total	Nonwhite	White
Never	_____	_____	_____
Almost never	_____	_____	_____
Sometimes	_____	_____	_____
Often	_____	_____	_____
Almost always	_____	_____	_____
	10	5	5

F. Do minority student and white student opinions differ concerning bias in the criminal justice system? If the opinions differ, how do they differ? Put the appropriate count in each cell in the table.

Biased CJS	Nonwhite	White	Total
No	――	――	――
Yes	――	――	――
Total	5	5	10

G. Briefly describe and interpret the results from your tables.
   1. Note the major differences between white and nonwhite respondents.

   2. If your findings are not as you expected, give a possible explanation for why you didn't find what you expected.

III. Consider the much talked about "three strikes you're out" sentencing policy. This policy suggests that chronic felons, defined as those receiving three felony sentences, be given life sentences without parole. Following is a scenario of an offender who would be serving life in prison if at the time of his third arrest a "three strikes you're out" sentencing policy had been in effect:

James is a 33-year-old African American male who has three prior drug felony convictions. He received his first adult conviction when he was 18 for possession of a controlled substance and his second conviction when he was 20 for possession and sale of marijuana. He is currently serving a five-year sentence for cocaine possession, his third drug offense. He was caught when the police stopped him for speeding. He voluntarily allowed the police to search him, and they found one gram of cocaine in his jacket pocket. James has been married for 13 years to the same woman and has two children (ages 10 and 12). He has an eighth grade education. When not serving time in prison, he works in construction as a welder's helper, earning $6 per hour. While in prison this time he is voluntarily participating in drug rehabilitation and a high school equivalency programs.

A. Given the case above and the information in the essay, what effect might policies like "three strikes you're out" have on the prison population, and minority prison populations in particular?

B. What might be an alternative to these kinds of policies?

PART II

SOCIAL INEQUALITIES

The essays in this part examine social problems related to various forms of inequality—economic and class, racial and ethnic, gender, age, sexual orientation, and disabilities. The first selection, by Jonathan H. Turner, explores how social inequality is perpetuated by powerful groups who exert influence over public policies so as to benefit upper-class interests. Leonard Beeghley then examines the historical dimensions of poverty in the United States to understand why a long-term decline in poverty has occurred; he also addresses why the U.S. poverty rate is so much higher than that of other industrialized societies.

Problems concerning race relations in the United States are the subject matter of two selections. In Charles Case's selection, historical trends and changes in the treatment of and the position of African Americans are discussed. The essay by Adalberto Aguirre, Jr., and David V. Baker, focuses more narrowly on the unequal treatment of African Americans in the courts, especially capital punishment cases.

The last five selections in this part concern relatively new social problems or new ways of viewing social problems. Elizabeth M. Almquist discusses how multiple types of inequality combine to disadvantage minority women in their access to rewarding employment opportunities. Dana Dunn and David V. Waller discuss why poverty is increasingly a female phenomenon in the United States. Joel Best examines how children's problems are constructed as social problems by focusing public attention on societal conditions that threaten children's well-being. The selection on sexual orientation and inequality by Kenneth Allan describes an emergent problem, the discrimination experienced by gays and lesbians. In the last selection in this part, Richard K. Scotch discusses the extent of disability in the population and the problems persons with disabilities confront, such as employment discrimination and access to health care.

9

Inequality and Stratification

Jonathan H. Turner

We can see the signs of inequality all around us: homeless people seeking warmth in cardboard boxes; affluent individuals in expensive cars garaged in clean and safe neighborhoods; poor children of color living in the filth of public housing projects and dodging the bullets and the cruel seduction of gang life; rural poor with dirt, tin roofs, parasites, and despair as integral parts of their lives; rich people with mansions, yachts, airplanes, and other possessions marking success; ordinary white-collar and blue-collar workers worried about job security, house and car payments, taxes, and their children's future. Indeed, more than any other advanced industrial society, America evidences the greatest degree of relative inequality. By official statistics, over 15 percent of Americans live in poverty, which translates into 39.3 million people; and if a more realistic standard of poverty were used, this figure would rise to perhaps as many as 45 million or 50 million people. At the other end of the spectrum, 1 percent of the population hordes close to 50 percent of all wealth, and the top 20 percent of the population possesses 75 percent of all wealth (Turner, 1994).

Inequality exists in all societies, so the problem is not inequality, per se, but the degree of inequality in American society and the clear trend toward increasing inequality in the decades ahead. Inequality is a tension-generating dynamo; it sets into motion individual misery and societal pathologies, such as high crime rates, unstable families, dependence on drugs, domestic and civil violence, and ethnic and racial conflicts, which become difficult to contain.

THE POOR IN AMERICA

Who are the poor who suffer most from inequality? Around 20 percent of the poor are children, and this figure represents the largest category of the poor. Twenty

years ago the poor elderly outnumbered the young who were impoverished, but over the last two decades, much income has been transferred to the elderly via Social Security programs. What the elderly have received, children have lost. Well over 50 percent of poor families are headed by a single female, indicating that children are poor because their broken families are in difficult straits (Turner, 1994).

Minorities are over-represented among the poor: 30 percent of African Americans, 17 percent of Hispanics, and 36 percent of Native Americans are poor (Aguirre and Turner, 1994); and because poor families tend to have more children than affluent families, even greater percentages of minority children are poor. For example, over 45 percent of all black children and 36 percent of Hispanic children live in poverty. Minority elderly are also more likely to be poor, indicating that the transfer of income to the elderly has bypassed much of its minority segment. For example, almost 34 percent of the black elderly fall below the poverty line (Wright and Devine, 1994: 8).

Close to half of poor family heads worked full-time, indicating that laziness is less of a problem than the public often thinks. The real problem is that wages are low, and the opportunities for higher wages in manual work have declined, forcing poor people to work hard for very little. For example, working even for an above minimum-wage salary—say $5 an hour—translates into $200 per week or $800 per month. Subtract from this Social Security contributions, and add to it the costs of health and dental care, which are rarely covered by benefits packages associated with minimum wage jobs, and it is abundantly evident that a poor person trying to support a family by working full-time is often unable to do so. Imagine trying to fund housing, food, clothing, transportation, health benefits, dental care, and utilities for a family on less than $800 a month in an urban area, where most poor now live.

IS POVERTY PERMANENT?

Americans believe that poverty is chronic among certain categories of poor, such as ethnic minorities. They fear that an "underclass" of poor people who are unemployable and welfare dependent, who are prone to produce single-parent families, and who are attracted to crime and drug use is now a permanent feature of American society. Yet the evidence on the poor does not fully support the media-driven hysteria over the issue of an underclass.

The actual data indicate that there is considerable turnover among the poor. From one third to one half of the poor in a given year are able to rise above the poverty line; approximately 15 percent will be poor for over a year, and 8 percent will remain poor from three to eight years. Only about 3 to 4 percent of the population will remain poor for a longer period of time (Turner, 1994). Do these more permanently poor constitute a dangerous underclass?

Again, the evidence does not fully support the public's view that there is a growing underclass. One early estimate of the urban underclass was 2.5 million individuals (Ricketts and Sawhill, 1988), but others (Gottschalk, 1987) could not find support for such high estimates. Christopher Jencks's (1991) review of the data on what the public sees as the syndrome of the underclass is instructive. After 1974, the proportion of single mothers collecting welfare began to decline; violent crime decreased in the 1980s, especially among blacks; dropout rates from school declined in the 1980s; and disparities between blacks' and whites' educational attainment decreased. Yet Jencks found other evidence supporting the public's perceptions: joblessness among black males increased; many black males who had worked at least episodically in the 1960s and 1970s had dropped out of the labor force; and babies born to single parents increased, especially among blacks where the rate is now well over 60 percent. Other issues relating to perceptions of a growing underclass could not be accurately assessed; drug use declined among high school students, but the number of hard-core users may have increased.

Thus, we are left with an intriguing question: Is there an underclass or not? In the first place, let us be clear on the origin of the term itself. The term *underclass* was a journalistic construction (Auletta, 1982); and although some social scientists began to argue for the existence of a large underclass (e.g., Wilson, 1987), the term perhaps exaggerates the situation. Joblessness, illiteracy, welfare dependency, drug use, unwed motherhood, and crime certainly exist among the poor, but whether this syndrome of pathologies is concentrated among a growing stratum of poor is not so clear. Moreover, even if we take the doubtful estimate of 2.5 million members of the underclass, there are well over 35 million poor who are not members of this underclass. In fact, when the public's attention focuses only on the underclass, it becomes more difficult to address the problems of the vast majority of poor who,

somehow, survive without manifesting the pathologies of the underclass.

THE HOMELESS IN AMERICA

The face of homelessness is changing. Homeless individuals and, increasingly, homeless families are one of the most visible signs of poverty in America. Migrating hobos and skid-row inhabitants had always been a feature of twentieth-century America, but in the 1980s as skid-row districts were declining, a new kind of homelessness emerged (Rossi, 1989). The old homeless had been mostly older white men with inadequate pensions who worked part-time and could usually find a place to sleep in a flophouse or fleabag hotel, whereas the new homeless include nonwhite minorities, younger men, and women (often with children) who often must sleep on the streets and who do not work (Barak, 1991; Lee, 1980). The increased visibility of the homeless, plus the problems in securing counts of their actual numbers (Wright and Devine, 1992), make it difficult to know how big a problem is at hand. Advocacy groups put the homeless on any given night at 1.5 million to 3.0 million, whereas government estimates point to a few hundred thousand. A good estimate places these figures at 750,000 to 1 million homeless each night, with a majority of these not being homeless for long periods of time. There is a constant turnover of the homeless as people fall into this state and then find ways to secure more permanent shelter. Various studies indicate that people become homeless because they can no longer rely on their families, whose patience and loyalty have been exhausted by chronic alcoholism, crime, mental illness, drug use, or other disabilities (Stagner and Richman, 1985; Rossi, 1989).

Yet more than personal failure is involved in creating the new homeless. The deinstitutionalization of the mentally disabled as well as those in drug and alcohol treatment centers has increased the ranks of the homeless in recent decades. Civic improvement projects, often carried out under the umbrella of a city or metropolitan redevelopment agency, have also increased the number of homeless by having the ironical effect of eliminating inexpensive housing in the cores of cities, forcing the poor onto the streets and increasing the rents of the domiciled poor to the point where they cannot afford to help friends and relatives. Along with this trend have been dramatic cutbacks in federal housing programs for the poor, pushing many more poor onto the streets. Decreasing welfare benefits in most states have also aggravated the problem, and once homeless, it becomes very difficult to secure welfare when a family does not have a permanent address or phone. And broader economic forces, especially the mechanization of low-skill and even temporary jobs, such as dishwashing and cleanup work, have decreased employment opportunities for the low-skilled poor.

Much like the perception of a large underclass, the

homeless are also highly visible, even though their numbers are small compared to the 40 million or so poor who manage to find housing. And much like the underclass, too much focus on the homeless deflects attention away from the much larger problem of poverty, which in turn is a result of broader patterns of inequality.

INEQUALITY: THE WEALTHFARE AND WELFARE SYSTEMS

The pattern of inequality in America—concentrated wealth at the top and a large poverty sector at the bottom—is mitigated by a number of intermediate social classes, whose profile is summarized in Table 9.1 (Turner and Musick, 1985, p. 186). The relative affluence of these strata reduces the tensions that inevitably accompany a large poverty sector by giving a sense that most Americans—from the upper white-collar affluent to the affluent blue collar—are doing well. These more affluent sectors often become the "shock troops" in sustaining the privilege of the rich and the despair of the poor. For as the affluent middle classes in America become fearful of their security, they almost always blame the "lazy poor" and the welfare system, while supporting governmental programs and tax policies that favor the rich. In the implicit bargain with the rich, the affluent retain their share of resources, while being given an opportunity to parade their superiority as "hard-working" citizens.

To understand inequality in America, then, we need to understand that joint systems of "wealthfare" for the rich (and their affluent allies) and "welfare" for the poor

TABLE 9.1
Social Class Structure in the United States

Class	Distinguishing Characteristics
The Elite	High income High-wealth holders Own or manage large corporations or important and strategic firms, govern major cities and states, or hold top-level elective and appointive government jobs High prestige and considerable political power *Examples*: president of Du Pont, prominent senator, chairman of Joint Chiefs, mayor of New York, secretary of state, head of Wall Street firm
The Upper Affluent	High income Sometimes high-wealth holders Possess highly paid professional entrepreneurial skills Relatively high prestige and some political power through professional or trade associations *Examples*: successful lawyer or doctor, college president, president of a state university, successful small-business owner
The White-Collar Affluent	Moderate to high income Modest wealth Professionals or middle- to lower-level bureaucrats in industry or government Moderate prestige and relatively little power outside the influence of the organization for which they work *Examples*: research chemist, school administrator, insurance salesman, government manager
The Lower White Collar	Moderate to low income Little wealth Relatively unskilled white-collar employees in government or industry Modest prestige and little power outside the organizations to which they belong *Examples*: secretary, department store sales clerk, file clerk, receptionist
The Blue Collar Affluent	Moderate to sometimes high income Moderate to little wealth Perform skilled and semiskilled salaried and commission work with their hands Modest prestige and little power *Examples*: plumber, carpenter, heavy equipment operator
The Lower Blue Collar	Moderate to low income Little wealth Perform salaried work with their hands Little prestige and power outside organizations to which belong (primarily unions)
The Poor	Unemployed, unemployable, or very low income Must receive public assistance Little power and severe stigma

now exist in America. Wealthfare policies maintain great privilege at the top and relative affluence for the middle; welfare policies sustain poverty.

The Wealthfare System.   Any long-term system involves established structures and relationships which are legitimated by moral beliefs. We need not see the structure and legitimacy of the wealthfare system as "evil," but we should recognize it for what it is and what it does. And, importantly, we should assess its opposite— welfare for the poor—only in the context of wealthfare for the rich.

This system benefiting the wealthy and affluent operates primarily through government policies that favor certain types of economic activity, that use the tax system as a way of concealing who is on the "government dole," and that hide the transfer of income to the "deserving affluent." Let us review some of the most prominent structural manifestations of these policies.

1.   The government collects taxes and then spends them—often wastefully in the public's mind. But these direct government expenditures overwhelmingly benefit the affluent—a fact which makes for the curious irony that those who most benefit from these expenditures are also the most critical of "government waste." Most expenditures go to two basic classes of beneficiaries: (a) bureaucrats of government in the form of salaries, and (b) owners, managers, and workers of government contractors. People usually complain about the former and conveniently ignore the latter. Thus, when government issues a contract for military hardware (airplanes, tanks, missiles, satellites), for civil engineering projects (dams, sewage-treatment plants, roads, bridges), for usable products (paper, paper clips, computers, desks, cars, buses), for buildings, and for many other activities, it is subsidizing a sector of the society—the owners, managers, and higher salaried workers of these businesses. There is nothing "wrong" with this situation, per se, for indeed these are necessary purchases, but we need to remain aware of what is involved: subsidy to the more affluent. And when we add to these private contractors the salaries to those directly employed by government, the scale of the subsidy is very evident.

2.   Government also uses taxes and laws to influence prices and profits in the marketplace. When, for example, import tariffs and taxes are imposed on foreign goods (cars, shoes, clothing, and other goods), they represent a subsidy to domestic owners, managers, and workers of companies who compete with foreign companies. When government purchases excess farm output, such as wheat, corn, dairy products, or when it pays farmers not to cultivate tracts of land, it is subsidizing the farming industry by keeping supply lower than it would otherwise be, and hence, demand and prices high. Again, in the abstract, there is nothing wrong with these practices; they may be essential, but they are also a subsidy to the more affluent in society, while imposing additional costs on the poor, who can ill afford to pay higher prices.

3.   The government uses the tax system as a vehicle for subsidizing certain categories of taxpayers by not collecting taxes that they would otherwise owe. These "loopholes," or more accurately "tax expenditures," take various forms:

   a. *Exclusions of certain forms of income,* such as sick pay, retirement account withholdings, some kinds of income earned abroad, exercise of stock options, employer contributions to pensions and medical coverage, a portion of Social Security income, interest income from some types of municipal bonds, certain kinds of expense accounts

   b. *Deductions from income,* like interest on home mortgages, entertainment of business clients, state and local taxes (from federal taxes) which reduce taxable income and the amount of tax paid

   c. *Tax credits,* or the direct subtraction from the taxes owed, of certain types of expenses, such as purchases of equipment by businesses

   d. *Special tax rates,* such as taxes on capital gains (the net profits from selling real estate, stocks, or any asset), where the tax rate is lower than the regular income rate for the rich, whose income is mostly from capital gains rather than salaries and commissions

   e. *Tax sheltering,* whereby credits, deductions, depreciation, and exclusion are allowed for certain kinds of economic activity and the income generated by that activity (although the new codes enacted in the 1980s dramatically reduced the ability to use tax shelters)

All of these types of tax expenditures may seem necessary and useful for encouraging particular kinds of economic activity, but they still should be viewed for what they are: subsidies to the more affluent that are hidden by the fact that the government does not write a wealthfare check to the beneficiary. For example, the ability to deduct from taxable income interest on home mortgages is a direct subsidy to the homeowner and to everyone else in the home-building industry (contractors, bankers, real estate agents, insurance companies, landscapers, etc.) because homes are being made easier to purchase. Again, this subsidy is perhaps necessary and desirable, but it is nonetheless wealthfare since only the more affluent sectors of the population own homes.

4. The biggest income-transfer payments in America are Social Security and Medicare. Its recipients—the elderly—are allowed to believe that these are "insurance benefits" or income from "government-kept savings" that they had deposited during their working years. In fact, recipients have virtually never paid into these systems what they get back because these systems were never designed in this way. Rather, they are structured so that younger workers pay the benefits of the retired. The constantly expanding array of these benefits is dramatically beyond the "safety net" that was their original intent. Therefore, the young today pay much more than previous generations, who have contributed comparatively little into these systems. The result is that the young are paying a tax so that the elderly can receive a benefit which is really a "welfare" payment but which is hidden under the presumption that this payment was "earned." In fact, it is government charity—probably a worthy and certainly a necessary one—but one that enables the elderly to avoid the stigma of being on the welfare dole.

A critical feature of wealthfare is that it allows those receiving it to maintain their dignity and, indeed, to proclaim their moral superiority as hard-working homeowners, as business owners, as deserving retired, as salt-of-the-earth farmers, as successful buyers and sellers of capital, and, in general, as worthy contributors to society. There is, then, no stigma for being on the wealthfare dole because these activities are legitimated by powerful beliefs, the two most important being: (1) "national-interest" beliefs maintaining that the subsidy is important for the interests of the society as a whole, and (2) "trickle-down" beliefs arguing that even as subsidies go to the rich and affluent, they eventually percolate down to the less affluent. The national-interest belief is more defensible than trickle-down, because clearly some kinds of activity are probably essential for a viable and productive society. But trickle-down is less justifiable because much of the subsidy is consumed in ways that benefit few others, with the trickle being more of an occasional drop. Yet the recent demand in Congress that capital gains taxes be lowered even more (from 28 percent to 15 percent) is justified by the idea that these "capitalists" will use their extra money to invest in activities that employ others. To some extent, this is true, but much of the extra money goes into highly speculative investments that employ few, into foreign markets that do not employ Americans, into luxury goods consumption whose manufacture employs small numbers, and into other activities that do not generate mass numbers of jobs.

The Welfare System. Even Franklin D. Roosevelt, who was the founder of the federal government's welfare system, was moved to proclaim in the depths of the Depression that "the federal government must and shall quit the business of relief." Thus, from the beginning Americans have not liked government aid to the poor, which has meant that benefits have been modest and monitoring of recipients has been high. Moreover, unlike those receiving wealthfare payments, welfare recipients are stigmatized as failures and, in the minds of many Americans, as unworthy of assistance.

The welfare system is complicated because federal, state, and county governments are all involved, but a general profile of the system looks like this:

1. The federal government mandates certain types of benefits and pays about half the costs; the states and counties pick up the rest.

2. Among the welfare programs there are two basic kinds.

    a. *Cash payment programs,* such as Aid to Families with Dependent Children (AFDC), providing monthly income to poor families with children, and Supplemental Security Income (SSI), giving cash assistance to the aged, blind, and disabled poor

    b. *In-kind assistance,* such as Medicaid, which provides medical assistance to the poor, and food stamps, which offer redeemable coupons to qualifying poor

Together, the four programs constitute about 60 percent of the total expenditures on welfare for the poor.

Around one third of those eligible for welfare receive none, out of ignorance, fear, or pride. Many categories of poor, such as single adults without children, are not eligible for any cash programs. In 1990 the federal total cost of all welfare programs was about $125 billion, including additional educational, service, and housing programs (Turner, 1994). Much of this sum is actually a wealthfare payment in the form of salaries, contracts, and grants to the nonpoor administrators and providers of services to the poor. And compared to the poor, wealthfare in the form of Social Security, Medicare (medical assistance to the nonpoor), and tax expenditures on the rich and affluent is about three times what is spent on the poor. Indeed, the $90 billion or so in tax expenditures for special treatment of income, plus the $47 billion for benefits in housing (mostly interest deductions on mortgages), are by themselves more than the federal government spends on all welfare programs to the poor. Add to these figures the contracts, subsidies, price policies, and other government wealthfare programs, and we can see that expenditures on wealthfare are perhaps as much as seven times what is spent on the poor.

Because the public is so concerned about "welfare cheaters," monitoring of recipients is high. An eligibility worker assesses need and determines benefits of those who apply, constantly forcing welfare recipients to prove their need. Past abuses of monitoring systems, such as midnight raids on AFDC mothers to see if "a man was in the house," have been corrected, and most of those assessing the eligibility of the poor are concerned and responsive. But, unlike tax expenditures and other wealthfare programs for the nonpoor, the monitoring is constant.

In contrast to beliefs about wealthfare, which extol the moral worth of recipients, those about welfare stigmatize the poor. Americans firmly believe that income should come from work—a situation that automatically stigmatizes the poor, while conveniently ignoring the subsidies that go to wealthfare recipients who happen to own a house, sell some stock, put untaxed money into a retirement account, or receive Social Security or Medicare. None of these wealthfare benefits comes from "work," but for those receiving welfare, 20 percent of whom work full-time and 30 percent part-time, benefits are usually seen by the public as undeserved. This is why "workfare," where the poor must work for their benefits (ignoring the fact that half of the recipients already *do* work) is so rhetorically popular with the public; and yet, similar cries for the elderly to work for Medicare or that other wealthfare recipients work for their benefits are rarely heard because there is an illusion that their benefits come from work.

Another stigmatizing belief is the perception that many, if not most, welfare recipients are cheaters and therefore misrepresent their needs. A variant of this belief is that "welfare queens" have additional children in order to increase their welfare benefits. Such beliefs give the impression that the poor are unworthy, not only because they do not work (ignoring again that one half of welfare recipients *do* work) but also because they have bad character. Some poor, no doubt, do have bad character; but so do some of those receiving wealthfare who cheat on their taxes, bilk the government on cost overruns, perform unnecessary medical procedures, and so on. Moreover, the most problematic poor—drug users, gang members, unemployable adults—do not receive any cash welfare (at best, they might get food stamps) because they are single; and yet, the public's distrust of them often works to penalize the children, elderly, and working poor.

THE POLITICS OF INEQUALITY

The dual wealthfare and welfare systems exist because the affluent and rich outnumber the poor and have more resources to devote (via lobbying and other activities) to exerting political influence. Moreover, the general despair of the poor keeps them from voting to the same degree as the more affluent, especially categories of the affluent like the elderly, who vote in such numbers that cuts in Social Security and Medicare become difficult. Unlike the more affluent, who have unions and professional associations to represent their interests in the political arena, the poor remain politically vulnerable. Only when the poor engage in campaigns of moral persuasion, such as the Civil Rights

Movement, or in large-scale collective outbursts of violence, such as the Los Angeles riots of 1992, does the public and government mobilize to help the poor. Thus, the respective subsidies to rich, poor, and affluent reflect the relative power of each.

The 1994 elections, which brought Republican majorities to both houses of Congress, represent a dramatic loss of sympathy for the poor. Indeed, the poor are implicitly blamed for the high costs of government, for high taxes, and for other ills of American society. Proposals to cut welfare, send poor children to orphanages, reduce government tax revenues, turn programs back to the states and counties, make the poor work (for whom is rarely specified), and cut off benefits after two years all signify distrust of, and hostility for, the poor. However, since wealthfare is a much greater proportion of the federal budget than welfare, it will be interesting to see if tax cuts and reductions of middle class entitlements will be politically possible to sustain. Even if much of the wealthfare system remains intact, as voters realize that it is *their* wealthfare "payments" that will be cut, programs for the poor will be the first to go or suffer the most severe cutbacks.

This conclusion need not argue against "welfare reform," which is long overdue. The current system clearly does little to eliminate poverty and its causes; rather it simply sustains mothers, children, elderly, and disabled at some minimal level. Over the years there have been many proposals from liberals and conservatives alike. Together, they point to several potential changes.

1. Some form of guaranteed income administered through the Internal Revenue Service as a "negative income tax" (that is, the less the poor earn, the more subsidy they receive up to a specified amount)

2. Some dramatic cutbacks in the bureaucracy of welfare such that monitoring costs are reduced (the guaranteed annual income would do this by having poor individuals fill out tax forms that would be spot-checked just like regular tax forms by the IRS)

3. Some system of universal child support, revolving around enforcement of child support obligations of divorced parents, subsidized day-care facilities for the poor so that their parents can seek and sustain work, and a revised or abandoned foster care system for children whose parents cannot take care of them (with orphanages being the most dramatic step)

4. Some combination of job training and workfare.

More radical proposals would not only eliminate AFDC, SSI, food stamps, Medicaid, and other mainstays of the current system but also force dramatic revisions of the Social Security system, such as requiring all workers to contribute, shifting the mix of benefits so that affluent and poor are treated alike, and changing the age at which benefits could be collected (Haveman, 1988). Just what emerges in the next decade from the heightened desire to "do something" about welfare is hard to predict, especially as the realities of tax cutting and budget reduction are faced. The relative power of various classes, as was summarized in Table 9.1, will be the best predictor of what will ensue.

CONCLUSION

A society revealing large-scale inequalities, especially inequalities associated with ethnic and racial groups, is in danger. America is thus living dangerously, because the current system for dealing with the needs of the poor fails to address its most volatile element: the young. It also fails to encourage people to work, while providing very little in the way of job training and real job opportunities. And, in the recent rounds of cutbacks in government programs, the truly disadvantaged sectors of the poor—the homeless, gang members, criminals, drug users, teen-age mothers, single-parent households—have all been victims of inattention.

Americans get highly moralistic about the poor and welfare; yet they do very little to help the poor manifest the morality—work, responsibility, and stable families—that the affluent insist the poor manifest. Americans simply stigmatize the poor, complain about high taxes (which, in fact, are not high compared to the rest of the industrial world), advocate workfare (without providing jobs with real futures), and demand that welfare benefits be cut. The neglect and failure to deal with realities of inequality, and the poverty sector that inequality has generated, assure that American society will experience great tension in the future.

REFERENCES

AGUIRRE, ADALBERTO and JONATHAN H. TURNER
1994 *American Ethnicity: The Dynamics and Consequences of Discrimination*. New York: McGraw-Hill.

AULETTA, KEN
1982 *The Underclass*. New York: Random House.

BARAK, GREGG
1991 *Gimme Shelter: A Social History of Homelessness in Contemporary America*. Westport, CT: Praeger.

GOTTSCHALK, PETER
1987 "Statement: Poverty, Hunger and the Welfare System." House Select Committee on Hunger, 99th Congress. Washington, DC: U.S. Government Printing Office.

HAVEMAN, ROBERT
1988 *Starting Even: An Equal Opportunity Program to Combat Our Nation's New Poverty*. New York: Simon & Schuster.

JENCKS, CHRISTOPHER
1991 "Is the American Underclass Growing?" in *C*. Jencks and P. E. Peterson, eds., *The Urban Underclass*. Washington, DC: Brookings Institution.

LEE, BARRETT
1980 "The Disappearance of Skid Row: Some Ecological Evidence," *Urban Affairs Quarterly* 16: 81–107.

RICKETTS, EROL R. and ISABEL SAWHILL
1988 "Defining and Measuring the Underclass," *Journal of Policy Analysis and Management* 7: 316–325.

ROSSI, PETER
1989 *Without Shelter: Homelessness in the 1980s*. New York: Priority Press.

STAGNER, MATHEW and HAROLD RICHMAN
1985 *General Assistance Profiles*. Chicago: Illinois Department of Public Aid.

TURNER, JONATHAN H.
1994 "Poverty and Inequality," in G. Calhoun and G. Ritzer, eds., *Introduction to Social Problems*. New York: McGraw-Hill Primis.

TURNER, JONATHAN H. and DAVID MUSICK
1985 *American Dilemmas: A Sociological Interpretation of Enduring Social Issues*. New York: Columbia University Press.

WILSON, WILLIAM J.
1987 *The Truly Disadvantaged*. Chicago: University of Chicago Press.

Wright, James D. and JOEL A. DEVINE
1992 "The United States Census Effort to Count the Homeless: An Assessment of Enumeration Procedures During 'S-Night' in New Orleans," *Journal of Official Statistics* 8: 211–222.

WRIGHT, JAMES D. and JOEL A. DEVINE
1994 "Poverty among the Elderly," *Journal of Long-Term Health Care* 13: 5–16.

EXERCISE 9

Name _____   Date _____

ID # _____   Class Time _____

Complete *one* of the two following exercises.

I. In the 1994 election, the House of Representatives candidates in the Republican party campaigned on a "Contract with America." Analyze this contract (secure a copy from the local Republican party organization or your university or public library) in terms of its effects on inequality and stratification. Review each component and indicate who benefits, and what its effect would be, or has been, on inequality.

II. Congress became so concerned with tax loopholes in the 1960s that it required the annual publication of a Tax Expenditure Budget. For the most recent year, examine this budget (available in most libraries, along with the regular budget) and assess who benefits from these expenditures. Also, analyze whether these expenditures are all in the national interest or if they will ever trickle down to the less affluent.

10

Poverty in the United States

Leonard Beeghley

Maria Sanchez telephoned the emergency room at Boston's City Hospital because her 9-month-old baby had diarrhea. A doctor told her to buy Pedialyte, water with electrolytes added, at a pharmacy. Alas, she did not have enough money for it. Although Medicaid will pay for over-the-counter drugs, a prescription is required. Instead of going to the hospital right away, Ms. Sanchez took the child home. The infant became worse, and the next day she took him to the emergency room. He later died (Klass, 1992).

This example, although extreme, illustrates the dilemmas the poor face. Ms. Sanchez had a medical emergency but no money. More affluent persons faced with the same problem would simply pay for the medicine or, if short of cash, use credit cards. This was not a choice for Ms. Sanchez. Rebuffed at the pharmacy, she had no car and no money to pay for transportation. Also, she spoke little English. Hospital bureaucracies are difficult to deal with, even for well-educated, reasonably affluent, English-speaking persons with insurance. For the poor, such organizations are even more intimidating. So, given these limitations, Maria Sanchez tried to care for the baby herself.

It is easy to view her decision harshly. And the harshness with which the nonpoor judge the poor ought to alert you to the way stereotypes ("they are lazy") mislead. In fact, Ms. Sanchez's decision does not seem irrational, given the difficulties she faced. For the poor, solving problems often requires a degree of wisdom and heroism that few possess.

The example also illustrates the dilemma faced by those who would help the poor. When physicians diagnose an illness, they confront not only a medical problem but also poverty. When teachers send work home or want a conference with parents, they confront not only education but also poverty. When counselors deal with a drug abuser, they confront not only self-destructive behavior but also poverty. It affects every dimension of life. If the physician

who talked to Ms. Sanchez on the telephone had told her to come for a prescription before going to the pharmacy, the baby's death might have been avoided. The physician, although well-meaning, did not appreciate the difficulties Ms. Sanchez faced. When would-be helpers are unfamiliar with the reality of poverty, they fail to recognize its connection to the problem at hand.

In order to consider such connections, a definition is necessary. In this chapter, poverty refers to a minimum income level below which individuals or families find it difficult to subsist. The word *subsist* should be taken literally; it is hard for poor people to obtain food, shelter, and medical treatment. Maria Sanchez provides an example of the last dilemma.

HISTORICAL TRENDS AND COMPARATIVE RATES OF POVERTY

Standards of living change over time. In 1900, only 1 percent of all families owned an automobile, which meant it had no impact on people's economic circumstances because social life was organized without requiring ownership of high-speed transportation (U.S. Bureau of the Census, 1975: 717). Today, those without a car find it difficult, and sometimes impossible, to get to and from work. Similarly, only 12 percent of the population had running water in their homes at the turn of the century, which meant that most people used outhouses to relieve themselves. Although this practice exposed people to disease and, hence, had negative health consequences, it was free. Today, it is impossible to use an outhouse in any city, where most people now live. The poor must pay cash for water, heat, electricity, and all other items necessary for living.

Such differences in the standard of living make assessing the long-term trend in the poverty rate tricky. One way to resolve this problem is to ask a simple question that stems from the definition offered earlier: What proportion of the population has difficulty subsisting? The answer provides estimates that take into account the changes mentioned above.

In *America's Struggle Against Poverty, 1900–1985*, James T. Patterson shows that between 40 percent and 60 percent of the population was poor around the turn of the century (1986). The poverty rate apparently began falling about this time, primarily due to industrialization and other factors described later. The poverty rate declined sharply during World Wars I and II, and an extreme rise occurred during the Depression. Apart from these spikes, the long-term trend in poverty has been downward. Immediately after World War II, the rate probably stood at 30 percent or less (CEA, 1969: 154).

The data in Table 10.1 take up the story as of 1960. Based on the government's official poverty line, they constitute the most realistic measure of poverty currently available (Beeghley, 1984; U.S. Bureau of the Census, 1994: 475; U.S. Bureau of the Census, 1995: 4).

Thus poverty declined to about 22 percent by 1960 and continued falling during that decade, reaching 11 to 12 percent in the 1970s. During the 1980s, however, the long-term trend reversed, with poverty rising to 13 to 14 percent. As of 1993, the rate stood at 15 percent. In monetary terms, the poverty line for a family of four was $14,764 in 1993 (U.S. Bureau of the Census, 1995: vii). The cutoff varies, however, by family size, being lower for a two-person family and higher for a six- to seven-person family. The line also varies by age of the household head, being slightly lower if the head is over 65 and higher if under 65. The threshold does not vary by region or rural-urban residence because the Census Bureau concluded that the problems in making such distinctions are too great. Taking these factors into account, the 15 percent of the U.S. population living in poverty in 1993 equaled about 36 million people. Of this total, approximately 14 million were children. Thus more than one in five young persons in the United States lived in poverty. It would be wise to consider the long-term consequences, both for the youth growing up in poverty and the larger society.

TABLE 10.1
The Poverty Rate in the United States for Selected Years, 1960–1993

1960	22%
1963	20
1966	15
1969	12
1972	11
1975	12
1978	11
1981	14
1984	14
1987	13
1990	14
1993	15

SOURCES: Beeghley, 1984; U.S. Bureau of the Census, 1994; U.S. Bureau of the Census, 1995.

TABLE 10.2
The Poverty Rate in Selected Countries for Selected Years in the 1980s

United States	1987	13%
Canada	1987	7
United Kingdom	1986	5
France	1984	5
Sweden	1987	4
Netherlands	1987	3
West Germany	1987	3

SOURCE: Committee on Ways and Means, 1993.

Although poverty fell over time in the United States, its decline in other societies has been even greater. Table 10.2 summarizes the poverty rate in selected countries. Because other nations do not have official poverty lines, it is necessary to look at the proportion of the population with incomes less than 40 percent of the median. The result provides an approximate comparison with the United States, as shown in Table 10.2 (Committee on Ways and Means, 1993: 1453). These data probably exaggerate the level of impoverishment in other nations because they provide more noncash benefits for all citizens, regardless of ability to pay. Thus not only are there fewer poor, but being impoverished in other Western societies is not nearly as onerous as in this country. Such comparative differences carry an important implication: The amount of poverty in modern societies reflects political choices. Public policies can be devised that put people to work, preventing them from being in situations like that of Maria Sanchez. This country, however, chooses to maintain a rather large impoverished population and to live with the consequences.

In order to understand poverty and, indeed, many other topics, it is useful to distinguish between micro- and macro-levels of analysis (Beeghley, 1996; forthcoming). At the micro-level, the question is why some individuals rather than others become poor. In this case, the explanatory variables are social psychological, either directly (as indicated by people's personal experiences) or indirectly (as indicated by their characteristics). At the macro-level, the question is why rates of poverty vary over time and across societies. In this case, the explanatory variables are structural; that is, they refer to networks of relationships and values that connect people to one another and to society. Such factors identify why so many or so few people act. The difference between micro and macro concerns can be illustrated by thinking about a house. One can ask why one individual rather than another enters a house, and the answer will be social psychological. Or one can ask why so many more people go through the front door rather than the back, and the answer will be structural. The following sections deal with these two issues.

INDIVIDUALS AND POVERTY

Some individuals are poor because they have job skills and levels of education that are commensurate with low wages. People with more education—who write well, speak a foreign language, learn the law, and fill prescriptions—have job skills. They rarely become impoverished. People without higher education—who type, operate cash registers, and repair cars—also have job skills, but they are more prone to poverty. Listed below are poverty rates among individuals aged 25 years and older by educational attainment (U.S. Bureau of the Census, 1993: 70):

Less than high school diploma: 26 percent

High school diploma: 10 percent

College diploma: 3 percent

But regardless of skill level, jobs do not always exist. Plants close, leaving entire communities out of work and those in this situation often become poor. Here are the poverty rates for individuals aged 16 and over by employment status (U.S. Bureau of the Census, 1993: 84):

Unemployed all year long: 23 percent

Employed part of the year: 14 percent

Employed full-time, year-round: 3 percent

In addition, divorce, separation, or abandonment often lead to poverty for mothers and children. Poverty rates among various types of families are listed below (U.S. Bureau of the Census, 1993: 6):

Female-headed families: 46 percent

Male-headed families: 22 percent

Two-parent families: 8 percent

Family instability among the poor is reinforced by the fact that Aid for Families with Dependent Children (AFDC), the nation's main public assistance program, generally goes to single parents. Although it cannot be shown that AFDC influences families to break up because there are so many intertwined factors involved, focusing benefits on single parents clearly does not encourage family stability. Impoverished single women do not have many realistic options. They can find a well-paying job or increase their skills, but these strategies depend on obtaining adequate child care or leaving youngsters without supervision. They can also, of course, find another husband to support them. These choices are difficult.

Poverty is thus a transforming event. Children whose parents go through the experiences described here learn quickly that life is neither predictable nor controllable. Such events can be defining episodes in people's lives. Not all of these people suffer hunger, but many do. Not all of the poor endure homelessness, but some do. Not all of them withdraw into drug abuse or join gangs and ex-

press their rage, but a few do. All of the poor, however, even those whose families remain stable, experience hardship and deprivation.

Such personal experiences, it turns out, are associated with specific characteristics such as race and age. The fact that certain racial and ethnic groups are more likely to be poor than others is well known. Here are the data (U.S. Bureau of the Census, 1993: xi):

African Americans: 33 percent

Latinos, all races: 29 percent

White, non-Latino: 10 percent

In considering these data, however, note that the pattern differs when absolute numbers are shown. The percentages refer to 10 million African Americans, about 6 million Latinos, and 24 million whites. Hence, in terms of absolute numbers, more whites are poor than any other group.

Young adults and the elderly usually find it difficult to earn a living. Here are the poverty rates for families headed by people at three different ages (U.S. Bureau of the Census, 1993: 10):

Head aged 18–24 years: 18 percent

Head aged 35–44 years: 10 percent

Head aged over 65 years: 13 percent

The reason families composed of young adults are more likely to be poor is they have not acquired education or job skills. As these are obtained, the probability of poverty declines. Thus, the decision to establish a household independently of one's parents at a young age dramatically increases the probability of poverty. One factor leading some young people to this decision is pregnancy. Yet the United States makes it relatively difficult for young persons to obtain contraception and thereby prevent pregnancy (Jones et al., 1986). This difficulty affects the poor most of all. Sadly, sometimes girls become sexually active and pregnant as a reaction to an abusive home life or other deprivations (Sgroi, 1984). In effect, they respond by confusing sexual intercourse with love and by conceiving a child as evidence of their humanity, their adulthood. Boys from impoverished backgrounds often react in similar ways. They get someone pregnant under the delusion that this indicates their manhood (Marsiglio, 1993). Another factor leading young persons to establish their own household is the desire to escape an impoverished home life (Rubin, 1976). Hence, young persons make unwise decisions in specific contexts in which their choices are limited and their experiences teach them (often falsely) that they will be better off forming their own families.

The common-sense approach to understanding poverty is to blame individual deficiencies: If only they would work harder, it is said, they could escape impoverishment. And there is truth to this adage, albeit partial truth. In reality, there are not enough jobs. If those out of work sought all the jobs available, they would overwhelm the vacancies at the lower skill levels (Kasarda, 1990). This fact means that advocating self-help strategies to eliminate poverty is not practical. Such proposals affirm dominant values without increasing understanding. Understanding occurs when the level of analysis shifts to the social structure.

SOCIAL STRUCTURE AND POVERTY

This section deals with two issues that follow from the historical and comparative data presented earlier. First, why did a long-term decline in poverty occur? Second, why is the U.S. poverty rate so much higher than that of other societies?

The Long-Term Decline in Poverty. Common sense, as mentioned above, suggests that people avoid poverty by working hard. Hard work, people are taught, produces success. Failure results from giving up. From this point of view, it is easy for those who achieve some success to attribute it to their work ethic. After all, they sacrificed while training, found a job, and labored for years to advance. Their lives confirm the idea that hard work pays off. By extrapolation, then, the conventional explanation assumes that in "a social context where plenty of opportunity existed," those who worked hard have been successful and those who are poor must not have worked very hard.

The phrase "a social context where plenty of opportunity existed" was placed in quotes to alert you to the structural question: What factors produced a context in which hard work could pay off? The answer is that the long-term fall in the poverty rate reflects:

1. Industrialization
2. Class differences in fertility rates
3. Declining discrimination

Industrialization. Industrialization refers to the transformation of the economy as new forms of energy were substituted for muscle power, leading to advances in productivity. However, this definition, while accurate, is also rather narrow. Industrialization occurred in the context of other basic structural changes. First, it was linked to the rise of capitalism, an economic system based on private ownership of the machines and techniques used to produce goods and services (Berger, 1986). Ownership produces a concern with profit, one motive for increasing productivity. Second, industrialization was also linked to the rise of work-centered values, sentiments that do not develop by accident. People are taught them at home and at school. They emerged as unintended consequences of the Protestant Reformation (Weber, 1968). Third, industrialization was linked to the value placed on personal freedom that arose in the West in the eighteenth century (Lenski, 1966). Free people choose for themselves what

to produce and buy. Finally, industrialization was based on advances in scientific knowledge that occurred over the past 400 to 500 years. The terms *industrialization* and *industrial society* then are often used as shorthand ways of describing a historical watershed: the rise of new kinds of societies in the West over the last few centuries.

Industrialization implies more than merely a change in economic organization. This change is of primary interest here. With industrialization, the proportion of white-collar jobs rose while farming jobs fell. Thus, the white-collar work force increased from 19 percent in 1880 to 58 percent in 1992, and the farm work force declined from 52 percent to 3 percent. The new job slots at the top of the class structure constituted a vacuum that had to be filled; they "pulled" people upward out of poverty because an industrial society requires managers, professionals, sales clerks, and clerical help. So people left farming and blue-collar jobs for better-paying ones. Poverty fell as a result.

Class Differences in Fertility Rates. The fertility rate refers to the average number of children born to each woman. Although a two-century decline in fertility has occurred (the "baby boom" generation being the exception), people from lower-class backgrounds have always displayed higher birth rates. This difference, greater in the past than today, meant that families in farming and blue-collar occupations had more children on average than those in white-collar occupations. In the context of industrialization, in which the number of farming and blue-collar jobs was declining, these "excess" young persons were "pushed" upward in the occupational hierarchy by population pressure. The result was upward mobility and, hence, a decline in the rate of poverty.

Declining Discrimination. Discrimination refers to the unequal treatment of individuals and groups due to their personal characteristics, such as race or gender (Beeghley, 1996). In the past, the unequal treatment of racial and ethnic minorities was deliberate and overt, often legal. For example, the denial of civil rights kept racial and ethnic minorities from full citizenship. Other problems followed: unequal medical treatment, housing segregation, school segregation, and occupational discrimination, to name some obvious examples. Hence, whites enjoyed tremendous advantages in a context of industrialization and class differences in fertility rates. Yet, while discrimination continues in all these areas, significant change has occurred. African Americans, Latinos, and Asian Americans (not necessarily Native Americans) suffer less discrimination now than in the past. The result has been a lower rate of poverty.

The unequal treatment of women was similarly deliberate and overt, and also legal (Beeghley, forthcoming). For example, access to higher education and professional schools was restricted for women. Their ability to obtain credit in their own name was limited. Traditional norms dictated that women should remain home, bearing and raising children, and taking care of their husbands. Hence, males enjoyed tremendous advantages in seeking economic success over most of this century. Yet, while unequal treatment remains widespread, women suffer less discrimination today than in the past.

It remains true that, regardless of industrialization and class differences in fertility, people (usually white males) only succeeded by hard work. These structural variables are important, however, because they provided a historical context in which hard work could pay off. A century ago, the vast majority of people worked either on the farm or in blue-collar jobs, using muscle power to produce goods, and most were poor. If the job structure had not changed then, these people and their descendants (most of you) would have remained hard-working farmers. In the real world, however, people's options changed. Although no one was forced to be upwardly mobile, both the jobs and the people to fill them existed. These facts had nothing to do with each individual's motives or abilities. In Emile Durkheim's phrase, they reflected a change "in the nature of society itself" (1982: 128). The result has been a decline in the proportion of poor people in all industrial nations, more so in Western Europe than the United States.

THE U.S. POVERTY RATE TODAY

Despite the reduction in poverty during this century, the United States maintains a higher rate than other Western societies. The hypothesis below accounts for this situation.

The rate of poverty in the United States reflects:

1. The reproduction of the class structure
2. The vicious circle of poverty
3. Macroeconomic policy
4. The structure of elections
5. The structure of the economy
6. Institutionalized discrimination

The Reproduction of the Class Structure. In the United States, as in all societies, class structure is stable over time. Evidence for this assertion comes from analyses of mobility, which document that most people end up in the same class as their parents (Beeghley, 1996). This stability exists because people at each level use their resources to protect their advantages and pass them on to their children (Weber, 1968). Thus, those who are most vulnerable to poverty, working-class families, tend to remain that way over time and across generations.

Working-class individuals cannot alter the class structure into which they are born. It exists as a reality independently of them, limiting their choices. Thus, while a few near the top of the blue-collar hierarchy who work hard and have ability will move into white-collar jobs, most (including many who work just as hard and have just as much ability) will remain about where they began.

Some of them will become impoverished during their lives. And, in turn, a small proportion of the poor become trapped.

The Vicious Circle of Poverty. Most poverty is short-term: people find jobs, remarry, change their economic circumstances, and thereby escape impoverishment (Duncan, 1984). But the economic situation of the poor sometimes combines with other aspects of life in a reciprocal cause-effect way, a vicious circle that produces persistent poverty. For example, while public aid alleviates some problems poor people face, it also keeps them poor because the penalties for obtaining jobs are so severe. Imagine a poor family in which a parent is offered work paying, say, $5.50 per hour, or $11,440 per year. If the parent takes the job, he or she will lose Medicaid benefits for the children. Thus, the poor often experience a serious dilemma—be unemployed and require public aid or accept a job and lose medical insurance. Sometimes people choose not to accept employment, not because they are lazy but because the structure of opportunities makes this choice rational.

Macroeconomic Policy. Macroeconomic policy refers to the way government regulates the economy, especially inflation and unemployment. Ideally, there would be minimal amounts of both. In practice, however, a trade-off usually occurs such that one is higher than the other (Heilbroner and Thurow, 1982). This means that all economic problems are political problems in which someone's interests must be harmed while others benefit. In general, unemployment hurts the poor more than inflation does. For example, a 1 percent increase in the unemployment rate raises the poverty rate by an almost identical .97 percent. In contrast, a 1 percent increase in inflation raises the poverty rate by only .12 percent (Blank and Blinder, 1986: 187). Thus, except for unusual circumstances, when macroeconomic policy decisions are made, the poor benefit when unemployment is kept low.

Since World War II, however, U.S. policy has focused primarily on reducing inflation (Hibbs, 1977). It has sought (not always successfully) lower levels of inflation, 3 to 4 percent, in exchange for higher levels of unemployment, 5 to 6 percent. In contrast, most Western European governments have sought (again, not always successfully) higher levels of inflation, 5 to 6 percent, in exchange for lower levels of unemployment, 3 to 4 percent. These different choices affect the level of poverty by restricting the number of jobs available. The U.S. emphasis on inflation reflects the political priorities of middle-class and rich persons. They generally do not worry about unemployment and do not suffer its consequences. Rather, they see the value of their salaries and return on investments fall due to inflation, even if it is only moderate. Therefore, their representatives act to prevent it.

The Structure of Elections. The phrase "their representatives" is deliberately provocative, suggesting that public officials make choices reflecting the interests of the most powerful segments of a society. The fact that public policy in the United States creates more poverty than in other nations indicates the dominance of middle-class and rich people. They participate in the political process at a much higher rate than the working class and poor, which means the poor are relatively incapable of protecting their interests. The reason has to do with the structure of elections (Beeghley, 1992). First, holding elections on working days (rather than weekends or holidays) limits the ability of working class and poor persons to vote. People who are most able to vote have jobs that are less physically demanding, enjoy personal leave time as a job perquisite, have child care available, own a car, and live in safe neighborhoods. Second, registration requirements limit the ability of the poor to vote. Across all social classes, about 80 percent of people who are registered vote. Those who find it most difficult to register are working class and poor. Besides voting, people also participate by contributing money. Upper-income persons, of course, always have an advantage here. Low voting rates add to it, while high rates would reduce it because politicians would have to appeal to the interests of the entire population in order to be elected. Since this is not the case, macroeconomic and public aid policies reflect the interests of the nonpoor.

The Structure of the Economy. Wage levels and job location affect the poverty rate. Sometimes hard work does not pay off simply because wages are low. A person employed full-time at the minimum wage of $4.35 per hour will earn only $9,048 annually before taxes. In addition, the number of high-wage blue-collar jobs has declined over the past 10 to 15 years (Blank, 1991). Thus, during the 1980s, the poorest 20 percent of the population saw their wages drop in real terms (i.e., after inflation), even though the economy expanded during this period.

The location of low-wage jobs also affects the poverty rate. In the past, cities were centers for the manufacture of goods, and people with little education and few job skills could find work. Since about 1970, however, hundreds of thousands of jobs have moved to the suburbs. Getting to them requires a long and expensive commute, usually by car. This job mismatch has especially affected African Americans, who find it hard to live in suburbia due to housing discrimination. The reasons for the relocation of jobs can only be guessed. One is probably cheaper land and easier access to transportation. Another is probably a corporate aversion to African American workers (Williams, 1987). Regardless of the reason, the result is massive unemployment in central cities, concentrated among minority people.

Institutionalized Discrimination. Although discrimination has declined over time, as mentioned earlier, it remains built into the social structure—often in ways that are unintended. For example, African Americans, Latinos, and whites usually participate in different social networks. Thus, whites work at different jobs, their children go to different schools, they live in different neighborhoods, and they attend different churches from minorities. In effect, these forms of segregation identify the boundaries of the networks in which members of each group participate.

Such boundaries indicate how the class structure affects interaction patterns, housing choice, educational attainment, occupational attainment, and every other aspect of life. The fact of segregation, of participating in different social networks, often produces discrimination, even if no individual intends to do so. One result is a higher rate of poverty among African Americans and Latinos.

We noted earlier that the impact of traditional norms has declined over the years, which produces greater opportunities for women. Nonetheless, many women still govern their lives by such traditions (Beeghley, forthcoming). For example, a significant proportion of women still do not work for pay, work part-time in order to fill family obligations, and depend on their husbands for their lifestyle even if employed. In addition, men continue to resist the reorganization of family life to promote equal opportunity. Moreover, many parents still teach their children, male and female, that traditional norms ought to guide their lives. One result is that women are less successful economically.

We are two nations: one poor, one nonpoor. When presented with the details of poor people's lives, nonpoor persons often react with sympathy and understanding (see Kotlowitz, 1991). The dilemmas faced by mothers like Maria Sanchez can be heart-rending. However, when discussing "the poor" without specifics, these same persons revert to stereotypes about "deservedness." The structural analysis presented here should alert you to the fact that poor individuals acting in their own self-interest cannot significantly reduce the level of poverty. No amount of moralizing about the importance of self-reliance and individual initiative will change that blunt fact.

REFERENCES

BEEGHLEY, LEONARD
1984 "Illusion and Reality in the Measurement of Poverty," *Social Problems* 31: 312–324.

BEEGHLEY, LEONARD
1992 "Social Structure and Voting in the United States: A Historical and Comparative Analysis," *Perspectives on Social Problems* 3: 265–287.

BEEGHLEY, LEONARD
1996 *The Structure of Stratification,* 2nd ed. Boston: Allyn & Bacon.

BEEGHLEY, LEONARD
Forthcoming *What Does Your Wife Do?: Gender and the Transformation of Family Life.* Boulder, CO: Westview Press.

BERGER, PETER M.
1986 *The Capitalist Revolution.* New York: Basic Books.

BLANK, REBECCA M.
1991 "Why Were Poverty Rates So High in the 1980s?" Working paper #3878. Cambridge, MA: National Bureau of Economic Research.

BLANK, REBECCA M. and ALAN S. BLINDER
1986 "Macroeconomics, Income Distribution, and Poverty," in S. H. Danziger and D. H. Weinberg, eds., *Fighting Poverty: What Works and What Doesn't.* Cambridge, MA: Harvard University Press.

COUNCIL OF ECONOMIC ADVISORS (CEA)
1969   *Economic Report of the President.* Washington, DC: U.S. Government Printing Office.

COMMITTEE ON WAYS AND MEANS (CWM)
1993   *1993 Green Book: Background Material and Data on Programs within the Jurisdiction of the Committee on Ways and Means.* Washington, DC: U.S. Government Printing Office.

DUNCAN, GREG
1984   *Years of Poverty, Years of Plenty.* Ann Arbor, MI: Institute for Social Research, University of Michigan.

DURKHEIM, EMILE
1982   *The Rules of the Sociological Method.* New York: Free Press, 1982 (originally published in 1985).

HEILBRONER, ROBERT L. and LESTER C. THUROW
1982   *Economics Explained.* Englewood Cliffs, NJ: Prentice Hall.

HIBBS, DOUGLAS A.
1977   "Political Parties and Macroeconomic Policy," *American Political Science Review* 71: 1467–1487.

JONES, ELISE, JACQUELINE D. FORREST, NOREEN GOLDMAN, STANLEY HENSHAW, RICHARD LINCOLN, JEANNIE I. ROSOFF, CHARLES F. WESTOFF and DEIRDRE WULF
1986   *Teenage Pregnancy in Industrial Countries.* New Haven, CT: Yale University Press.

KASARDA, JOHN D.
1990   "Structural Factors Affecting the Location and Timing of Urban Underclass Growth," *Urban Geography* 11: 234–264.

KLASS, PERRY
1992   "Tackling Problems We Thought We Solved," *The New York Times Magazine,* December 12: 54–64.

KOTLOWITZ, ALEX
1991   *There Are No Children Here.* New York: Doubleday.

LENSKI, GERHARD
1966   *Power and Privilege.* New York: McGraw-Hill.

MARSIGLIO, WILLIAM
1993   "Adolescent Male's Orientation Toward Paternity and Contraception," *Family Planning Perspectives* 25 (January–February): 22–31.

PATTERSON, JAMES T.
1986   *America's Struggle Against Poverty, 1900–1985.* Cambridge, MA: Harvard University Press.

RUBIN, LILLIAN
1976   *Worlds of Pain.* New York: Basic Books.

SGROI, SUZANNE, ed.
1984   *Handbook of Clinical Intervention in Child Sexual Abuse.* Lexington, MA: D. C. Heath.

U.S. BUREAU OF THE CENSUS
1975   *Historical Statistics of the U.S.: Colonial Times to 1970.* Washington, DC: U.S. Government Printing Office.

U.S. BUREAU OF THE CENSUS
1993   *Poverty in the United States: 1992.* Current Population Reports, Series P60-185. Washington, DC: U.S. Government Printing Office.

U.S. BUREAU OF THE CENSUS
1994   *Statistical Abstract of the United States, 1994.* Washington DC: U.S. Government Printing Office.

U.S. BUREAU OF THE CENSUS
1995   "Income, Poverty, and Valuation of Noncash Benefits, 1993," *Current Population Reports,* P60-188. Washington, DC: U.S. Government Printing Office.

WEBER, MAX
1968   *Economy and Society.* Totowa, NJ: Bedminster Press, 1968 (originally published in 1920).

WILLIAMS, BRUCE B.
1987   *Black Workers in an Industrial Suburb: The Struggle Against Discrimination.* New Brunswick, NJ: Rutgers University Press.

EXERCISE 10

Name _____   Date _____

ID # _____   Class Time _____

I. Assume you are not a student. You have no savings or goods to sell. Assume you have a job that pays the minimum wage, $4.35 per hour, and that you work full-time, 52 weeks per year (there are no paid vacations). You receive no company benefits such as medical insurance. Assume you are married and have two children, both of whom are younger than 10 years old. Your spouse is unemployed and takes care of the children full-time (it does not matter which sex the spouse is). Because your family is intact, assume you are not eligible for AFDC or Medicaid. You are, however, eligible for food stamps. Assume you have a tenth-grade education.

A. In the space provided, prepare a comprehensive and detailed list of expenditures that shows how you will budget your money in this situation. Do not just fantasize; be realistic with your monthly estimates. If you move, deposits must be paid on all utilities and rental units. Also keep in mind that social security taxes are withheld from your check.

Budget Items	Amount
Food	
Housing	
Transportation to work	
Utilities	
Clothing	
Medical treatment	
Children's school expenses	
Other	
Other	
Total monthly expenses	
Monthly income	

B. Now describe in detail what your life would be like with these financial constraints.

II. Develop two roles: you as a poor person and you as an upper-middle-class person. Work on language, costume, body language, and so forth to make these presentations convincing.

A. Select one or a matched pair of organizations. Present yourself to a representative of that organization with an unusual request. Select your request so that it is neither illegal nor very expensive or time-consuming to the organization. However, your request should not be part of the organization's routine performance. For example, purchase a pound of fish from a supermarket, then ask that it be ground into fishburger. (Your cat will love you!) Use your imagination. Select a plausible request but an odd one. For purposes of this assignment, it is less useful to ask to drive a new Mercedes or be shown a house because the salespeople may be treating you differently in each role based on a reasonable evaluation of your ability to purchase these items.

B. Present yourself twice, once as each person. Use the next two pages to describe the similarities and differences in treatment and outcome. How do you think poor people feel? What effect will this kind of treatment have on the poor when it is repeated over time?

C. Summarize your experience (e.g., how others treated you) as a poor person.

D. Summarize your experience (e.g., how others treated you) as an upper-middle-class person.

11

Racist and Egalitarian Ideologies in Modern American Culture

Charles Case

The history of America is a history of the gradual extension of citizenship rights and equal opportunities to a greater number of groups and categories of our residents. In colonial America, full participation in political and civic affairs was generally afforded only to white, land-owning males who were members of the appropriate religious denomination. More than three hundred years later, very substantial progress has been made toward making equal rights and equal participation available to virtually all categories of American residents. Still, very substantial inequalities in opportunities and conditions for vast numbers of minority group members remain a fact of life in present-day America.

This essay will examine the present condition of minorities in America with a particular focus on African Americans. We will discuss the major forces that have created, increased, or diminished racial inequality throughout history and in the present era. Examples will be presented of areas where traditional American minority groups have substantially increased their power, influence, opportunities, and participation. Examples will also be presented of aspects of present-day American culture and society where vast numbers of minority group members have made little or no progress toward equal conditions of life, opportunities, power, and influence.

A BRIEF HISTORY OF AFRICAN AMERICANS

The first 250 years of American history saw very little progress toward racial equality for African Americans. With rare exceptions, all African Americans were slaves until the conclusion of the Civil War in 1865. After emancipation, there were efforts by the federal government to assure voting and other rights of citizenship to the former (male) slaves. These efforts were so successful that by 1868, many formerly confederate states had more black registered voters than white voters. Hundreds of newly

emancipated black citizens were elected to local and state government positions, including two lieutenant governors and several U.S. congressmen. Reconstruction was effectively ended by the Compromise of 1877. Very briefly stated, the 1876 election was a brokered deal in which Southern white Democrats gave the presidency of the United States to the Republican candidate, Rutherford B. Hayes, instead of the Democratic candidate, Samuel Tilden, who won the popular vote. In return, the Republicans agreed to use their control over the federal government, courts, and military to ensure complete autonomy for the white (Democratic) political establishment of the former confederacy. They also promised to remove the federal troops that had been sent to protect the rights of the former slaves.

For the next 70 years the federal government and federal courts lived up to their pledge of "home rule." This was a period of declining national political influence in the Southern states and one of increasing "states' rights" or local governance. For the states of the former confederacy this resulted in "Jim Crow" laws, violence, terrorism, poll taxes, literacy tests, and other tactics employed to systematically prevent African Americans from achieving the slightest semblance of equality in power, status, or opportunities. From the 1870s to the 1950s, white mobs lynched (tortured and killed) over 3,000 African Americans for such offenses as attempting to bring a lawsuit against a white man, making boastful remarks, being a witness, trying to act like a white man, looking at a white woman "the wrong way," and attempting to vote (from unpublished records at Tuskegee Institute, cited in Cox, 1948). Sharecropping largely replaced slavery as the means for obtaining virtually free agricultural labor.

For the hundreds of thousands, and eventually millions, of African Americans who left the South seeking a better life in the industrial cities of the North and West, conditions were little better. Industrialists recruited many of the migrants as strike-breakers in the labor wars of the emerging labor union movement. However, most black workers were unemployed again as soon as the strike was settled. The deep and lasting hostility that resulted between organized labor and African Americans was one reason why labor unions continued to be among the most racially segregated American institutions up to the 1970s. The virtual exclusion of African Americans from labor unions removed an important rung from the ladder of upward mobility that had been available to other ethnic minorities.

Overall, very little progress toward equal opportunities or equal participation in American society was achieved between the end of slavery and World War II. In 1941, things began to change significantly. President Roosevelt began the process of ending racial discrimination in Civil Service and other government employment. In 1948, President Truman ordered an end to racial discrimination in the United States armed services. In 1954, the U.S. Supreme Court ruled that racial segregation in public schools violated the constitutional guarantee of equal protection under the law provided by the Fourteenth Amendment. Thus, by the 1950s, the movement toward greater levels of equal participation and opportunities for African Americans became a nationwide effort. Since then, relatively rapid progress toward racial equality has been achieved through the tactics of civil rights organizations (demonstrations, protests, boycotts, lawsuits, etc.), court rulings, state and federal civil rights legislation, mass media attention to racial injustices, and shifts in public opinion toward greater support for racial equality.

Attitudes of white Americans toward racial equality have changed dramatically over the past 50 years. Figure 11.1 shows changes in attitudes between 1942 and 1980. In 1942, the majority of all Americans, both Southern and non-Southern, opposed the racial integration of their blocks and schools. By 1956, most non-Southerners favored integration, but among Southerners, segregation was still supported by an overwhelming majority. By 1980, the majority of Americans in all regions expressed support for racial equality. Figure 11.2 shows trends in egalitarian attitudes and interactions between 1972 and 1993. We see that support for equal treatment for African Americans continues to increase among Southern and non-Southern respondents. By 1993, racist attitudes are expressed by relatively few Southern and very few non-Southern respondents. Figure 11.2 also shows the percentage of white Americans who report having integrated neighborhoods, churches, and dinner tables. Although a great deal of segregation still exists today, clearly both the attitudes and behaviors of Americans are moving toward racial equality.

THE DETERMINANTS OF RACIST IDEOLOGIES

The United States of America has always taken pride in being the premier democracy in the world. The Constitution and Bill of Rights guarantee equal justice for all and the protection of individuals' rights and freedoms. The main tenets of egalitarian ideology are that all humans are equal in basic human qualities and potentials and that it is

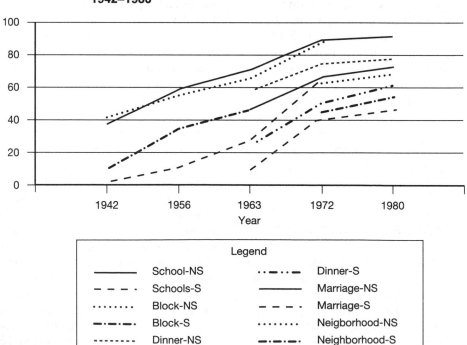

FIGURE 11.1:   Trends in Egalitarian Attitudes in the South and Non-South, 1942–1980

SOURCE: Charles E. Case and Andrew M. Greeley, "Attitudes Toward Racial Equality," *Humboldt Journal of Social Relations* 16 (1990): 67–94.

FIGURE 11.2:   White Americans with Egalitarian Attitudes and Interactions by Year and Region

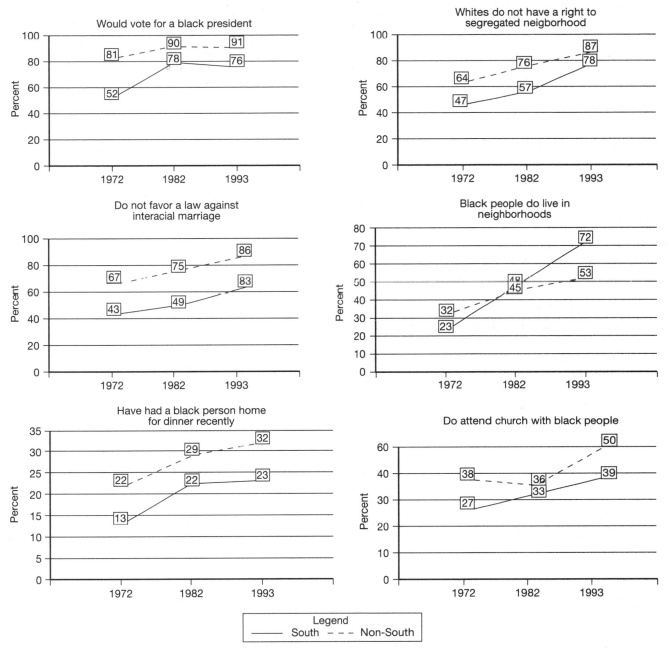

SOURCE: NORC, General Social Services.

logically and morally appropriate to afford equal opportunities and rights to all people (Case and Greeley, 1990). Given the legal underpinnings of democracy and the pervasiveness of the egalitarian ideology, it is very difficult to rationalize such practices as slavery, the virtual extermination of Native Americans, the incarceration of Americans of Japanese descent during World War II, and numerous other atrocities against minority group members throughout United States history. Such practices share a common strategy and result; by portraying minorities as subhumans unqualified for the rights of "real" humans (white males), they maintain or increase significant advantages for members of the majority group at the expense of those in the minority group. This is the sociological concept of racism.

Racism is a set of beliefs that seeks to justify the atrocious treatment of those who are the target of racist ideologies. The major elements of racist (and similarly sexist) ideologies include: (1) the belief that huge differences in basic human qualities exist among various racial, ethnic, and gender groups; (2) the belief that these differences are biologically and genetically determined and represent the will of God; (3) the belief that minority group members are naturally inferior to majority group members in mental, physical, moral, and emotional characteristics and potentials; and (4) the belief that equal treatment or equal opportunities for these "inferior" beings is illogical, unwise, and against the will of God.

As much as the beliefs or assertions of racist ideology challenge the egalitarian ideal, egalitarian beliefs and values likewise challenge racist ones. Indeed, the history of American race and ethnic relations has been as much a struggle between these ideologies—racism and egalitarianism—as it has been conflict among racial and ethnic groups. The two are deeply intertwined. Ironically, it is precisely our nation's history of high ideals and commitment to the principles of democracy and equality that have led to the often frenzied efforts to promote racist ideology and to silence egalitarian ideology in order to justify gross lack of democracy and equality that has been afforded minorities throughout our history. But ideological conflicts are only part of the picture. To fully understand the determinants of racial inequality, a number of other social factors must be considered.

The progress and lack of progress toward racial equality in the United States are also the result of four social factors that determine and represent relationships between majority and minority groups; ideology, power, conditions of life for minority groups, and interactions between minority and majority group members. Each of these social factors is both a result of and an influence upon each of the other key social factors.

The control of ideas (ideology) in any group or society is largely the consequence of the power or powerlessness of the various groups or elements in that group or society. Those who control political discourse, economic resources, the media, religious discourse, or educational institutions, or who have the resources to simply shout down or silence the opposing perspectives are able to ensure that the ideas, values, and beliefs favorable to their interests will prevail. Reciprocally, the relative inability to influence the prevailing ideas results in the perpetuation of powerlessness and the inability to successfully argue the case for equality of conditions and opportunities.

The ability to deny equal rights and opportunities to minority group members results in greater power and advantage for many members of the majority group. The lack of opportunities for minority groups assures a vast pool of cheap and exploitable labor for the benefit of the privileged group. Powerless and often desperate, minority persons can be employed to do much of the unpleasant, dirty, and dangerous work for minimum wage or less, creating huge profits for their employers. Besides providing cheap labor in the fields, factories, and fast food outlets of the privileged class, minorities often provide personal servitude for the advantaged group. This is well illustrated by the large number of elected officials and political appointees, who have recently been found to have had "undocumented aliens" (illegal immigrants) working in their homes. As long as all high-status positions in business, government, religion, education, and other institutions are reserved for privileged members of the majority group, the likelihood of success for the privileged group is greatly increased at the expense of subordinate minorities.

Equal-status interactions among members of various groups have long been understood to be one of the most effective means for reducing stereotypes and prejudices (e.g., Stouffer et al., 1949). At the other end of the spectrum, those groups and individuals that interact only with members of their own race, gender, or status group are largely incapable of viewing others as equal in human qualities and potentials (Fuchs and Case, 1989). For this reason, in times and places where extreme inequality and racism have prospered, segregation between majority and minority groups has been zealously imposed. Any interaction that did occur was in the clearly unequal status relationships between master and servant, rapist and victim, and so forth. The most forbidden relationships in systems that sought to impose extreme racism were (or are) marriage and dating relationships. We now know that only carefully guarded ignorance can preserve the racist assertion that various groups differ in basic human qualities.

The exclusion of African Americans from higher-status positions and roles in politics, business, education, sports, and other institutions reinforces the naive belief that African Americans lack the capacity to perform in these roles. Similarly, a large population of highly visible minorities living in poverty reinforces racist beliefs that "these people are different from us." Those who are highly racist are also the most likely to avoid interaction with members of minority groups and to oppose the integration of neighborhoods and institutions such as schools and churches.

Thus, inequality of opportunity and power, racist ideologies, and noninteraction among minority and majority group members all feed upon or reinforce one another. Figure 11.3 shows statistical evidence of the relationship between racial interaction and egalitarian attitudes. Approximately 30 percent of white Americans who report having segregated neighborhoods, churches, and dinner tables, give nonegalitarian responses on the question of support for laws against interracial marriage and on the question of whether whites have a right to maintain segregated neighborhoods. Of those who report racially integrated interactions in each of these three areas of their lives, few or no respondents voice support for racist perspectives.

PROGRESS AND RESISTANCE TOWARD EQUALITY FOR MINORITIES TODAY

The pace of movement toward increased egalitarianism and a reduction in racism and racial inequality has accelerated over the last few decades. Such progress is, of course, too fast for some but painfully slow for those who have lived their lives waiting and struggling for equality. Despite the efforts of persons of good will, progress has been resisted and undermined at every step of the way. Some of this resistance has come from avowedly racist individuals and organizations; some has been due to the mutual reinforcement of the four previously mentioned com-

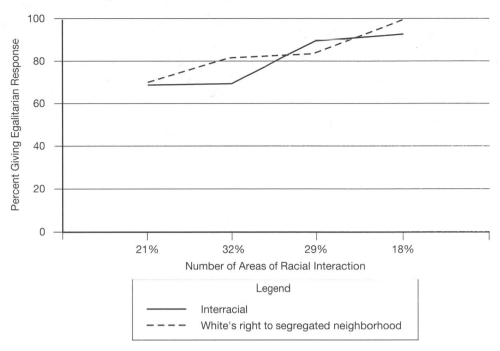

FIGURE 11.3: Egalitarian Attitudes by Amount of Interracial Contact

Number of Areas of Racial Interaction

Legend
—— Interracial
- - - - White's right to segregated neighborhood

ponents of inequality (ideology, power, conditions of life, and interactions).

The proverbial "glass half empty and half full" analogy accurately describes the present state of racial equality in America. African Americans and other minorities have made significant progress in virtually every area of society but still face significant inequalities. In politics, black mayors, judges, and police chiefs, are no longer a rarity. Between 1963 and 1993, over 12 million African Americans became registered voters, and the number of black elected officials increased from approximately 300 to over 8,000. Nonetheless, the highest political offices in the land—the presidency and vice-presidency, chief justice of the Supreme Court, and nearly every state governorship continues to be "for whites only." In entertainment and the mass media, we find popular African American superstars in music, sports, television, movies, and journalism, yet control of these industries continues to be overwhelmingly in the hands of white males.

Within virtually every area of American culture and society, positive role models and symbolic portrayals of harmonious equal-status interactions between members of minority and majority groups are abundant. At the same time, stereotypical and negative portrayals of minority persons as criminals, ghetto dwellers, and low-status individuals are potent images. Today, the proportion of African American families classified as middle income has increased to over 40 percent, up from 20 percent in 1968. Yet the approximate average black family yearly income, $19,000, lags far behind that of white families, $32,000 (U.S. Bureau of the Census, 1990). Over three times as many black families live below the poverty level as white families, and 57 percent of black children

live in poverty, compared to 38 percent of white children (CNN news, May 21, 1992). Forty years after the federal courts outlawed school segregation, an incredible 73 percent of black and Hispanic children attend segregated (predominantly minority) schools (Farley, 1995). The amount of tax money spent per child in wealthy, predominantly white suburban schools is approximately twice the amount spent in the central city schools that teach most of our nation's poor minorities (Kozol, 1991).

The United States is, and always has been, a land of contradictions. No other industrialized nation of the world has such concentrations of wealth and privilege and at the same time such concentrations of poverty and despair. Both racist and egalitarian ideologies have always been major features of our cultural landscape. While both sets of beliefs still persist (often within the same person), we have made very significant progress away from racism and toward egalitarianism. The remaining racial inequalities in the United States will not disappear automatically. Achieving true democracy and equality of opportunities for all Americans will require a widespread understanding of the forces that create inequality and a concerted effort to continue the struggle that so many have fought over past generations to overcome racism and injustice. The struggle will continue one institution, one symbol, one interaction, and one person at a time.

REFERENCES

CASE, CHARLES E. and ANDREW M. GREELEY
1990 "Attitudes Toward Racial Equality," *Humboldt Journal of Social Relations* 16: 67–94.

CNN News
May 21, 1992.

Cox, Oliver C.
1948   *Caste, Class and Race: A Study in Social Dynamics.* Garden City, NY: Doubleday.

Farley, John E.
1995   *Majority-Minority Relations,* 3rd ed. Englewood Cliffs, NJ: Prentice Hall.

Fuchs, Stephan and Charles E. Case
1989   "Prejudice as Lifeform," *Sociological Inquiry* 59: 301–317.

Kozol, Jonathan
1991   *Savage Inequalities.* New York: Crown Publishers.

Stouffer, Samuel A., E. A. Suchman, L. C. DeVinney, S. A. Star and R. N. Williams
1949   *The American Soldier, Vol. 1, Adjustment During Army Life.* Princeton, NJ: Princeton University Press.

U.S. Bureau of the Census
1990   *Statistical Abstract of the United States, 1990,* Washington, DC: Government Printing Office.

EXERCISE 11

Name _____   Date _____

ID # _____   Class Time _____

I. *Viewing Images and Messages of Racial Egalitarianism or Nonegalitarianism on Television.* Both racist and egalitarian ideas and symbols can be found in every part of American history and culture. Each portion of the following exercise is intended to have you examine some part(s) of your cultural environment for examples of both racist and egalitarian messages, symbols, and interactions.

A. Watch (and perhaps videotape) two-minute segments from ten different television shows (you may include advertisements). Using the data coding sheet below, analyze the people, symbols, messages, and interactions that you see in the television segments. In the parts labeled 1, 2, and 3, put "hash marks" in the appropriate box for each person or character, each message that you see and hear. In part 4, mark the number of each type of interaction among the people or characters in the segments you observe. You will probably see several of each type in each two-minute segment, so be prepared to make many hash marks recording each occurrence.

	African American	White	Other
1. How many people or characters from each category did you see?			
2. The central figure, star, leader, or most important person in each scene is . . .			
3. The "bad guy," criminal, or other person shown in a negative role is . . .			

4. How many of each of the following types of interactions did you observe?

	No interaction between black and white characters	Equal status interactions between blacks and whites	High-status whites and lower-status blacks	High-status blacks and lower-status whites
Number of occurrences				

B. What do you conclude from your television observations about the images and messages about racial equality and racial inequality in America today? For example, which groups are over-represented and under-represented in egalitarian or racially stereotyped roles? Is there a pattern with respect to the portrayal of minorities in positive or negative roles? Summarize your research findings in one or two short paragraphs in the space provided below.

II. *Detecting Egalitarian and Nonegalitarian Racial Expressions in Everyday Life.* Racially egalitarian and racially nonegalitarian expressions may take any of a number of different forms. In addition to their expression in the mass media, such expressions may occur in the words of a casual conversation, in an "innocent" joke, on a bumper sticker, in the way that people work or play together, in the political arena or economic sphere—practically anywhere.

A. You are to carry this observation sheet with you for one day. Record in the table below specific examples of racially egalitarian and nonegalitarian messages, symbols, and behaviors you experience directly or observe in the course of your day. Also, record the specific location where each observation was made.

	Messages	Symbols	Behavior	Location
Racial equality				
Racial inequality				

B. Now that you are more sensitive to different expressions of racial equality and inequality, the second part of this observation exercise asks you to identify specific examples of such expressions in different settings. Find examples of equality and inequality expressions in at least four of the six situations in the table below. (You may provide an example from some other area of social life not noted in the list and have it count as one of the four required examples.) *Note that the examples you provide here should be different from the examples you used to answer part A of this exercise.*

	Equity	Inequality	Location
School			
Family			
Neighborhood			
Work			
Church			
Politics			
Other			

12

Racism, Capital Punishment, and the U.S. Supreme Court

Adalberto Aguirre, Jr., and David V. Baker

The criminal justice system is a racist institution used by white society to safeguard its social, political, and economic interests from minority group infringement. As a result, the policies and behavior of criminal justice agents frequently victimize minorities. In the following pages we examine the extent to which the racist application of capital punishment in U.S. society victimizes nonwhite minorities and show that the degree of equality one receives in the American criminal justice system is directly linked to one's race and ethnicity.

Criminal law has long been recognized as "an instrument of the state and ruling class to maintain and perpetuate the existing social and economic order" (Quinney, 1974: 16). Loh (1984: 194) notes specifically that "capital statutes served the interests of private property and commerce against those who might seek to undermine them." Historically, economic and social conditions in the U.S. society have influenced the character of capital statutes. Capital statutes, for example, reflected the economic interests associated with the growth of slavery and the development of the Southern plantation economy. Slave stealing, concealing slaves with intent to free them, inciting slaves to revolt, and circulating seditious literature among slaves were among North Carolina's capital crimes in the late 1830s (Bowers, 1974). Such statutory developments suggest that the death penalty served to protect and control the institution of slavery in the South. The history of capital punishment in the United States, then, is the history of an extremely efficient institutional means of protecting dominant group interests.

The President's Commission on Law Enforcement and Administration of Justice pointed out in 1967 that "there is [now] evidence that the imposition of the death sentence and the exercise of dispensing power by the Courts . . . follow discriminatory patterns. The death sentence is disproportionately imposed and carried out on the poor, the Negro, and the members of unpopular groups." Former U.S. Supreme Court Justice Arthur J. Goldberg

(Goldberg and Dershowitz, 1970: 1784) argued three years later that the Court should declare capital punishment unconstitutional based on the Eighth and Fourteenth Amendments to the federal Constitution because it is "highly suspect under the standards of degrading severity and wanton imposition." However, the Court did not address racial discrimination in the application of the death penalty until 1972. Since 1972, policy and legal experts have debated how strong empirical evidence must be for the Court to accept that racial factors influence the way the state imposes the death penalty. The American Society of Criminology introduced and recommended the following resolution in 1987, in Montreal, Canada, at its annual meeting:

> Be it resolved that because social science research has demonstrated the death penalty to be racist in application . . . , the American Society of Criminology publicly condemns this form of punishment, and urges its members to use their professional skills in legislatures and courts to seek a speedy abolition of this form of punishment.

Most recently, retired U.S. Supreme Court Justice Harry A. Blackmun held that after a 20-year struggle with the issue of capital punishment, the Court should recognize that "the death penalty experiment has failed" and that it is time for the Court to abandon the "delusion" that capital punishment could be consistent with the Constitution. He specifically argued that:

> Twenty years have passed since this Court declared that the death penalty must be imposed fairly and with reasonable consistency or not at all (*Furman v. Georgia*), and, despite the effort of the states and courts to devise legal formulas and procedural rules to meet this daunting challenge, the death penalty remains fraught with arbitrariness, discrimination, caprice and mistake (1994).

Nearly 4,100 prisoners in the United States have been executed since 1930.[1] Fifty-three percent of these prisoners were black and 46 percent were white. Racial disparity in capital sentencing is glaringly apparent among executions for rape. Of the 455 executions for rape during this period, 89 percent were black prisoners and about 10 percent were white prisoners. U.S. Department of Justice data show that southern states have administered over 98 percent of all black executions. Barlow (1993) points out that no white executions have occurred for the killing of a black since 1976. Further, only 30 executions in the history of capital punishment in the United States involved a white defendant sentenced to death for killing a black.

Given that blacks have consistently represented about 11 percent of the total U.S. population since 1930, these figures suggest that blacks have suffered from discriminatory treatment in the imposition of the death penalty. The rate of execution for blacks has been over five times that of whites. Black execution rates for rape, however, have been nine times the execution rate of whites. Our purpose here is to review empirical studies that reveal that the death penalty has been disproportionately applied to blacks convicted of rape and murder. These studies establish pervasive evidence that racial disparity in the death penalty amounts to discretionary and discriminatory application of the penalty in U.S. criminal justice.

SOCIOLOGICAL INVESTIGATION OF RACISM AND CAPITAL PUNISHMENT

Many studies have documented evidence of racial discrimination in the imposition of the death penalty on blacks. We review these studies in their historical context—whether they were conducted before, during the interim, or after the U.S. Supreme Court decisions in *Furman v. Georgia* (1972) and *Gregg v. Georgia* (1976). The *Furman* decision held that all death penalty statutes in the United States were unconstitutional because they allowed discretionary and discriminatory application of capital punishment. Such application, argued the Court, amounts to cruel and unusual punishment violating the Eighth Amendment to the U.S. federal Constitution. The *Furman* decision did not abolish capital punishment in the United States. The court argued that the death penalty is not inherently cruel and unusual punishment but held that the capricious manner in which the state applied the penalty in the cases before the court was unconstitutional. In the *Gregg* decision, the court attempted to curb the discretionary and discriminatory application of the death penalty to blacks by providing for guided discretion in capital sentencing. The court affirmed the death sentences in the cases under review in *Gregg*. The Court affirmed the cases because Georgia had directed attention to the circumstances of the crimes and provided for consideration of mitigating factors designed to protect against arbitrary imposition of the death penalty.

Pre-*Furman* Studies. Brearley (1930) completed the earliest study on black-white differentials in the administration of justice in 1930. He found that 52 percent

of the 407 homicide cases in South Carolina prosecuted between 1920 and 1926 resulted in guilty verdicts. Of the convictions, 64 percent involved black defendants and 32 percent involved whites. Brearley attributes this finding to racial prejudice by white jurors and court officials, and to blacks' low economic status, which inhibits the process of securing "good" criminal defense lawyers.

Mangum (1941) studied racial disparity in capital cases in several southern states. He reported that between 1920 and 1938, 74 percent of all black and 50 percent of white death sentences were carried out. In 1938, Missouri executed 83 percent of all blacks and 75 percent of all whites sentenced to death. From 1909 to 1938, Missouri carried out 52 percent of all black and 39 percent of all white death sentences. From 1915 to 1937, Oklahoma executed 39 percent of all blacks and 34 percent of all whites sentenced to death. South Carolina executed 72 percent of all blacks and 41 percent of all whites sentenced to death from 1912 to 1938. Mangum also discovered that, between 1928 and 1938, Tennessee executed 67 percent of all blacks and 35 percent of all whites sentenced to death. Virginia executed 83 percent of all blacks and 79 percent of all whites sentenced to death from 1924 to 1938.

In 1941, Johnson conducted a study on race and capital punishment. He studied 220 homicide cases in Virginia, 95 homicides in Georgia, and 330 homicide cases in North Carolina between 1930 and 1940. His study shows that blacks who killed whites suffered the death penalty more than blacks who killed blacks. For example, in Virginia and Georgia, 27 percent of all black offenders with white victims received the death penalty, yet only 16 percent of all white offenders with white victims received the death penalty. Only 3 percent of all black offenders with black victims received the death penalty, and no white offender with a black victim received the death penalty.

Garfinkel's (1949) investigation of 821 homicide cases in North Carolina between 1930 and 1940 also established that there is a statistically significant association between the race of the defendant and that of the victim. Garfinkel found that 94 percent of all cases involving blacks who killed whites resulted in a first-degree murder indictment, yet only 28 percent of all cases involving whites accused of killing blacks ended in a similar indictment. Also, only 15 percent of all cases involving blacks accused of killing whites resulted in an acquittal. Garfinkel found that 10 percent of the blacks who killed whites received life imprisonment, but none of the whites who killed blacks received life imprisonment.

Johnson (1957) studied rape cases that resulted in death sentences in North Carolina between 1909 and 1954. He found that 56 percent of all persons executed were black and 43 percent were white. Johnson's study concluded that blacks were far more likely to suffer the death penalty for rape than whites convicted of rape. The Florida Civil Liberties Union (1964) reported similar findings from a study conducted in 1964. In Florida, between 1940 and 1964, 54 percent of all blacks who raped white women received the death penalty. During the same period, only one of the eight white males convicted of raping black females received the death penalty.

The Ohio Legislative Service Commission conducted a study in 1961 that found 37 percent of all death penalty sentences in 1950 were for black offenders. When compared to blacks, the study found that whites were more likely to have their sentences commuted to life imprisonment. Wolfgang et al.'s (1962) study of 439 men sentenced to death in Pennsylvania for murder between 1914 and 1958, found it statistically significant that only 11 percent of blacks convicted of murder had their sentences commuted to life imprisonment. About 20 percent of all cases involving white prisoners, however, resulted in commuted sentences.

A variety of other researchers have found that several other states disproportionately apply the death penalty to blacks. Carter and Smith (1969) found that black executions comprised 22 percent of all executions in California between 1938 and 1963. Similarly, Koeninger (1969) found that between 1924 and 1968, Texas disproportionately executed blacks, the young, the poor, and the ignorant. Koeninger found that of the 460 persons executed in Texas during that period, about 59 percent were black.

In March 1972, Wolfgang testified before a congressional subcommittee for a moratorium on capital punishment.[2] The testimony presented evidence supporting a contention of racial discrimination in the imposition of the death penalty. With the aid of the NAACP Legal Defense and Education Fund, Inc., and Professor Anthony Amsterdam, Wolfgang collected data on over 3,000 rape convictions between 1945 and 1965 in 11 southern states: Alabama, Arkansas, Florida, Georgia, Louisiana, Mississippi, North Carolina, South Carolina, Tennessee, Texas, and Virginia. Wolfgang and his associates examined over two dozen variables measuring nonracial factors concerning disproportionate application of the death penalty for blacks. The variables included the circumstances of the offense (the degree of force employed by the defendant to commit the crime, the amount of physical harm suffered by the victim, and whether the crime was committed during the commission of another crime); the character of the victim (age, marital status, dependent children, chastity); the characteristics of the defendant (age, marital status, occupation, prior criminal record); the nature of the relationship between the defendant and the victim (prior acquaintance, prior sexual relations); and the circumstances surrounding the trial that led to the conviction of the defendant. He found that none of the nonracial variables could explain the higher conviction rate for blacks and concluded that only race could account for the disproportionate application of the death penalty to blacks convicted of rape.

Zimring et al. (1976) collected data on 204 homicide cases in Philadelphia in 1970. Less than 20 percent of the cases analyzed had interracial defendant-victim combinations. Sixty-five percent of those involving black defendants with white victims ended in a death sentence or life imprisonment. However, only 25 percent of all felony defendants convicted of killing blacks were sentenced to death or life imprisonment.

Kleck (1981), who has critically evaluated studies on racial discrimination in the death penalty conducted before the *Furman* decision, makes two observations about these various studies. First, he argues that although studies show conclusive patterns of racial discrimination against blacks in the use of the death penalty, these patterns most often occur in southern states. On this point, however, Kleck is incorrect. While racial disparities in imposing the death penalty are more pronounced in the South, several studies show that patterns of racial discrimination in presentencing, sentencing, and postsentencing decisions are not restricted to southern jurisdictions (Gross and Mauro, 1984, 1989; Bedau, 1964, 1965; Bowers and Pierce, 1980; Kalven, 1969; Carter and Smith, 1969).

The second observation made by Kleck is that black murder defendants with black victims are the least likely defendant-victim category associated with the death penalty outside the South. This observation has substantial merit, as noted above. In explaining the lenient treatment of black murder defendants convicted of murdering a black victim, Kleck suggests that "interracial crimes are considered by [the] predominantly white social-control agents to be less serious offenses, representing less loss or threat to the community than crimes with White victims" (1981: 800).

According to our review of pre-*Furman* studies on capital punishment, the state executes black prisoners in a discretionary and discriminatory manner. This practice is not isolated in the South, however. Racial discrimination in capital punishment is a national phenomenon. Moreover, these studies illustrate the extent to which racism permeates the U.S. criminal justice system.

Furman v. Georgia. With *Jackson v. Georgia* (1972) and *Branch v. Texas* (1972), the U.S. Supreme Court held by a bare majority in *Furman* that the imposition of the death penalty as currently administered in the United States amounted to cruel and unusual punishment as prohibited by the Eighth and Fourteenth amendments. The holding not only set aside the sentences of *Furman, Branch,* and *Jackson* but also vacated some 120 other cases before the Court. Similarly vacated were some 645 cases involving death row inmates in prisons throughout the nation (Ehrhardt, 1973; McDonald, 1972). The Court overruled the death penalty statutes of 40 states, the District of Columbia, and the federal government as defective and unconstitutional pursuant to *Furman.*

The five-to-four decision contains nine different opinions with five separate one-vote opinions comprising the majority view. Justices Brennan and Marshall found the death penalty per se unconstitutional because it is cruel and unusual punishment pursuant to the Eighth Amendment. Justices Douglas, Stewart, and White did not find capital punishment per se unconstitutional but argued instead that capital punishment is invalid because the state applies it in an arbitrary and capricious manner. Chief Justice Burger and Associate Justices Powell, Rehnquist, and Blackmun argued that abolition of the death penalty is strictly a matter for Congress to decide.

Despite the overwhelming importance that the issue of racial disparity had on the finding in *Furman,* only five of the nine justices approached the issue of racial discrimination in the imposition of the death penalty. Justice Douglas cited empirical findings from several different studies showing that it is the poor and blacks who are more likely to suffer imposition of the death penalty than other groups. The justices concluded that the capital statutes before the Court were discriminatory. Relying on similar research findings, Justice Marshall argued that capital punishment is unconstitutional because it is "imposed discriminatorily against certain identifiable classes of people" and that it is "morally reprehensible" to American values (*Furman v. Georgia,* 1972: 363–369). Justice Stewart disagreed with Justices Douglas and Marshall that racial discrimination proves to be a factor in imposing the death penalty. He did argue, however, that the justices "have demonstrated that, if any basis can be discerned for the selection of these few to be sentenced to die, it is the constitutionally impermissible basis of race" (p. 310). Of the dissenters, Chief Justice Burger and Justice Powell mentioned the relationship between racial discrimination and use of the death penalty. While both justices found the evidence of racial discrimination against blacks particularly valid, they believed that the proper role of the Court was not to decide public policy.

The essence of the *Furman* decision is that for the first time the U.S. Supreme Court formally recognized that the U.S. reserved capital punishment for a select group of people—namely, blacks, the poor, and the powerless. Two facts concerning the application of the death penalty resulted from the *Furman* decision. First, the Court recognized that while the death penalty per se is not unconstitutional, the manner in which the penalty had been applied in the past is because it denies the sentenced equal protection under the law and amounts to cruel and unusual punishment. Second, the Court made it clear that policy makers must devise guidelines that will secure restricted discretion in remanding prisoners to death.

Post-*Furman*, Pre-*Gregg* Studies. Researchers conducted several studies on racial discrimination between the *Furman* decision in 1972 and the *Gregg* decision in 1976. Riedel (1976) compared the racial composition of offenders under the sentence of death in December 1971 (pursuant to pre-*Furman* capital statutes) with those under the sentence of death as of December 1975 (pursuant to mandatory and discretionary post-*Furman* capital statutes). He not only found that the racial disparity affecting death row inmates in the pre-*Furman* era remained unchanged in the post-*Furman* period but also that the black defendant–white victim category was the defendant-victim racial classification with the highest rate of death sentences imposed. Riedel reported that 53 per-

cent of the death row inmates in December 1971 were nonwhite and that this figure rose to 62 percent in December 1975. The percentage of nonwhites in death row populations in the South declined from 67 percent to 63 percent during this period. However, the western region increased its percentage of black death row inmates from 26 percent to 52 percent. From these figures, Riedel concluded the statutes enacted before and after the *Furman* decision produced the same degree of racial disproportion in death sentences.

Riedel also found that 87 percent of the death sentences were for white-victim murders and 45 percent were for the murder of white victims by black defendants. The degree of racial disparity in death sentences is even more pronounced in this period (1971–1975), and the black defendant–white victim category comprised the smallest proportion of the total number of murder cases.

In a study of first-degree murder prosecutions in Dade County, Florida, from 1973 to 1976, Arkin (1980) reported that black defendants who murdered whites were more likely to be sentenced to death than white defendants. Arkin's data reveal juries were four times more likely to convict black offenders with white victims of first-degree murder charges than blacks with black victims. While the black-defendant–white-victim category of criminal offense comprised only 21 percent of the 350 murder cases prosecuted, 50 percent of the cases resulting in death penalty sentences came from that category of offender.

In sum, these two studies show that the *Furman* decision had little or no diminishing effect on racial discrimination in the imposition of the death penalty. These studies show that the state still used the death penalty to protect a specific class of individuals—namely whites—from criminal victimization. Juries overwhelmingly convicted and sentenced to death black defendants whose victims were white compared to other defendant-victim racial categories.

Gregg v. Georgia. When the *Furman* decision was first handed down by the U.S. Supreme Court, many scholars interpreted the finding as the abolition of capital punishment in the United States (Gross, 1985). Yet in 1976, the Court granted certiorari to *Gregg v. Georgia* (1976) and its two companion cases: *Proffit v. Florida (1976)* and *Jurek v. Texas* (1976). In *Gregg,* Georgia provided the Court with a set of procedural safeguards designed to guide the discretion of the sentencer (whether judge or jury). The Georgia post-*Furman* statute provided for bifurcated trials, defined aggravating circumstances, and provided for automatic appellate review of all capital sentences. The state argued in *Gregg* that bifurcated trials guard against irrelevant evidence influencing the sentencing decisions. [Bifurcated trials involve one trial for the determination of guilt and another trial for rendering an appropriate punishment.] The Georgia statute made it mandatory that the state could not impose the death penalty unless a jury unanimously and beyond a reasonable doubt found that the offender aggravated the circumstances of the crime. Georgia also required that the Georgia Supreme Court review capital cases to determine whether the evidence supported the jury's finding of an aggravating circumstance and whether the imposition of the death penalty was excessive or disproportionate to the penalty imposed in similar cases (Galloway, 1978). In *Woodson v. North Carolina* (1976) and *Roberts v. Louisiana* (1976), decided the same day as *Gregg,* the court declared that the capital punishment statutes in North Carolina and Louisiana were unconstitutional because they did not leave room for the consideration of individual mitigating circumstances. Thus, the Court argued in *Gregg* that capital punishment does not necessarily amount to cruel and unusual punishment in the presence of procedural safeguards that curb arbitrary and capricious application of the death penalty.

Post-*Gregg* Studies.   Within the past several years, empirical analyses have revealed that the guidelines established in Gregg have failed to eliminate racial disparities in capital cases. Bowers and Pierce (1980) extensively analyzed data collected after the *Gregg* decision for patterns of death sentencing in Florida, Texas, Ohio, and Georgia from 1972 to 1977. Seventy percent of all death sentences imposed in the United States during this period occurred in these states. Bowers and Pierce found that the decision to execute in these states reflects the same arbitrariness and discrimination that has characterized imposition of the death penalty in the past (before the *Furman* and *Gregg* decisions). In each of these states, killers of whites were sentenced to death more than killers of blacks. Also, black defendants with white victims were more likely to receive the death penalty than white defendants with black victims.

Radelet (1981) examined whether race remains a significant factor in the processing and outcome of post-*Furman* homicide cases in Florida between 1976 and 1977. He discovered that the blacks accused of murdering whites were more likely to be sentenced to death than blacks accused of murdering blacks. Radelet explains that this trend is due primarily to higher probabilities that blacks accused of murdering whites would be indicted for first-degree murder. When controlling for the race of the victim, however, Radelet's data did not clearly support the hypothesis that the defendant's race is strongly associated with the probability of a first-degree murder indictment or imposition of the death penalty. Rather, "relative equality in the imposition of the death penalty appears mythical since prosecutors are more likely to obtain first-degree murder indictments for those accused of murdering white strangers than for those accused of murdering black strangers (1981: 926).

In 1981, Zeisel published his analysis on the composition of Florida death rows from 1972 to 1981. He found that Florida continues to discriminate against black defendants convicted of killing white victims in imposing the death penalty. Zeisel points out that this pattern of systematic discrimination based on the race of the defendant and the victim is consistent with pre-*Furman* studies: The percentage of offenders on Florida's death rows who killed blacks (12 percent) was still considerably below the 47 percent who had killed whites.

Using data on 1,400 homicide cases in Florida between 1973 and 1977, Radelet and Pierce (1985) examined disparities between police reports and court records on "felony," "possible felony," and "nonfelony" homicides. Among defendant-victim categories, black defendants with white victims were considerably more likely to have their cases upgraded to a felony charge, and least likely to have their cases downgraded to a lesser charge as they moved through the judicial process.

In South Carolina, Paternoster (1983) found that when the race of the offender and the race of the victim are considered together a clear pattern of racial disparity in prosecutors' decisions to seek the death penalty is evidenced. Paternoster argued that substantial racial disparity continues to exist in that blacks who kill whites have over 4.5 times greater risk of having the death penalty sought than do black killers of blacks. Whites who kill blacks are (1.12 times) more likely to have the death penalty sought by the prosecutor than whites who kill other whites. The race of the victim may be a more important consideration of public prosecutors than is the race of the offender, concludes Paternoster. Again, post-*Furman* capital punishment statutes fail to remedy the problem of racial discrimination influencing imposition of the death penalty in capital cases.

Radelet and Vandiver (1983) examined the degree to which the Florida Supreme Court has achieved the goals of "consistency and fairness" in capital sentencing. They were also concerned with whether the extralegal factors of the defendant's race and/or the victim's sex correlate with the court's decision to uphold the death sentence of a convicted capital offender. Their concern arose from Justices Brennan and Marshall's dissenting opinion in *Proffit* that a state supreme court's review of capital sentences would ensure "evenhanded and consistent" application of the death penalty sentences. Radelet and Vandiver found that the Florida Supreme Court affirmed 52 percent of the 145 death sentence cases examined by the court. Of the 70 remaining cases resulting in a favorable decision for the defendant, 43 percent were resentenced to life imprisonment, 26 percent were remanded to the trial court for resentencing, and 32 percent were sent back to the trial court for new trials.

Their conclusion was that white defendants are more likely to receive a favorable decision than black defendants, and that defendants with male victims were more likely to receive a favorable decision than defendants with female victims. The victim's sex significantly modified the impact of the defendant's race, and vice versa. About 40 percent of the 23 convicted black defendants with female victims received a favorable decision, and half the 36 blacks convicted of killing a man received positive outcomes from the court. This pattern reverses with white defendants. Among the 36 appeals by defendants with female victims, about 61 percent resulted in a favorable ruling. But the 23 cases involving black defendants with female victims were least likely to receive a favorable decision. These findings overwhelmingly suggest the possibility that capital punishment is applied discriminatorily to this category of offense. According to Radelet and Vandiver (1983), the Florida Supreme Court fails to correct the disparities of the trial courts in their decisions on direct appeal.

Gross and Mauro (1984) conducted an extensive study of sentencing under post-*Furman* death penalty laws in Arkansas, Florida, Georgia, Illinois, Mississippi, North Carolina, Oklahoma, and Virginia. While the data permitted separate analyses for Georgia, Florida, and Illinois, death sentences for the states of Arkansas, Mississippi, North Carolina, Oklahoma, and Virginia were analyzed collectively. In Georgia, Florida, and Illinois, they found that while blacks and other racial minorities comprised more of the homicide victims than whites, the risk of a death sentence was far lower for suspects charged with killing blacks than for defendants charged with killing whites. For the state of Georgia, defendants who killed whites were almost ten times more likely to be sentenced to death than defendants whose victims were black. In Florida, the killers of whites were eight times more likely to be sentenced to death. And in Illinois killers of whites were about six times more likely to be sentenced to death.

When controlling for the race of the victim, Gross and Mauro found that blacks who killed whites were far more likely to be sentenced to death than whites who killed whites. In Georgia, about 20 percent of the death sentences were imposed on black defendants with white victims, and about 1 percent of the homicides involving black defendants and black victims ended in death sentences. In Florida, some 14 percent of black defendant–white victim cases led to a death sentence, while only about 1 percent of black defendant–black victim category of offenders received a death sentence. In Illinois, about 8 percent of the black defendants with white victims received the death penalty, and about 1 percent of blacks who killed other blacks were sentenced to death. Gross and Mauro also found a consistent pattern of racial disparity in death sentences for which data was analyzed collectively (Oklahoma, North Carolina, Virginia, Mississippi, and Arkansas).

McCleskey v. Kemp.

In 1978, Warren McCleskey, a black man, was convicted in Fulton County, Georgia, of murdering a white police officer during an armed robbery of a furniture store. The conviction was in keeping with the Georgia statute, under which a jury cannot sentence a defendant to death for murder without a finding that the crime was aggravated by at least one of ten particular circumstances. McCleskey failed to present any mitigating evidence to the jury and was subsequently sentenced to death.

On appeal to the U.S. Supreme Court, McCleskey claimed that the Georgia capital sentencing process is administered in a racially discriminatory manner violating the Eighth Amendment protection against cruel and un-

usual punishment, and that the discriminatory system violates the Fourteenth Amendment guarantee to the equal protection of the law. McCleskey proffered the results of the Baldus et al. (1983) study in support of his claim. In 2,484 murder and nonnegligent manslaughter cases in Georgia between 1973 and 1979, defendants who killed whites were sentenced to death in 11 percent of the cases, while defendants who killed blacks were sentenced to death in only about 1 percent of the cases. Researchers discovered that the death penalty was imposed in 22 percent of the cases where the defendant was convicted of murdering a white, 8 percent of the cases with white defendants and white victims, 3 percent of the cases with white defendants and blacks victims, and only 1 percent of the cases involving black defendants and black victims. Baldus et al. controlled for some 230 nonracial variables and found that none could account for the racial disparities in capital sentences among the different racial combinations of defendant-victim. Killers of whites were 4.3 times more likely to be sentenced to death than killers of blacks, and black defendants were 1.1 times more likely to be sentenced to death than other defendants.

McCleskey argued that race affected the administration of capital punishment in two distinct ways. First, the race of the offender was related to the likelihood of receiving the death penalty, and second the race of the victim also affected the probabilities of being sentenced to death. McCleskey held that he was discriminated against by the Georgia system of imposing the death penalty because he was a black man who killed a white.

In April 1987 the U.S. Supreme Court handed down its decision. Associate Justice Powell delivered the opinion of the court and was joined by Chief Justice Rehnquist and Justices White, O'Connor, and Scalia. Justices Brennan, Blackmun, and Stevens filed dissenting opinions, with Justice Marshall joining in part. The question before the court in *McCleskey* was "whether a complex statistical study that indicates a risk that racial consideration enters into capital sentencing determinations . . . is unconstitutional under the Eighth and Fourteenth Amendments" (*McCleskey v. Kemp,* 1987: 1). The essence of the majority opinion in *McCleskey* is that there are acceptable standards of risk of racial discrimination in imposing the death penalty. The court held that the Baldus study simply shows that discrepancies appear to correlate with race in imposing death sentences, but the "statistics do not prove that race enters into any capital sentencing decisions or that race was a factor in petitioners' cases."

To Justices Brennan, Marshall, Blackmun, and Stevens, "McCleskey has clearly demonstrated that his death sentence was imposed violating the Eighth and Fourteenth Amendments," and that "[n]othing could convey more powerfully the intractable reality of the death penalty: that the effort to eliminate arbitrariness in the infliction of that ultimate sanction is so plainly doomed to failure that it—and the death penalty—must be abandoned altogether" (*McCleskey v. Kemp,* 1987: 39). The dissenters argued that whether *McCleskey* can prove racial discrimination in his particular case is totally irrelevant in evaluating his claim of a constitutional violation because the court has long recognized that to establish that a pattern of substantial risk of arbitrary and capricious capital sentencing suffices for a claim of unconstitutionality. The dissenting justices also called into question the effectiveness of the statutory safeguards designed to curb discretionary use of the death penalty.

CONCLUSION

This discussion has examined several of the more important studies conducted on the extent to which arbitrariness and discrimination have characterized the imposition of capital punishment in the United States. Two substantial conclusions emerged: First, despite the attempts by the U.S. Supreme Court in *Furman v. Georgia* and *Gregg v. Georgia* to thwart racial discrimination in the use of capital punishment, the death penalty continues to be imposed against blacks in a discriminatory manner. Second, the specific finding by many studies that blacks who victimize whites consistently have the highest probability of receiving a capital sentence substantiates the claim that capital punishment serves the extralegal function of majority group protection; namely, the death penalty acts to safeguard (through deterrence and retribution) that class of individuals (whites) who are least likely to be victimized. Our review suggests that the U.S. Supreme Court moved from a position of formally recognizing that imposition of the death penalty is imbued with racial prejudice (i.e., *Furman*), to a position of sanctioning racial prejudice as a cost of imposing the penalty (i.e., *McCleskey*). It appears from the cases handed down from the court that racism is viewed as a legitimate penological doctrine. For the advocates of racial ethnic equality, the death penalty cannot be morally justified on the premise that racial oppression, subjugation, and social subservience are legitimate liabilities of maintaining social order. Social order under these circumstances amounts to social order predicated upon racism.

NOTES

1. Excluded from this figure are 160 military executions conducted between 1942 and 1961. Also, the federal government will execute its first inmate in 32 years on March 30, 1995. The last federal inmate executed by the federal government was Victor Feuger, who was hanged in Iowa in 1963 for murder and kidnapping. David Chandler is the first federal defendant sentenced to death pursuant to the Anti-Drug Abuse Act of 1988. That act made the murders associated with a continuing criminal enterprise a capital offense at federal law. See "First Federal Execution Since 1963 Scheduled," *The Los Angeles Times,* March 14, 1995.

   The most comprehensive list of executions conducted in the United States has been compiled by Espy and Smykla (1987)—better known as *The Espy File.* This data set contains information on 14,570 executions performed under civil authority in the United States from 1608 to 1987. These data are available from the Inter-University Consortium for Political and Social Research (ICPSR) in Ann Arbor, Michigan.

2. See the *Hart-Cellar Hearings,* March 16, 1972, pp. 174–180, 182, 183.

REFERENCES

ARKIN, S.
1980 "Discrimination and Arbitrariness in Capital Punishment: An Analysis of Post-*Furman* Murder Cases in Dade County, Florida, 1973–1976," *Stanford Law Review* 33: 75–101.

BALDUS, D., C. PULASKI and G. WOODSWORTH
1983 "Comparative Review of Death Sentences: An Empirical Study of the Georgia Experience," *Journal of Criminal Law and Criminology* 74: 661–770.

BARLOW, H.
1993 *Introduction to Criminology,* 6th ed. New York: Harper-Collins.

BEDAU, H.
1964 "Death Sentences in New Jersey: 1907–1960," *Rutgers Law Review* 19: 1 ff.

BEDAU, H.
1965 "Capital Punishment in Oregon: 1903–1964," *Oregon Law Review* 45: 1–39.

BLACKMUN, HARRY A.
1994 *The New York Times,* February 23, 1994, p. A10.

BOWERS, W.
1974 *Executions in America.* Lexington, MA: D. C. Heath.

BOWERS, W. and G. PIERCE
1980 "Arbitrariness and Discrimination Under Post-Furman Capital Statutes," *Crime and Delinquency* 26: 563–635.

BRANCH V. TEXAS
1972 408 U.S. 238.

BREARLEY, H.
1930 "The Negro and Homicides," *Social Forces* 9: 247–253.

CARTER, R. and L. SMITH
1969 "The Death Penalty in California: A Statistical Composite Portrait," *Crime and Delinquency* 15: 63–76.

EHRHARDT, C.
1973 "The Aftermath of Furman: The Florida Experience," *Journal of Criminal Law, Criminology, and Police Science* 64: 2–21.

ESPY, M. WATT and JOHN ORTIZ SMYKLA
1987 *Executions in the United States, 1608–1987: The Espy File.* Ann Arbor, MI: Inter-university Consortium for Political and Social Research.

FLORIDA CIVIL LIBERTIES UNION
1964 Pamphlet.

Furman v. Georgia
1972 408 U.S. 238.

GALLOWAY, J.
1978 *Criminal Justice and the Burger Court.* New York: Facts on File.

GARFINKEL, H.
1949 "Research Notes on Inter and Intra-Racial Homicides," *Social Forces* 27: 369–381.

GOLDBERG, A. and A. DERSHOWITZ
1970 "Declaring the Death Penalty Unconstitutional," *Harvard Law Review* 83: 1784.

GOODMAN, D.
1987   "Demographic Evidence in Capital Sentencing," *Stanford Law Review* 39: 499–543.

Gregg v. Georgia
1976   428 U.S. 153.

GROSS, S.
1985   "Race and Death: The Judicial Evaluation of Evidence of Discrimination in Capital Sentencing," *University of California Davis Law Review* 18: 1275.

GROSS, S. and R. MAURO
1984   "Patterns of Death: An Analysis of Racial Disparities in Capital Sentencing and Homicide Victimization," *Stanford Law Review* 37: 127–153.

GROSS, S. and R. MAURO
1989   *Death and Discrimination: Racial Disparities in Capital Sentencing.* Boston: Northeastern University.

Jackson v. Georgia
1972   408 U.S. 238.

JOHNSON, E.
1957   "Selective Factors in Capital Punishment," *Social Forces* 35: 165–169.

JOHNSON, G.
1941   "The Negro and Crime," *Annals of the American Academy of Political and Social Science* 217: 93–104.

Jurek v. Texas
1976   428 U.S. 262.

KALVEN, H.
1969   "A Study of the California Penalty Jury in First-Degree Murder Cases," *Stanford Law Review* 21: 1297–1301.

KLECK, G.
1981   "Racial Discrimination in Criminal Sentencing: A Critical Evaluation of the Evidence with Additional Evidence on the Death Penalty," *American Sociological Review* 46: 783–804.

KOENINGER, R.
1969   "Capital Punishment in Texas, 1924–1968," *Crime and Delinquency* 15: 132–141.

LOH, W.
1984   *Social Research in the Judicial Process: Cases, Readings, and Text.* New York: Russell Sage Foundation.

McCleskey v. Kemp
1987   481 U.S. 279.

McDONALD, L.
1972   "Capital Punishment in South Carolina: The End of an Era," *South Carolina Law Review* 24: 762–794.

MANGUM, C.
1941   *The Legal Status of the Negro.* Chapel Hill, NC: University of North Carolina.

OHIO LEGISLATIVE SERVICE COMMISSION
1961   *Capital Punishment.* Staff Research Report No. 46.

PATERNOSTER, R.
1983   "Race of Victim and Location of Crime: The Decision to Seek the Death Penalty in South Carolina," *Journal of Criminal Law and Criminology* 74: 754–785.

Proffit v. Florida
1976   428 U.S. 242.

QUINNEY, R.
1974   *Critique of Legal Order: Crime Control in Capitalist Society.* Boston: Little, Brown.

RADELET, M.
1981   "Racial Characteristics and the Imposition of the Death Penalty," *American Sociological Review* 46: 918–927.

RADELET, M. and G. PIERCE
1985   "Race and Prosecutorial Discretion in Homicide Cases," *Law and Society Review* 19: 587–621.

RADELET, M. and M. VANDIVER
1983   "The Florida Supreme Court and Death Penalty Appeals," *Journal of Criminal Law and Criminology* 73: 913–926.

REIDEL, M.
1976   "Discrimination in the Imposition of the Death Penalty: A Comparison of the Characteristics of Offenders Sentenced Pre-Furman and Post-Furman," *Temple Law Quarterly* 49: 261–286.

Roberts v. Louisiana
1976   428 U.S. 325.

WOLFGANG, M., A. KELLEY and H. NOLDE
1962   "Comparison of the Executed and the Commuted Among Admissions to Death Row," *Journal of Criminal Law, Criminology, and Police Science* 53: 301–311.

Woodson v. North Carolina
1976   428 U.S. 280.

ZEISEL, H.
1981   "Race Bias in the Administration of the Death Penalty: The Florida Experience," *Harvard Law Review* 95: 456–468.

ZIMRING, F., S. O'MALLEY and J. EIGEN
1976   "The Going Price of Criminal Homicide in Philadelphia," *University of Chicago Law Review* 43: 227–252.

EXERCISE 12

Name _____   Date _____

ID # _____   Class Time _____

I. Analyzing the foundations or evidence for the claims people make about social issues is an important part of understanding controversies about public issues. In the case of law and social science, the evaluation of prior cases and research is necessary for one's own argument to be successfully received. This exercise asks you to first summarize some of the evidence utilized in this article.

A. In the chart below, summarize the findings of any five of the studies cited and discussed by Aguirre and Baker that deal with capital punishment and the issue of race.

	Author	Date	Finding
Example:	Johnson	1941	Study of homicide cases in three southern states which shows that black offenders with white victims were most likely to receive the death penalty

B. In the chart below, summarize several of the Supreme Court cases cited and discussed by Aguirre and Baker. Then answer the questions that follow the chart.

Case Name	Date	Finding

C. How do the studies and cases cited by Aguirre and Baker support their claim that the criminal justice system is racist in terms of discrimination in the application of the death penalty to blacks in the United States?

D. What are the policy implications of Aguirre and Baker's conclusions?

E. Discuss the advantages and disadvantages of basing legal decisions on scientific studies.

II. Aguirre and Baker have focused their study on the racist application of capital punishment to African Americans convicted of murder and rape in the United States. Select a different minority group (e.g., Hispanics, Asian Americans, Native Americans) and locate evidence from research that addresses the imposition of the death penalty on this group. You may either identify an article on your own or review one of the following articles: A. Aguirre, Jr., and D. V. Baker, "The Execution of Mexican American Prisoners in the Southwest," *Social Justice* 16 (4): 150–161 (1989); A. Aguirre, Jr., and D. V. Baker, "A Descriptive Profile of Hispanic Penal Populations: Conceptual and Reliability Limitations in Public Use Data," *The Justice Professional* 3 (4): 189–200 (Fall 1988); Donald E. Green, "American Indian Criminality: What Do We Really Know," in Donald E. Green and Thomas V. Tonnesen, eds., *American Indians: Social Justice and Public Policy* (Madison, WI: University of Wisconsin System), pp. 223–270. Summarize the findings of this research. Be sure to include the complete citation for the article you select.

13

Who's the Boss?
Race, Ethnicity, and Gender
in Managerial Jobs

Elizabeth M. Almquist

Each year, *Fortune* magazine's survey reveals almost no women or minorities among the chief executive officers (CEOs) of the 500 largest corporations in the United States. Yet women do hold 38 percent of all executive, administrative, and managerial (EAM or, simply, managerial) jobs in this country and comprise 46 percent of all employed persons, while race and ethnic minorities hold 13 percent of all EAM positions and make up 20 percent of all employed persons.

A sketch of the occupational pyramid of power shows managerial and elite professional jobs in the top layers of the pyramid, carrying considerably more prestige, pay, and authority than jobs farther down. Managerial jobs are further divided into multiple layers, with the tiny group of CEOs of the largest corporations occupying the apex of the pyramid. One pattern occurs throughout: the higher the level, the fewer women and minorities (Almquist, 1987; Reskin and Ross, 1992).

Inequality in access to these powerful and highly rewarding positions is the topic of this chapter. Once held almost exclusively by white men, these jobs are now held by increasing numbers of women and minorities. Today, white men comprise only 43 percent of all employed persons but hold over half of the EAM jobs. The following discussion focuses on conditions that foster or impede the movement of minority women and men into managerial jobs, while the exercise at the end asks you to analyze the consequences of such job holding.

MINORITY GROUPS AND MANAGERIAL WORK

This research covers the 12 largest race and ethnic minority groups in the United States, whose characteristics and experiences in the United States differ enormously. Education level, population size, proportions of foreign born, circumstances of entering the country, industry, and work setting all affect movement into top jobs in multiple and

intersecting ways. The analysis addresses each of these factors, using data from the U.S. Bureau of the Census (see Tables 13.1 and 13.2).

College degrees are useful, though not indispensable, criteria for entering EAM jobs. Employers have been reluctant to place nonwhites in positions of authority over whites, and research consistently demonstrates that the larger the population of a minority group, the greater is the bias and discrimination against it (Healy, 1995). Immigrant groups are typically small in number, yet they include different mixes of qualifications and resources. "Voluntary" immigrants (e.g., Chinese, Koreans, and Asian Indians) frequently possess strong educational credentials and sometimes have startup capital to open their own businesses. Refugee groups (e.g. Vietnamese, some of Other Hispanics) typically lack these resources. Indigenous groups (e.g., Native, African, and Mexican Americans) are much larger in population and have experienced a long, unrelenting history of systematic discrimination in school and at work. In between are other groups—Cubans, Puerto Ricans, Japanese, Filipinos—with mixed levels of resources and diverse patterns of immigration and employment.

Some minority group members achieve occupational success by building (typically small) businesses. They may specialize in serving customers from their own groups or they may seek other clients and customers. In either case, they typically operate in highly competitive industries where individual stores and firms emerge and fail rapidly. They succeed in part by using family members and by hiring recent immigrants from their native countries, all of whom work very long hours at relatively low wages. The owner, most often a man, is classified as holding an EAM job; his wife is usually a service or sales worker.

Lack of capital prevents establishing one's own business. Some groups, notably African and Native Americans, find more possibilities in government work. But

TABLE 13.1
Characteristics of Minority Groups, 1990

Group	Total Population[a]	Percent Foreign	Percent College Gradates[b] Women	Men	Ratio
African American	18,630	5.4%	14%	12%	114
Native American	1,395	2.3	8	7	108
Chinese	1,309	69.3	50	56	90
Filipino	1,079	64.3	42	32	130
Japanese	725	32.4	47	50	94
Asian Indian	576	75.9	55	63	88
Korean	580	72.6	35	49	70
Vietnamese	423	79.9	17	24	74
Mexican	8,808	33.2	7	7	100
Puerto Rican	1,796	1.3[c]	12	11	114
Cuban	883	71.7	24	21	112
Other Hispanics[d]	3,538	54.0	14	15	97

SOURCE: U.S. Bureau of the Census, C-P-1, 1990 Census of Population, Characteristic, 1993.

[a]Total population is given in thousands.
[b]College graduates are among people aged 25 and older. The ratio is the percent of women who are college graduates divided by the percent of men who are college graduates, and multiplied by 100 to remove the decimal point.
[c]Puerto Ricans are U.S. citizens and are not considered foreign born.
[d]Other Hispanics include everyon who indicated Hispanic origin on the census form other than Mexican Americans, Puerto Ricans, and Cubans.

most people from all groups end up as private wage or salary earners working for someone else. The variable "employment setting" shows the distribution of each group across self, government, and private employment, allowing us to examine its impact on managerial employment. Similarly, manufacturing industries hire many workers and few managers, which leads to the prediction that groups that are highly concentrated in manufacturing will have few EAM jobs.

It is important to note that the labor force data used here do not measure specific job levels (e.g., whether a person is CEO of a giant corporation versus manager of a fast-food restaurant); they reveal only access to the large, general EAM category. Moreover the data do not tap the processes by which people are sifted and sorted into jobs. The ultimate job placement of all workers depends on dozens of choices made by the workers themselves and on employer decisions regarding how many people of what background will be employed in which positions. When employers do hire minority managers, they often place them in situations where they supervise other minority workers, deal with minority clients, or work in support-

TABLE 13.2
Employment Patterns of Minority Groups, 1990

Group	Industry: Percent in Manufacturing	Class of Worker* Private	Government	Self
African American	15%	73%	24%	3%
Native American	16	71	23	6
Chinese	19	78	15	8
Filipino	16	80	16	3
Japanese	14	73	19	8
Asian Indian	18	78	15	7
Korean	15	72	9	20
Vietnamese	37	84	10	7
Mexican American	21	83	12	5
Puerto Rican	20	78	19	3
Cuban	17	82	7	11
Other Hispanics	19	83	11	6

SOURCE: U.S. Bureau of the Census, 1990 Census of Population.

*Class of workers categories are private wage and salary workers, government employees, and self and unpaid family workers.

staff positions outside the central production and decision-making arenas of the corporation. These enclaves and niches offer few chances to move into middle and upper-level management. Finally, community protests and federal mandates to offer equal employment opportunity had some CEOs scrambling to place more minorities in management positions in the 1960s and 1970s (Collins, 1989). African Americans made important job gains at that time, but the pace of change slowed dramatically in the 1980s as federal pressure to promote equal opportunity eroded (Jacobs, 1992).

GENDERED ROUTES AND BARRIERS TO MANAGEMENT

Gender figures prominently in all matters relating to work. Regardless of the extent to which women and men pursue different fields, they experience unequal access to highly valued jobs.

Reskin and Roos (1990) examined the mass movement of women into the labor force over the last three decades and their deployment across different jobs. Contrary to media depictions and popular opinion, women made few inroads into the ranks of the elite professions but made significant gains in several EAM jobs and in other areas widely scattered throughout the occupational pyramid. Bankers, bakers, and bus drivers are some fields where women gained more jobs than would be predicted simply on the basis of increased numbers in labor force. In each occupation in which women gained jobs, demand for workers had increased at the same time the occupation became deskilled or routinized and lost prestige. Men sought out other jobs that were not becoming deskilled; this left several fields more accessible to women.

How might we account for women making relatively large inroads in EAM jobs? Women's changed career aspirations, seen partly in the strong push many exerted to enter work at managerial levels, is a primary reason. Women increasingly sought and earned M.B.A.s as well as advanced degrees in education and public administration, thereby positioning themselves for movement into EAM jobs. Employers overcame some traditional reluctance to place women in positions of authority over men as the demand for EAM workers in middle- and lower-management levels grew. Federal and state policies pressured corporations to hire more women in management, and in some instances, men sought jobs in other fields, leaving the area open to new recruits. A case study of bank managers (Bird, 1990) reveals that the prestige of banking declined as CEOs sought increasingly to compete with other financial institutions (e.g., credit-card companies). CEOs reasoned that "friendly" people (women) with titles (loan officer) would attract more customers, so they assigned large numbers of women to these ranks, especially in branch banks, but they kept major decision making within the central banks. Women gained managerial titles but few opportunities to advance into upper management.

INDICATORS OF ACCESS TO TOP JOBS: THE ORI AND THE GENDER RATIO

This analysis asks if different groups experience differential access to EAM jobs, and if women and men within the same group have differential access. The Occupational Representation Index (ORI) measures access by weighing each group's share of the top jobs against its share of the total labor force. ORI scores for EAM jobs (see Table 13.3) are computed by dividing a group's share of EAM jobs by its share of all employed persons in the United States and multiplying by 100 to eliminate the decimal point. For example, African American men hold only 2.78% of the EAM jobs, but they are 4.66% of all job holders. Their ORI score = (2.78/4.66) × 100 = 60.

ORI scores smaller than 100 indicate the group is under-represented in managerial jobs compared to its representation in the total labor force. ORI scores above 100 indicate the group is over-represented in EAM jobs. ORI scores of exactly 100 indicate the group is represented in the same proportion in managerial jobs as it is in all jobs.

Are women as well represented in EAM jobs as men from the same group? Generally not. To systematically compare women and men, we compute the gender ratio that divides women's ORI scores by men's ORI scores and multiply the result by 100 to eliminate the decimal point. For instance, African American women's ORI score of 56, divided by men's ORI score of 60 and multiplied by 100, is 93, suggesting the women are close to achieving parity with men. By contrast, Chinese women have a higher ORI score (91) than black women, but Chinese men's score (133) is higher still. The gender ratio for Chinese is only 68, showing that Chinese women do not fare very well

TABLE 13.3
Occupational Representation Index Scores Executives, Administrators, and Managers, 1990[a]

	ORI Scores		Gender Ratio
	Women	Men	
African American	56	60	93
Native American	72	71	101
Chinese	91	133	68
Filipino	50	66	77
Japanese	84	180	47
Asian Indian	67	132	51
Korean	73	140	52
Vietnamese	33	46	72
Mexican American	46	50	92
Puerto Rican	63	62	101
Cuban	75	108	69
Other Hispanics	56	72	78
Nonhispanic Whites[b]	90	126	71

SOURCE: U.S. Bureau of the Census, 1990 Census of Population.

[a]Includes all administrative, executive, and managerial occupations except the cluster of management-related occupations, such as accountants and public relations officers, which are excluded from these figures.
[b]Nonhispanic whites are included for comparison only.

compared to men in their group. Across all groups, the higher the ORI scores, the smaller the gender ratio. In groups achieving a strong share of EAM jobs, men's access is much greater than women's. See Table 13.3 for gender ratio scores.

Minority Groups and Managerial Jobs. Which minority groups have obtained more managerial jobs than other jobs in the total labor force? Japanese, Korean, Chinese, Asian Indian, and Cuban men (but not women) have ORI scores above 100. Women from these groups also have high ORI scores compared to women from other groups, but none exceeds 100. Vietnamese, Mexican Americans, African Americans, and Puerto Ricans have low ORI scores for both women and men, but higher gender ratios.

Comparing Tables 13.1, 13.2, and 13.3 shows that minority groups with high ORI scores and low gender ratios tend to be small in population, and to *not* be strongly concentrated in manufacturing or private wage and salary employment. Instead, they are groups with high proportions of college graduates who are more likely than other groups to have large numbers of self-employed workers. Groups that are less well represented in EAM jobs (low ORI scores, but higher gender ratios) have the opposite patterns: they are large groups who are heavily concentrated in manufacturing and in private wage employment; they have fewer college graduates and very few self-employed workers. Table 13.4 reveals these patterns clearly, by showing the rank order correlation between each background variable and women's ORI scores, men's ORI scores, and the gender ratio of ORI scores.

A correlation is a statistical measure of the extent to which changes in one variable are accompanied by changes in the other variable, as well as the direction in which those changes go. Correlations can range from −1.00 to +1.00. To interpret them, consider both the sign and the size of the correlation. A plus sign means a group with a high value on one variable typically also has a high value on the other variable; a minus sign means that high values on one variable are accompanied by low values on the other variable. For example, the positive correlation between percent who are self or unpaid family workers and women's ORI score indicates that the more often members of a group are self-employed, the higher is their access to managerial jobs. In contrast, women's ORI scores are negatively correlated with the percent who are private wage and salary workers, meaning that the more a group is in private wage and salary work, the lower is women's access to managerial jobs.

The size of the correlation must also be considered. Values below .300 show that the two variables are only weakly connected, while values above .300 show a stronger link between the two. The largest correlation in the entire table (−.925, between percent college graduates and the gender ratio) suggests a very strong connection such that the more highly educated members of a minority group are, the greater is the gender gap in attaining managerial jobs. I speculate that more affluent and highly educated groups invest more in sons than in daughters. They send children of both sexes to college but are more likely to push sons to obtain advanced degrees (see education data in Table 13.1), to choose sons to inherit the family business, and to stress family for women and career for men

TABLE 13.4
Correlates of ORI Scores: Executives, Administrators and Managers, 1990

Variable	ORI Scores		Gender Ratio
	Women	Men	
Population size	−.189	−.418	+.713
Percent foreign born	−.031	+.208	.538
Industry percent in manufacturing	−.500	−.314	+.445
Class of workers:			
Percent private wage and salary workers	−.528	−.568	+.136
Percent government employees	+.207	−.142	+.276
Percent self and unpaid family workers	+.708	+.797	−.809
Percent college graduates[a]	+.437	+.694	−.925
Earnings of year-round full-time workers[b]	+.577	+.738	−.907
Percent families with income below poverty level	−.259	−.774	+.832
Percent family households headed by women	−.543	−.897	+.854
Fertility rate	−.510	−.774	+.832

[a]Percent college graduates is measured for the entire group, not separately for women and men.
[b]Women's earnings are correlated with women's ORI scores; men's earnings are correlated with men's ORI scores and with the gender ratio of ORI scores.

(Almquist, 1995). But in interpreting any of these results, please be cautious. These are only correlations, and we need more evidence to explain why they exist.

These variables are cross-sectional, observed at one point in time. I assume that the first several variables in Table 13.4—population size, class of worker, college graduates—represent factors that influence access to managerial jobs, and that the last four variables—earnings, poverty level, family households that are female headed, fertility—measure the results of unequal access to these jobs (Almquist, 1995). But influence could easily flow in the opposite direction. For instance, groups with high rates of poverty have a great deal of difficulty in educating their children, so poverty could be as much a cause as a result of access to EAM jobs. Throughout, we must be careful in making assumptions about how and why any variables are connected.

With all these caveats, what can we tell from Table 13.4? First, women's ORI scores are little influenced by the size of the population, but men in the larger groups are less likely to be represented in EAM jobs. Further, the larger groups are precisely the ones in which the gender ratio is higher while the ratio is lower among the smaller groups. A high gender ratio indicates that women's ORI scores are close to men's while a low gender ratio indicates that women fall far behind men in achieving access to managerial jobs. The percent who are foreign born has little impact on ORI scores, probably because immigrants are a mix of volunteers and refugees with both high and low levels of resources. Note that groups with large numbers of foreign-born persons—primarily Asian groups—exhibit low gender ratios.

Employment setting also affects ORI scores. The more groups are self-employed, and the more they avoid private employment and manufacturing industries, the higher are their ORI scores, and the less likely women are to achieve access to EAM jobs on a par with men. Finally, the higher the proportion of college graduates, the higher are their ORI scores and the lower the gender ratio.

Throughout, variables which increase access of women and men to managerial jobs also deflate the gender ratio. In other words, the more access a minority group has to managerial jobs, the greater is the inequality between women and men in access. If you are a member of a minority group that has favorable opportunities for acquiring top jobs, you also have brothers, husbands, and friends who are much more likely than you to do so.

CONCLUSION

The purpose of this research is neither to fuel the flames of prejudice nor to ignite controversy between groups. Instead, it is designed to explore the contours of the pyramid of occupational power and the placement of various groups within it. A similar, separate analysis of access to the elite professions in medicine, science, and engineering revealed very similar patterns. The only difference is that men were much more fully represented in the elite professions than women, and the gender ratios were therefore much smaller than for managers. These findings depict a pyramid in which various groups have varying levels of access to top jobs, and varying degrees of occupational gender inequality.

White men have been raised to believe that job achievement is a major mark of their success as a man, and that if they work hard, they are entitled to expect occupational rewards. The socialization is so intense that it is small surprise that they sometimes feel beleaguered by issues of gender inequality and threatened by the misinformation that other groups are taking over the top jobs. Women and minority people of both sexes have made some progress over the past two decades, but the groups who are strongly represented in top jobs are also extremely small in population; women and minorities of both sexes are highly concentrated in the lower ranks of any occupation, and white men still retain the largest share of top jobs.

The findings presented here demonstrated neither bias against nor favoritism toward any group or individual of either sex. They do show sizable differentials in access to top jobs, and they show, as you will discover in the exercise, that who gets to be the boss does matter in terms of income, poverty, and family composition—all factors which have serious consequences for the quality of life and the perpetuation of social problems.

REFERENCES

ALMQUIST, ELIZABETH M.
1987 "Labor Market Gender Inequality in Minority Groups," *Gender and Society* 1: 400–414.

ALMQUIST, ELIZABETH M.
1995 "The Experiences of Minority Women in the United States: Intersections of Race, Class and Gender," in Jo Freeman, ed. *Women: A Feminist Perspective*. Mountain View, CA: Mayfield, pp. 573–606.

BIRD, CHLOE
1990 "High Finance, Small Change: Women's Increased Representation in Bank Management," in B. F. Reskin and P. A. Roos, *Job Queues, Gender Queues*. Philadelphia: Temple University Press, pp. 145–166.

COLLINS, SHARON M.
1989 "The Marginalization of Black Executives," *Social Problems* 36: 313–317.

HEALEY, JOSEPH F.
1995 *Race, Ethnicity, Gender and Class*. Thousand Oaks, CA: Pine Forge Press.

JACOBS, JERRY A.
1992 "Women's Entry into Management: Trends in Earnings, Authority, and Values Among Salaried Managers," *Administrative Science Quarterly* 37: 282–301.

RESKIN, BARBARA F. and PATRICIA A. ROOS
1990 *Job Queues, Gender Queues: Explaining Women's Inroads into Male Occupations*. Philadelphia: Temple University Press.

RESKIN, BARBARA F. and CATHERINE E. ROSS
1992 "Jobs, Authority, and Earnings Among Managers: The Continuing Significance of Sex," *Work and Occupations* 19: 342–365.

EXERCISE 13

Name _____   Date _____

ID # _____   Class Time _____

I. This exercise is designed to assess the consequences of unequal access to managerial jobs for earnings, poverty status, household composition, and birth rates. Begin by examining the table below.

Earnings, Poverty Status, and Household Composition of Minority Groups, 1990

Group	Earnings Rate[a]			Below Poverty Level[b]	Women Heads[c]	Fertility Rate[d]
	Women	Men	Ratio			
African American	59%	70%	84%	26%	51%	2,205
Native American	52	69	75	27	33	2,312
Chinese	73	99	74	11	15	1,703
Filipino	68	82	83	5	22	1,898
Japanese	76	117	65	3	17	1,470
Asian Indian	68	113	60	7	8	2,034
Korean	59	89	66	15	16	1,776
Vietnamese	59	79	78	24	21	1,836
Mexican	49	59	83	23	23	2,173
Puerto Rican	59	70	84	30	44	1,904
Cuban	57	77	74	11	21	1,375
Other Hispanics	51	67	76	18	29	1,709

SOURCE: U.S. Bureau of the Census, 1990 Census of Population.

[a]Earnings rate represents the earnings of year-round, full-time workers, expressed as a percentage of the earnings of year-round, full-time white, non-Hispanic male workers. The earning ratio = women's earnings expressed as a percentage of men's earnings within each group.
[b]Below poverty level indicates the percent of families whose incomes are below poverty level.
[c]Women heads represents the percent of all family households that are headed by women. Other family households are headed by men, or by two parents.
[d]Fertility rate is the number of children ever born per 1,000 women aged 35 to 44.

A. Make a list of the four or five groups with high earnings. Make a separate list of groups with low poverty rates, few households headed by women, and low fertility rates.

List 1   *List 2*

1. Are the two lists the same? Why or why not?

B. Now list groups with low earnings. Make a second list of groups with high poverty rates, many households headed by women, and high fertility rates.

List 1   *List 2*

    1. Are the two lists similar? Why or why not?

C. Reexamine ORI scores in management from Table 13.3. List the four or five groups in which women and men have high ORI scores compared to other groups.

List

    1. Is this list similar to the groups you listed in step A.1? Explain why.

D. List the four or five groups in which women and men have low ORI scores compared to other groups.

List

    1. Are these the same groups you listed in step B.1? Why or why not?

E. With the comparisons in parts A through D accomplished, you are prepared to interpret the correlations in the bottom part of the table on the first page of this exercise. Write sentences describing the relationships between ORI scores and earnings, poverty, and household composition. *Example:* The ORI scores for both women and men are negatively correlated with poverty rates, which means that the more access a group has to managerial jobs, the lower are its poverty rates.

F. Discuss the implications of these findings for the quality of life and the perpetuation of social problems. Do not assume that high fertility rates and women-headed households are problematic; focus more on earnings and poverty.

14

The Feminization of Poverty*

Dana Dunn and David V. Waller

Women in the United States are at far higher risk of poverty than men, and they represent an increasing share of the poverty population. Recognition of this fact led Diana Pearce (1978) to coin the term, "feminization of poverty." The phrase refers not only to women's disproportionately high rate of poverty but also to the poverty of dependent children in female-headed, single-parent families. Whilewomen as a group are at higher risk of poverty than men, certain categories of women are especially likely to be impoverished. Minority women, elderly women who are widows, and women who are single mothers have the highest rates of poverty.

Currently, about two out of every three impoverished adults in the United States are women. Sixteen percent of women in the United States lived below the poverty line, compared to 12.3 percent of men (U.S. Bureau of the Census, 1993). The gender-poverty ratio, the ratio of women's to men's poverty rates, was 1.30 for the United States in 1991, which means that women are 31 percent more likely to be poor than men (Caspar, McClanahan and Garfinkle, 1994).

More than one out of five children live in poverty, and over 50 percent of all children in female-headed families are poor (Kemp, 1994). In terms of absolute numbers, in 1991 over 13 million children lived in poverty (Polakow, 1993). Child poverty is not evenly distributed by race/ethnicity. Among children under six years of age in female householder families, the poverty rate for whites is over 60.5 percent, nearly 73.1 percent for African Americans, and 71.8 percent for Hispanics (U.S. Bureau of the Census, 1993).

CAUSES OF THE FEMINIZATION OF POVERTY

There are two key contributors to women's disproportionately high rates of poverty: the earnings gap between

* Adapted and reprinted from *Ready Reference: Women's Issues* by permission of the publisher, Salem Press, Inc. Copyright 1996 by Salem Press, Inc.

the sexes and the high number of female-headed households.

The Earnings Gap. Sex differences in earnings occur in almost every occupation and in every country throughout the world. The disparity in earnings between the sexes is calculated by dividing women's earnings by men's to yield a percentage known as the earnings ratio. In 1992, the pay gap in the United States was 67 percent, indicating that for every $10,000 paid to the average man only $6,700 was paid to the average woman (U.S. Bureau of the Census, 1994). This gender gap in pay has long historical roots in the United States. During the early years of industrialization, working women earned only about a third of the average male wage. More recently, from 1950 to 1980, women's earnings fluctuated to around 60 percent of men's earnings. From 1980 to 1990 the earnings gap narrowed slightly, less than one cent per year. The gender gap in pay among whites is larger than that for blacks and Hispanics, due to the fact that minority men's wages are lower on average than white men's. As a group, women are more than twice as likely as men to have wages at or below the official minimum wage.

Numerous factors contribute to the sex gap in pay. First, men spend more time at work than women. The fact that men work more hours overall than women explains only a small portion of the earnings gap, however. If the sexes were to work equal numbers of hours, over three quarters of the pay gap would remain. Differences between the sexes in terms of level of education, amount of job experience, and job stability also contribute to the earnings gap. Recent research indicates that these productivity-related differences between the sexes also explain only a small portion of the sex gap in pay.

Sex discrimination, while illegal, contributes to pay differences between women and men. The Equal Pay Act of 1963 required the employers pay "equal pay for equal work"; however, data still show that there are differences in pay received by women and men in similar jobs, even when controlling for education and experience. It has been suggested that some employers circumvent such legislation either by assigning slightly different job titles to men and women performing the same job, or by making sure that there is something slightly different about the actual work performed by men and women so it can be claimed that the work is not equal. In 1970, the court's attempt to address such evasive strategies—essentially declaring that work does not have to be identical, but only substantially equal—helped somewhat to reduce pay discrimination.

The gender gap in pay that results from the above-mentioned factors is small compared to that which results from occupational segregation. Occupational sex segregation refers to the fact that most women workers are concentrated in occupations that are predominately female. Despite the fact that the gap between male and female labor force participation rates is the lowest it has ever been, most women continue to work in a rather narrow range of occupations traditionally defined as "female occupations." Employment segregation by sex declined slightly during the 1980s; still, nearly half of all employed women today work in occupations that are over 75 percent female. In fact, over 50 percent of all employed women would have to change occupations for women to be distributed across occupations in the same manner as men. Occupational segregation by sex creates wage disparities between the sexes because female-dominated occupations pay less than male-dominated occupations. The low pay in female-dominated occupations cannot be explained by their demand for skill, experience, education, or training. This type of systematic undervaluing of women's jobs is a prevalent form of pay discrimination that is immune to pay equity legislation.

More than one third of all employed women perform clerical work, the single largest employment category for women. Clerical work is often disparagingly referred to as the "pink collar ghetto" because low wages are typical of this kind of work. The second largest employment category for women, service work (e.g., food service, health care services, personal services, private household service occupations), is also typically low-wage work.

Three explanations have been offered for why women cluster into traditionally female-dominated, low-wage occupations: gender-role socialization, work-place discrimination, and family obligations. Gender-role socialization contributes to labor market segregation by encouraging young females to prepare for and pursue traditional women's occupations. Work place discrimination concerns the barriers to employment women face in certain occupations, such as the preferences of employers and/or male employees that result in selective hiring on the basis of sex. The traditional role in the family may also serve to restrict women's occupational choices and cause them to cluster in occupations that are more compatible with the requirements of child rearing and family obligations.

Legislative and policy initiatives can help to reduce the amount of gender segregation in the work place and the systematic devaluing of women's jobs—both require-

ments for a significant reduction in the female poverty rate. Advocates of comparable worth legislation argue that employers should be prevented from considering the sex composition of a job when setting wage rates. If female-dominated occupations were carefully evaluated with respect to the contributions they make and paid accordingly, the average wage for such jobs would climb markedly. Raising the wages associated with traditionally female jobs would encourage more men to enter the positions, and over the long run, lead to a reshuffling of male and female workers and less work place segregation. While no targeted legislation is yet in place to force or to create incentives for private enterprise to establish equitable pay scales for female- and male-dominated positions, the federal government and a number of state governments have begun the process of adjusting their own pay scales to eliminate the earnings gap.

Female-headed Households. In the United States 17.5 percent of all families are headed by a female householder, and these households have a poverty rate (34.9 percent) that is 5.6 times higher than that for married-couple families (6.2 percent). Female-headed households represent 52.4 percent of all poor families, while the poverty rate for all families was 11.7 percent in 1992 (U.S. Bureau of the Census, 1993).

Two separate sets of phenomena are responsible for the high and rising number of female-headed households. Among the elderly, differences in life expectancy between the sexes, combined with the fact that women tend to marry partners who are older, results in high rates of female-headed households. Among younger women, the growing number of births to single women, trends toward later marriage, and high rates of divorce and separation create high rates of female-headed households.

The negative economic consequences of divorce are greater for women than men. For example, of all divorced or separated persons 16 years and older living in families, the poverty rate is 32.4 percent for women and 13.2 percent for men. If there are no children under 18 years of age in the family, the poverty rate is 6.8 for men and 16.8 for women; if there are children in the family, the poverty rate never tops 19 percent for divorced or separated men but increases to 39 percent for such women; and if one or more child is under the age of 6, the poverty rate increases to 58.1 percent for divorced or separated women (U.S. Bureau of the Census, 1993).

As noted above, female-dominated jobs often do not pay sufficient wages to support a family above the official level of poverty. When divorce involves children, women are typically awarded custody. Working women with children below school age need affordable child care. The lower labor force participation rate for divorced women with children under 6 years of age than for other divorced women is due, in part, to the inability of many such women to afford child care. Low and infrequently received spousal and child support payments also augment the negative effects of marital disruption on the economic well-being of women with children.

The poverty rate of female-headed households among minority groups varies. The poverty rate for whites is 30.2 percent, 53.7 percent for African Americans, and 51.2 percent for Hispanics. If children under 18 years of age are present, the rates of poverty increase to 40.3 percent, 60.4 percent, and 58.5 percent for whites, African Americans, and Hispanics, respectively (U.S. Bureau of the Census, 1993). Minority status worsens the economic position of such women because it limits their options for marriage or remarriage through its effect on minority men. High rates of unemployment, death, and imprisonment among African American males, for example, limit the supply of potential marital partners for African American females. Minority women also experience greater discrimination in labor markets than whites.

The primary policy strategy that has been employed to improve the economic situation of female householders with children involves the provision of government income support. Aid to Families with Dependent Children (AFDC), more commonly known as welfare, is the primary governmental program available for income support. AFDC specifies a maximum amount that can be earned by working mothers before they become ineligible for benefits. Some critics of AFDC argue that the amount is far too low and that working mothers earning above this amount are often unable to rise above the poverty line. Other critics of AFDC argue that public support encourages births out of wedlock.

Child support enforcement policies are also being implemented in many states to encourage noncustodial fathers to participate in the support of their children and thereby reduce poverty in female-headed households. These programs range from garnishment of wages to revocation of driver's licenses of men who do not pay the court-awarded amount of support. The lack of federal policies providing for interstate enforcement mechanisms of such programs is an important obstacle limiting their success.

CONCLUSION

The feminization of poverty concept has recently been criticized for distorting and oversimplifying the phenomenon of poverty. Burnham (1983) identified four problems with the feminization of poverty approach: (1) the misidentification of gender, rather than class, as the primary determinant of poverty; (2) the neglect of class differentiation among women; (3) the obscuring of racial stratification by class; and (4) the neglect of poverty among men of color. Some critics argue further that attention to the feminization of poverty has been disproportionately focused on the new poor—middle-class white women who experienced economic trauma as a result of divorce.

Despite these recent criticisms of the feminization of poverty concept, women's disproportionately high rates of poverty are a reality. In the absence of specific policy initiatives designed to alleviate the poverty of poor women and their dependent children, the suffering of millions will be a continuing feature of U.S. society.

REFERENCES

BURHAM, L.
1983   "Has Poverty Been Feminized in Black America?" *Black Scholar* March–April: 14–24.

CASPAR, LYNNE M., SARA S. MCCLANAHAN, and IRWIN GARFINKLE
1994   "The Gender Poverty Gap: What We Can Learn from Other Countries," *American Sociological Review* 59: 594–605.

KEMP, ALICE ABEL
1994   *Women's Work: Degraded and Devalued*. Englewood Cliffs, NJ: Prentice Hall.

PEARCE, DIANA
1978   "The Feminization of Poverty: Women, Work and Welfare," *Urban and Social Change Review* 11: 28–36.

POLAKOW, VALERIE
1993   *Lives on the Edge: Single Mothers and Their Children in the Other America*. Chicago: University of Chicago Press.

U.S. BUREAU OF CENSUS
1993   "Poverty in the United States, 1991," *Current Population Reports* (Series P-60, No. 185). Washington, DC: U.S. Government Printing Office.

U.S. BUREAU OF THE CENSUS
1994   *Statistical Abstract of the United States, 1994*. Washington, DC: U.S. Government Printing Office.

EXERCISE 14

Name _____   Date _____

ID # _____   Class Time _____

I. With the recent changes in the composition of the U.S. House and Senate and the presidential election of 1996, several policies and legislative initiatives are currently being debated that will affect the poverty rate for females. Your task is to identify at least one specific policy or legislative initiative (such as efforts to reform welfare for the poor) and to discuss the implications for women.

    A. Staple a recent newspaper article to this page which features a specific reform initiative you believe may have an impact on women's poverty. (Be sure to include the publication date and the name of the newspaper from which the article came.)

    B. Explain in two or three sentences the rationale for the proposed initiatives.

    C. Identify one or more ways in which women's poverty may increase as a result of the initiative.

II. It can be argued that the feminization of poverty directly affects everyone, even those so fortunate as to personally escape the ravages of poverty. The fact that one out of every five children today is growing up in poverty means that the nonpoor in the next generation of adults will be surrounded by those who have grown up in poverty circumstances. Reflect on how the feminization of poverty today will affect our future.

    A. List and briefly discuss three social problems that will be created or made worse by the feminization of poverty.

        1.

        2.

        3.

B. Now describe actions that could be taken to address the future problems described in part A above.

1.

2.

3.

C. In your opinion, is it more cost effictive to make efforts to reduce women's poverty today, or to wait and address the resulting social problems at some future point? Explain your answer in the space below.

15

Constructing Children's Problems

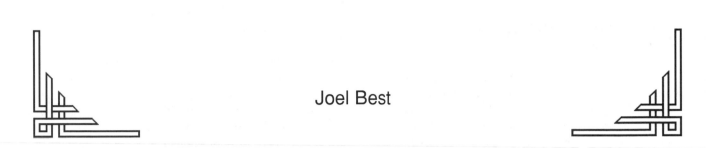

Joel Best

Children and adolescents under the age of 18 make up a quarter of the U.S. population—about 67 million young people in 1993. As minors, they are subject to many requirements and restrictions that do not apply to adults. The law requires (with exceptions, mostly for adolescents) that children live with their families, obey their parents, and attend school, while prohibiting (again with some exceptions) children from voting, drinking, driving, and most forms of employment. However, these inequities attract little notice; they are taken for granted as arrangements for the children's "own good."

Our culture defines children as innocent and vulnerable, as needing special protection. According to historians, this sentimental vision of childhood emerged and spread over the past two centuries. As time passed, people spoke less of children's ability to contribute to the family economy and more of their need for nurturing. The sentimental vision originated among the more privileged classes, then slowly spread throughout society (Shorter, 1977; Zelizer, 1985). Today, virtually everyone accepts the idea of childhood as a time of innocence and vulnerability needing protection.

Our idea about children as especially vulnerable makes it easy to describe social problems in terms of children by focusing public attention on some societal condition that threatens children's well-being. History reveals many examples of such reform campaigns: Charles Dickens's novels portrayed the brutal treatment of children in early industrial society; the nineteenth century featured great social movements to make schooling compulsory, to abolish child labor, and to establish systems of juvenile justice; and the twentieth century saw further efforts to extend child protection and improve child welfare.

Sociologists sometimes speak of these reform campaigns as "constructing social problems" (Spector and Kitsuse, 1977). This rather peculiar phrase is meant to suggest that social problems have to be recognized as troubling. A definition that some condition is a social

problem must be developed—or constructed—through people's efforts. Someone must identify the condition as a problem and bring it to others' attention; people must redefine what has gone unnoticed or been taken for granted as something troubling, something that demands action. In short, there must be *claims* that the condition is a social problem.

If many social problems come to our attention through such claims, then examining claims can help us understand the process of social problems construction. In particular, three issues merit examination. First, *who makes the claims,* and why are they the ones to draw attention to the problem? Second, *how do claims characterize the problem*—what sort of problem is it? Third, *what specific elements make the claims persuasive?* The answers to these questions will reveal patterns in the construction of social problems involving children.

WHO MAKES THE CLAIMS?

Various sorts of people can make claims, calling attention to children's problems. Activists or children's advocates, such as the Children's Defense Fund or Action for Children's Television, seek to mobilize support for a various children's issues. Lawyers, physicians, and researchers may use their professional authority to support their definitions of children's problems. In some cases, government agencies may organize campaigns to arouse public concern. While some of these claims concern problems that primarily affect children, such as child abuse or the quality of children's television programming, others address broader problems, but use children as examples in order to elicit a sympathetic response. For example, even though relatively few of the homeless are children, homeless advocates often use children to illustrate the problem.

Most people who make social problems claims are not completely disinterested. They stand to gain money, influence, or prestige if their claims become widely accepted. Successful activists may attract more members and contributions to their causes, and their views receive more respectful attention from the media and officials. Similarly, professionals and officials who have their claims accepted often find themselves in charge of dealing with the problem. For this and other reasons, it is important to keep these interests in mind when evaluating social problems claims.

HOW DO CLAIMS CHARACTERIZE THE PROBLEM?

In the contemporary United States, four main images characterize children in social problems claims (Best, 1990). The first image is the *rebellious child*. Rebellious children break adult rules. They run away from home, have sex, break the law, and adopt disturbing tastes in music and dress. Rebellion is probably the central image in claims about adolescents, but it is less important in discussions of younger children. The sentimental view of childhood insists that children—particularly the innocent young—are basically good, and they are unlikely to rebel unless they somehow are corrupted.

The second image is the *deprived child*. Deprived children face poverty, family problems, or other disadvantages. Ordinarily, children—especially younger children—are not blamed for these deprivations, even for circumstances for which adults are normally held responsible. For example, adults who are poor or divorced usually receive at least part of the blame for their problems, but the children of poor or divorced parents get only sympathy.

The *sick child* in need of treatment is a third image. This image covers a wide range of medical problems. Successful treatments for polio, whooping cough, smallpox, and other once-devastating childhood diseases have encouraged reformers to mount campaigns against other illnesses, such as sudden infant death syndrome and muscular dystrophy. Furthermore, the successes of medical treatment have led some advocates and medical practitioners to redefine other problems in medical terms. This process of *medicalization* involves claims that some social problems are best understood as medical conditions; for example, attributing students' problems in school to such medical conditions as hyperkinesis or dyslexia (Conrad and Schneider, 1992).

The *child-victim* is the fourth image. Child-victims are threatened by kidnappers, child molesters, and other adult deviants. Like deprived and sick children, child-victims are not held responsible for their plight; their vulnerability is consistent with the sentimental view of childhood. Because the child-victim menaced by an adult deviant is an emotionally powerful image, claims sometimes use the language of victimization to describe children threatened by disease, poverty, or other impersonal social conditions.

WHAT SPECIFIC ELEMENTS MAKE THE CLAIMS PERSUASIVE?

People who make claims hope to persuade and convince us that some condition is a social problem that requires action. Claims about children's problems often contain persuasive elements that draw upon our culture's sentimental view of children. For instance, many claims use disturbing *horror stories* to illustrate the nature of the problem (Johnson, 1995). Because our culture favors a sentimental view of childhood, examples that emphasize children's suffering make claims more persuasive, and the more extreme the example the better. Often, social problems claims imply that their examples are typical, although, of course, extreme examples are by definition atypical.

Claims also tend to *emphasize the problem's effects on younger children*. Younger children are especially sentimental figures in our society, and social problems claims frequently play to that sentimentality. For example, in 1992, high-school-aged adolescents (15 to 19 years old) were eight times more likely to be homicide victims than younger children, yet discussions of drive-by shootings, guns in schools, and related problems frequently used examples involving young victims to illustrate these problems. Such claims may be effective at arousing public concern, but they accomplish this by distorting the nature of the problem.

In addition to disturbing examples, most social problems claims feature *statistics*. Since most claims seek to attract more attention to neglected problems, and since officials do not keep careful records of conditions they are neglecting, there rarely are accurate, authoritative statistics available (Best, 1990). As a result, many claims offer "guesstimates" or "ballpark figures." And, since a big number seems to reveal a big problem that demands action, social problems claims tend to use statistics that exaggerate the problem's size. For example, during the 1980s, the missing children movement estimated that strangers kidnapped up to 50,000 children per year. Researchers sponsored by the federal government later concluded that the number of serious stranger kidnappings per year was 200 to 300; that is, the movement's estimates had been about 200 times too high.

Social problems claims also tend to *ignore social patterns*. Claims often suggest that social problems threaten everyone. For example, discussions of child abuse regularly mention that abuse affects children of all races, all classes, and so on. This is no doubt true in the sense that a few children of millionaires suffer abuse. But such claims gloss over what we know about patterns of abusive behavior. Some children are far more likely to experience abuse than others; evidence shows, for example, that poverty and single-parent families greatly increase children's risk of being abused. But talking frankly about these patterns may make it harder to arouse public concern; some people may refuse to become involved because they don't believe the problem affects people like them. Fearing this reaction, people constructing social problems avoid discussing patterns of risk, or imply that the risks are the same for everyone. Again, this may increase support for their claims, but it gives the public a distorted sense of the problem.

Other claims *focus on the effects on children of broader problems.* This is another way the sentimental view of childhood shapes social problems claims. For example, the most successful social movement organization against drunk driving is Mothers Against Drunk Driving (MADD). As its name suggests, MADD began as a group of parents who had had children killed by drunk drivers, and its early claims emphasized child-victims. Of course, children composed only a small minority of those injured by drunk drivers, but MADD's focus on child-victims encouraged a sympathetic response to the organization's cause. Similarly, recent books use threats to children to talk about the broader problems of homelessness (Kozol, 1988), urban poverty (Kotlowitz, 1991), and even the threat of nuclear war (La Farge, 1987).

Social problems claims also *use children to talk about the future.* Because most children will outlive most adults, children seem to embody the future. Social problems claims that refer to children as "our most valuable resource" or "the leading endangered species of today" remind us that children are our link to the future and warn us that the future seems uncertain. A variety of contemporary claims warn that the future is threatened by public debt, nuclear war, epidemic disease, economic collapse, pollution, resource depletion, or overpopulation. Such claims often warn that, while today's adults may die before such calamities occur, our children—or at least our children's children—will suffer the consequences. This is, of course, yet another way children's sentimental meaning is used to influence how we think about social problems.

In sum, claims about social problems involving children adopt a variety of persuasive elements to arouse concern. Campaigns to construct social problems may incorporate several or even all of these elements. Consider, for example, the alarm about "crack babies" in the mid-1980s. The press carried horror stories about suffering infants and the prospect that they would be permanently damaged; experts offered statistical estimates for the numbers of children affected and the long-term costs of caring for them; some claims suggested that crack use (and its associated problems, including crack babies) were spreading to all segments of society; officials used crack's threat to infants to justify tough policies against the adults who smoked crack; and some claims even foretold a future with a nation ruined by drugs (Litt and McNeil, 1994). As the years passed, most of these warnings proved to be exaggerated. There were fewer crack babies than predicted, and relatively few of them suffered long-term damage; crack use largely remained confined to urban ghettoes; and so on. But the original claims portrayed crack as a terrible threat to the children of the United States. Like many claims about children's problems, the construction of the crack crisis drew upon the sentimental view of childhood.

CONCLUSION

The examples of the construction of children's social problems suggest that, as citizens, we need to think critically about social problems claims. This means, first, recognizing that social problems are constructed, that they are brought to our attention by people who want to persuade us and who design their claims to be persuasive. Thus, when we hear social problems claims, we should ask questions: Who are the people making the claims, and why are they speaking out? How is the problem defined and described? What evidence is offered for this description? What values do the claims invoke in order to persuade us? What policies are recommended as solutions to the problem? Do those policies fit the problem as it has been constructed? Do the policies seem likely to work?

In asking these questions, we need not become hostile or cynical. The point is not that social problems claims are always false or exaggerated. But most of what we know about social problems depends on meanings others construct; we learn from news stories, talk shows, everyday conversations, sociology textbooks, and a variety of other sources that construct social problems. The information provided by these sources needs to be evaluated. In order to understand and respond to social problems, we need to think critically about the claims we encounter.

REFERENCES

BEST, JOEL
1990 *Threatened Children.* Chicago: University of Chicago Press.

CONRAD, PETER and JOSEPH W. SCHNEIDER
1992 *Deviance and Medicalization,* 2nd ed. Philadelphia: Temple University Press.

JOHNSON, JOHN M.
1995 "Horror Stories and the Construction of Child Abuse" in Joel Best, ed., *Images of Issues,* 2nd ed. Hawthorne, NY: Aldine de Gruyter.

KOTLOWITZ, A.
1991 *There Are No Children Here.* New York: Doubleday.

KOZOL, JONATHAN.
1988 *Rachel and Her Children.* New York: Crown.

LA FARGE, P.
1987 *The Strangelove Legacy.* New York: Harper & Row.

LITT, JACQUELYN and MAUREEN MCNEIL
1994 "Crack Babies and the Politics of Nurturance," in Joel Best, ed., *Troubling Children.* Hawthorne, NY: Aldine de Gruyter.

SHORTER, EDWARD
1977 *The Making of the Modern Family.* New York: Basic Books.

SPECTOR, MALCOLM and JOHN I. KITSUSE
1977 *Constructing Social Problems.* Menlo Park, CA: Cummings.

ZELIZER, VIVIANA A.
1985 *Pricing the Priceless Child.* New York: Basic Books.

EXERCISE 15

Name _____   Date _____

ID # _____   Class Time _____

I. Locate a discussion in the mass media of some social problem involving children. Find an example of print journalism, such as a newspaper or magazine article, or a segment of electronic media, such as a televised news broadcast or an episode of a talk show. (If you decide to examine a television segment, it will help to make a videotape, so that you can view it more than once.) Avoid choosing a very brief discussion; a discussion which is too short will make it difficult to complete the exercise.

    A. In the space below, identify the social problem being discussed.

    B. Give a citation for your discussion (e.g., for a periodical article, include the author's name, article title, periodical title, date, and pages; for a television broadcast, give the name of the program, station, and date of broadcast).

    C. In the discussion you selected, who makes claims about the social problem?

    D. What qualifications do they have to make these claims?

    E. How might those who make these claims benefit if others accept their claims?

    F. How do the claims characterize children (e.g., as rebellious, deprived, etc.)?

G. Does the discussion include any of the following elements? If yes, describe below.

   1. Horror stories

   2. Emphasis on young children

   3. Statistics

   4. Claims that obscure social patterns

   5. Emphasis on children to discuss a broad problem which also affects adults

   6. Emphasis on an uncertain or dangerous future

H. Does the discussion's construction of the problem depend on a sentimental view of children? Explain.

16

Sexual Orientation and Inequality

Kenneth Allan

Between 1983 and 1993, the United States military discharged over 14,000 men and women from active service because they were not heterosexuals. On January 29, 1993, the President of the United States announced that the Defense Department's longstanding ban on homosexuals, that is, gays and lesbians, in the military would be lifted within six months. The President's proposed policy was called by some observers the ". . . gravest challenge ever to . . . [t]he last refuge of traditional masculinity" (Henry, 1992). In response to strong opposition from within the military and from political opponents, the President detailed the revised compromise policy of "don't ask/don't tell" just six months after the initial policy lifting the ban on homosexuals was introduced. By January 1994, just one year since the President initiated the change in policy at the Department of Defense, the U.S. Court of Appeals for the District of Columbia upheld the earlier rules banning homosexuals from serving in the military.

The attempts to change Pentagon policies regarding the treatment of homosexuals in the military so far have been ineffectual. Yet the efforts to change Pentagon policies and the public furor surrounding those efforts have helped to bring to the public forum the issues of discrimination concerning homosexuals and the broader issue of sexual orientation and inequality in society. Inequalities involving race, gender, or class are familiar concerns. Similarly, we usually understand sexuality as a social problem in terms of such pressing issues as abortion, pornography, or sexually transmitted diseases. In these terms, sex and inequality, as such, are not particularly new topics. Until recently, sexual orientation has not been a matter of public discourse. In the last two decades, in connection with the medical condition Acquired Immune Deficiency Syndrome (AIDS), homosexuality has entered the public sphere as never before in the United States; and only recently has sexual orientation been discussed publicly as a social inequality issue.

In this essay the connection between inequality and sexual orientation is discussed. The inequalities associated with sexual orientation and the discriminatory treatment of homosexuals are the result of factors deeply embedded in the culture of the United States. I argue that the discrimination and prejudice directed toward homosexuals is rooted in the way in which we categorize people as heterosexual and homosexual. Before these issues are discussed, I first examine how people attempt to understand the "cause" of homosexuality and how this is connected to different groups' attempts to define homosexuality.

WHAT'S IN A NAME? DEFINING HOMOSEXUALITY IN AMERICA TODAY

In addressing the connection between homosexuality and inequality, we are concerned with the differential treatment of a group as a consequence of their sexual orientation and with the social process of defining sexual orientation. The process of defining a group is a socially constructed one. The definition that emerges influences people's beliefs, values, and behavior toward the group. Though it is possible to define the meaning and treatment of homosexuality in an infinite number of ways, there are basically only a few beliefs about homosexuality in the culture of the United States today. For decades, the definition of homosexuality by the medical establishment has influenced the general public's beliefs and norms regarding the definition of homosexual behavior and people's reaction to it. Until 1973, the American Psychological Association (APA) defined homosexuality as a psychological illness. This definition led to various "treatments" in hopes of producing a "cure." For example, lesbians were forced to submit to hysterectomies and estrogen treatments. Homosexual males were subjected to castration, aversion therapy, transorbital lobotomy, and electroshock treatment.[1] Despite these treatments, very few homosexuals were ever "cured." In 1973, the APA removed homosexuality from its list of mental disorders. Yet homosexuality is still viewed by many people as a sickness, reflecting, in part, the decades of influence on public opinion of the medical community.

Beliefs about homosexuality today center on the controversy over whether homosexuality is a sexual preference (a lifestyle) or a sexual orientation (a biological tendency). Those who argue that homosexuality is a sexual preference view homosexual behavior as a choice; thus, they advocate making gays and lesbians responsible for their sexuality. If homosexual behavior is a choice, then the discrimination that gays and lesbians suffer is their responsibility, not society's. Politically active gays and lesbians disagree, preferring to define homosexuality as an orientation or a biological drive. Some recent scientific research has indicated that there may indeed be a biological component that creates dispositions for both homosexuality and heterosexuality. In the mid-1960s, it was discovered that the brain is inherently "female" and it requires the presence of testosterone to be masculinized. That discovery led to research aimed at uncovering possible dimorphic qualities of the brain. In 1990, a cluster of brain cells, the suprachiasmatic nucleus, was found to be structurally different according to whether the person was heterosexual or homosexual. Additional research in 1991 revealed that the hypothalamic structure of the brain was also different for heterosexual and homosexual men.[2] These studies have not as yet been confirmed, and some scientists are skeptical of the results. Yet they do suggest that biology may play a role in shaping sexual orientation. Research also suggests that people are not biologically influenced to be *exclusively* homosexual or heterosexual.

In the United States we generally believe that homosexuality is a sickness, a choice, or is biologically motivated. But the question "What motivates an individual to be a homosexual?" is rather different from "What criteria do we use to define someone as a homosexual?" *Webster's Dictionary* defines "homosexuality" as having sexual desire or relations with members of the same sex. It is typically argued that about 10 percent of any given population is homosexual. But if we take this definition seriously, then 10 percent is indeed a conservative or low estimate, at least in the United States. For example, during the late 1940s, Alfred Kinsey and his associates interviewed 12,000 men and found that 37 percent admitted to having at least one overt homosexual experience that led to orgasm. And 25 percent of the men had fairly frequent homosexual experiences that lasted at least three years (Kinsey, Pomery, and Martin 1948). Of the 8,000 women that Kinsey interviewed, 28 percent said that they had felt sexually attracted to another woman, 19 percent had some sexual contact with another woman, and 13 percent had experienced orgasm through homosexual relations (Kinsey, Pomery, Martin, and Gebbhard, 1953). If we define a "homosexual" as someone who has had one same-sex experience or has felt attracted to the same sex, then somewhere between a quarter to a third of the population is homosexual.

A study conducted in the early 1990s, the Janus survey (1993), found that 22 percent of the male respondents had at least one homosexual experience. Of those men, 5 percent had only one experience, 56 percent reported occasional experiences, 13 percent frequent, and 26 percent ongoing homosexual relations. The same study reports that 17 percent of the women surveyed had at least one homosexual experience. Of those women, 6 percent had only one experience, 67 percent reported occasional experiences, 6 percent frequent, and 21 percent ongoing homosexual relations. A recent study of sexual behavior in America conducted by sociologists from the University of Chicago and the State University of New York (Laumann, 1994) suggests that the actual percentage of the population engaging in homosexual relations is considerably lower. In their findings 5 percent of men reported having had a sexual encounter with another man as an adult, while 2.8 percent reported that they were homosexual or bisexual. Similarly, 4 percent of women reported having had a sexual encounter with another female, while 1.5 percent reported that they were homosexual or bisexual.

The wide disagreement among the few studies discussed here are not the result of faulty research design or misrepresentation of the results. The variation results from differing definitions of homosexuality across the studies. In some studies a single sexual encounter with a person of the same sex defines one as a homosexual. In others, multiple same-sex experiences are required for someone to be considered homosexual. The period of time elapsed since a same-sex encounter also influences the definition in some research on homosexuality. Still other studies consider the more subjective experience of "desire" in the defining process. For our purposes, the point is that what constitutes a homosexual is socially constructed and arbitrary.

Not long ago, these issues were not even in question. The place of homosexuality in America was simply taken for granted. Now, because of the general movement toward equality in the United States and the importance of defining social categories, the course of gay and lesbian behavior and the definition of what constitutes a homosexual are both hotly contested. The answers to these questions have not yet been determined, and it doesn't look like the answers are just around the corner. This current state of definitional flux indicates that we, as a society, are experiencing change; sexual orientation and stratification is an emerging social problem. In addition to the social and personal benefit of greater equality, the emergence offers us, as social scientists, the opportunity to observe the process of social change. In order for a system of stratification to exist, there must also exist a cultural scaffolding that reflects and reinforces the social structure of inequality. This cultural scaffolding can take the form of laws that institutionalize inequality or social categories that set the parameters for "normal" interaction.

HOMOSEXUALITY AND STRATIFICATION

Stratification is defined by Farley as "a system whereby scarce resources, such as wealth, income, status, and power are distributed unequally" (Farley, 1987). While accurate, Farley's definition does not capture a central aspect of stratification. Stratification is not simply the unequal distribution of scarce resources; it is the perpetuation or maintenance of that distribution. The word "stratification" comes from the Latin root *stratum*, meaning a covering; stratification is a system of inequality that provides a covering or a barrier between one group and another and prevents easy movement between groups, thus preventing easy access to scarce resources. The maintenance of inequality depends on both macro-level (large scale) and micro-level (small scale) dynamics of stratification.

The macro-level scaffolding that recreates stratification is supported by social institutions. Two institutions most affect the level of inequality experienced by homosexuals: religion and law. In the history of the world's religions, homosexuality has been variously treated as normal, sacred, and profane. For instance, among many North American Indian tribes, homosexuals, or "gender mixers," were viewed as having a spiritual gift that went along with their sexuality. They were also used as mediators of gendered relations between men and women. Another illustration is found in Plato's Greek creation myth, *Symposium*. The myth depicts three kinds of humans: men attracted to men, women attracted to women, and heterosexuals. It is the two groups of homosexuals that are viewed in more positive terms of love and affection. In the United States, like many countries in the Western world, Judeo-Christian culture influences our understanding of "normal" sexual behavior. According to the Old Testament, homosexuality is a sin that is condemned and made punishable by death (see, for example, Leviticus 18:22; 20:13).[3]

Often, laws regulating homosexual behavior are implicit. Gays and lesbians are implicitly excluded from marriage rights and insurance coverage; by definition they are not "man and woman." And while there are no laws that forbid an individual to be a homosexual, there are laws that forbid such practices as oral and anal sex in which homosexuals generally engage. These laws exist in spite of the high percentages of heterosexuals that engage in or approve of both practices.[4] An important constitutional test of sodomy law came in 1986. Two Georgia men were observed by a policeman having anal sex in the home of one of the participants; the policeman was there on another matter. The men were convicted of sodomy in Georgia but appealed to the United States Supreme Court (*Bowers v. Hardwick*). The Court upheld the conviction, often using biblical language in rendering its opinion, and the Georgia state law that makes "any sexual act involving the sex organs of one person and the mouth or anus of another" a felony punishable by up to 20 years in prison.

Of perhaps greater significance is the apparent emergence of a movement at the state level to pass laws that counter local ordinances aimed at protecting the civil rights of homosexuals. In 1992, 53 percent of Colorado supported such a law, Amendment 2, that would have nullified local county and city ordinances that protected gay and lesbian civil rights. The Colorado Supreme Court struck down Amendment 2 as unconstitutional in October 1994. Two additional states, Oregon and Idaho, recently placed similar laws on their ballots. Despite their failure to pass the first time round, their presence is an indicator that structural inequality aimed at homosexuals is not a dead issue. Conversely, there are only two states that currently have laws prohibiting discrimination against gays, Wisconsin and Massachusetts.

In addition to macro-level structures, stratification systems are also recreated in micro-level interaction (Collins, 1988). For example, laws are interpreted and enacted by human actors in real situations. In every micro-level encounter there are particular social categories that inform and frame mundane, daily interactions. In order for stratification to occur, these defining cultural categories must be in place. It is important for us to understand the connection between these two levels. Although debate about the relationship between micro and macro phenomena is an enduring one in sociology, Figure 16.1 helps to clarify the relationships between these phenomena and interaction (i.e., an "encounter").

Every encounter between two or more individuals is framed by both the macro- and micro-level structures, as noted by arrows a and b in Figure 16.1. Very few of us are powerful enough as individuals to directly affect macro-level structures. But we can affect micro-level structures in a somewhat more direct way. Think of micro-structures as emerging from encounters or interaction (arrow c in Figure 16.1). For example, as we repeatedly meet the same people under similar circumstances, a micro-structure emerges—a friendship, an acquaintance, a business relationship, etc.. This micro-structure consists of the personal definitions and behavioral expectations we have formed regarding these individuals. For example, on the first day of your Social Problems class you probably did not know exactly what to expect. Chances are you had never met the professor or most of your classmates and perhaps you had never taken a sociology class. You probably did have some idea of what to expect, but these expectations were based on prior classes you had taken at a university (micro-structure) and the general normative ex-

FIGURE 16.1: The Relationships Between Macro and Microstructures

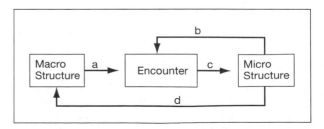

pectations of classroom behavior in an American university (macro-structure). But as the semester progressed, you got to know your professor and fellow students as individuals, and you all formed expectations of one another and the class as a whole. These expectations form a micro-structure that frames further encounters with those individuals and the class.[5]

Micro-structures not only frame further encounters, they can also affect macro-structures (arrow d in Figure 16.1). As micro-structures involve more and more people, over greater distances and longer periods of time, they affect the existing macro-structures or become macro-structures themselves. As an illustration, let's suppose that a professor is tired of trying to motivate students to learn material, and she decides that one of the main problems is the fact that students are expected to be passive receptors rather than active creators of knowledge. In an attempt to address this situation, she begins to conduct her classrooms as exploration centers. On the first day of class, she sets the parameters: This is the area we are going to discover. These are the questions we are going to answer. But she doesn't tell the students the answers. In fact, she may not even know the answers. She instead enables the students to creatively discover answers, and she facilitates their formation of further questions. Let's pretend further that this style of discovery is quantifiably successful, and other teachers begin to implement the strategy. Soon, teachers at other schools begin to experiment with the format, and it eventually comes to the attention of the state school board. The state school board then establishes a policy that all classrooms will be run using this format. In our imaginary scenario, what started out as a micro-structure of teacher/student expectations became a macro-structure affecting more and more classrooms and was eventually institutionalized in the form of state school policy.

I have to admit that this model is oversimplified. For one thing, it has no consideration of power and vested interests. A small number of people with significant resources can stop the process or can initiate processes of their own that become macro-structures. Keeping this caveat in mind, the model does give us a heuristic device to understand how both macro- and micro-structures affect every encounter in which you are involved, and how what you do in everyday interaction can affect even the macro-structures of our society.

In every social encounter we categorize people. Categorization is a process that allows us to quickly determine how we should behave toward the other and how the other should behave toward us. We categorize others based on information that they provide; for example, hair, dress, language, and so on. Once a categorization is made, we expect ("demand" may be a better word) certain behaviors from them based on that categorization. This process allows us to enter into social interactions with a fair degree of certainty, but it also creates tension when individuals do not meet the expectations of the category that they have claimed. Erving Goffman (1963) noted that

these expectations have a righteousness about them. When individuals do not live up to their categorization, others in the encounter become righteously indignant, and the individual becomes stigmatized.

Cultural categories are found at both the micro- and macro-levels of society. Macro-level categories are those categories that seem to apply in almost every encounter. These ubiquitous categories and their expectations are macro in the sense that they have the weight of people, space, and time, but they are dependent upon micro-interaction to recreate them. One of these macro categories, and one of the first categorizations we make, is gender. When making this categorization is difficult, as in the case of a baby or an androgynous adult, the interaction is awkward until the categorization is made of the person in question. One of the expectations that goes along with gender is sexuality. In most meetings between members of "the opposite sex" an evaluation takes place. Is this person available? Do I find this person attractive? Is this person interested? Do I have a chance? Thousands of tiny clues are noticed and cataloged, decisions are made, and actions follow (ask for a phone number, date, etc.).

In meetings between members of the same sex, we set aside sexuality, at least in terms of availability of the other. But if we are wrong, and the person to whom we have categorized as "same sex" turns out to be sexually available, we tend to experience what Goffman (1963) described as "righteous indignation." At times such indignation may be expressed violently. In 1988 the Institute for Justice stated that homosexuals were probably the most frequent victims of hate crimes but that such violence often goes underreported. Until 1990 "undercounting" of crimes against homosexuals also contributed to the inability to estimate the number of crimes against homosexuals. What changed in 1990 was that on April 23 the President of the United States signed into law the Hate Crimes Statistics Act in which homosexuals were for the first time identified as a category against which hate crimes could be perpetuated.[6]

Prior to the act, violence against gays and lesbians was not distinguished by the federal government as a hate crime. Because of these factors affecting the reporting of hate crimes involving homosexuals, most of the national data currently available is based on self-reports. Comparing the available data, it is fair to estimate that between 15 percent and 20 percent of all homosexuals will experience some form of physical violence, and about 70 percent will experience verbal abuse.[7] Even if the "categorized" homosexual is not victimized in an encounter, he or she is likely to be stigmatized as not meeting the norm of sexuality. As a result, many homosexuals attempt to "pass" as heterosexual. It takes, on the average, five years for individuals to "come out" to the straight community once they have acknowledged their own homosexuality. This type of categorization and the inequality it creates will probably continue until the category of gender is redefined.

CONCLUSION

This essay examined data concerning sexual orientation and stratification and discussed a theoretical perspective that accounts for how the process of stratification works. The perpetuation of inequality requires institutional structures such as laws and other institutional arrangements that structure and pattern face-to-face encounters, that is, micro-interactions. The maintenance of structures of inequality also requires micro-level encounters to reproduce the cultural categories that provide the scaffolding for the social structure. Significantly, the theoretical perspective developed here to help understand the maintenance of inequality also contains the elements of change. Thus if it is true that each of us and the people we interact with on a daily basis recreate the existing stratification system, then it is also true that each of us can contribute to changing this structure, albeit in limited ways—one encounter at a time.

NOTES

1. For a graphic depiction of the abuses suffered by homosexuals at the hands of medical science, see the 1992 documentary film *Changing Our Minds* by James Harrison.

2. For an accessible account of the scientific research on the biological foundation of homosexuality in the popular press, see Chandler Burr (1993).

3. It is interesting to note that *onanism,* the contraceptive practice of withdrawal before ejaculation, is condemned in like manner in biblical scripture (see, for example, Genesis 38:9–10).

4. According to the Janus survey (1993), 88 percent of men and 87 percent of women think that oral sex is "very normal" or "all right"; 29 percent of men and 24 percent of women surveyed think that anal sex is "very normal" or "all right."

5. A nice example of this process in the popular media is the initial interaction and subsequent restructuring of expectations in the movie *The Dead Poets Society.*

6. Currently, 22 states have hate crime laws, but 13 of them exclude homosexuals.

7. As of 1995, the statistics are different for men and women, with men suffering higher rates of physical abuse than women. The best treatment of this issue is Herek and Berrill, eds., *Hate Crimes* (1992).

REFERENCES

Bowers v. Hardwick
1986   478 US 186 (1986).

BURR, CHANDLER
1993   "Homosexuality and Biology," *The Atlantic Monthly* 271, no. 3 (March): 47–65.

COLLINS, RANDALL
1988   *Theoretical Sociology*. San Diego: Harcourt Brace Jovanovich.

FARLEY, JOHN E.
1987   *American Social Problems; An Institutional Analysis.* Englewood Cliffs, NJ: Prentice Hall.

GOFFMAN, ERVING
1963   *Stigma: Notes on the Management of Spoiled Identity.* New York: Simon and Schuster.

HENRY, WILLIAM A., III.
1992   "Clinton's First Fire Fight," *Time* 140, n. 22: 42.

HEREK, GREGORY M. and KEVIN T. BERRILL, eds.
1992   *Hate Crimes*. Newbury Park, CA: Sage.

JANUS, SAMUEL S. and CYNTHIA L. JANUS
1993   *The Janus Report on Sexual Behavior*. New York: John Wiley.

KINSEY, ALFRED C., WARDELL B. POMERY and CLYDE E. MARTIN
1948   *Sexual Behavior in the Human Male*. Philadelphia: W. B. Saunders.

KINSEY, ALFRED C., WARDELL B. POMERY, CLYDE E. MARTIN and PAUL H. GEBBHARD
1953   *Sexual Behavior in the Human Female*. Philadelphia: W. B. Saunders.

LAUMANN, EDWARD O.
1994   *The Social Organization of Sexuality: Sexual Practices in the United States*. Chicago: University of Chicago Press.

EXERCISE 16

Name _____   Date _____

ID # _____   Class Time _____

I. The author argued that sexual orientation and stratification is an emerging social problem. A phenomenon may become defined as a social problem if (1) it is widely regarded as undesirable or a source of difficulties; (2) the condition is defined as being caused by the actions or inactions of people or society; and (3) the condition is seen as affecting a significant number of people.

A. Discuss the case of sexual orientation and stratification in light of each of these conditions. (*Hint:* To answer one of the conditions you may have to do some library research to collect data to make the needed comparisons.)

1.

2.

3.

B. Does the case of sexual orientation and stratification satisfactorily meet the criteria of a social problem? Defend your answer. Use the space below to answer these questions.

1. Circle either: Yes or No

2. State your supporting argument.

II. Watch the movie *Philadelphia*.

A. Pick a scene from the movie and describe an encounter or interaction that is most salient to you regarding the treatment of gays.

B. Describe the encounter with respect to the use of categories and expectations.

C. What changes would have to occur at the micro-level of interaction for Tom Hanks's character to have been treated differently?

17

Disability

Richard K. Scotch

THE EXTENT OF DISABILITY

In 1990 there were over 35 million Americans with disabilities, greater than the number of elderly persons or African Americans—26 million and 28 million, respectively (LaPlante, 1991). Statistical estimates of the number of disabled people in the United States vary, depending on how disability is defined. For example, the Americans with Disabilities Act of 1990 estimated that there are 43 million Americans with disabilities, based on an extrapolation of figures from the National Health Interview Survey (NHIS). Using a somewhat more restrictive definition, the Institute of Medicine estimates that about 35 million people experience limitations in at least one major life activity such as working, caring for oneself, walking, seeing, or hearing (Institute of Medicine, 1991). If we broaden the definition to include common illnesses such as arthritis and hypertension, more than half of the working-age population and nearly 80 percent of persons age 60 and older, a total of over 120 million people, have at least one chronic health condition (LaPlante, 1991: 61).

Different impairments affect people at different stages of the life cycle. Young adults are most likely to experience limitations caused by spinal cord injuries, orthopedic impairments, and paralysis, while middle-aged and older adults are more likely to be limited by chronic diseases, especially heart and circulatory problems (Institute of Medicine, 1991). As with many health problems, people with disabilities are more likely to be older, have lower incomes, and be members of minority groups than people without disabilities.

The number of Americans reporting disability (as measured by the NHIS) increased rapidly in the 1970s, particularly among middle-aged men. The prevalence of disability has increased at a slower but fairly constant rate since 1981. Interpretations have varied for the increase in the 1970s, which was associated with rising claims for government disability benefits. Some have linked it to decreasing stigma associated with government assistance and reductions in the work ethic. Others have connected it to better access to medical care that was associated with better awareness of chronic conditions. Verbrugge (1984) has argued that increasing chronic illness is linked to reductions in mortality, with people living longer overall due to earlier detection of illness and treatment of conditions that might otherwise have been fatal. Yelin (1992) has linked increased disability claims to changes in the structure of the American economy, with long-term reductions in high-paying, skilled blue-collar employment leading middle-aged men with few job alternatives to use disability programs as a way out of the work force.

The Institute of Medicine estimates the annual costs associated with disabilities to be more than $170 billion. These costs include health care, benefit payments, and the lost productivity both of the person with a disability and of family caregivers. The costs of disability to our society have increased even faster than its prevalence, rising from 1.9 percent of all money spent in the U.S. economy (GNP) in 1970 to 4 percent in 1986 (Berkowitz and Greene, 1989). In response to disability, an enormous rehabilitation industry has developed, consisting of hospitals and other health care facilities, a vast network of home health and transitional care providers, major segments of the pharmaceutical and medical equipment industries, insurers, public charities, and research organizations (Albrecht, 1992).

CONCEPTIONS OF DISABILITY

Virtually everyone has some mental image connected with the term "disability." The nature of this image has important implications for people who have one. Paul Higgins (1992) has described several different ways of thinking about disability. In nonindustrial societies, disability was often understood as the result of evil spiritual forces.

Blindness, epilepsy, or missing limbs could be interpreted as punishment for sin. Alternatively, disabilities have also been seen as divine gifts, evidence of God's special attention. In either case, people with disabilities have been perceived as fundamentally different from other human beings.

More recently, disability has been defined medically as a long-term impairment or chronic condition that interferes with everyday activities. This medical model of disability implies that the disability is the product of a broken or malfunctioning body part or system, a biological incapacity that is inherently pathological but may be fixed by medical and rehabilitative experts. An individual with a disability is thus inherently flawed and in need of medical intervention and/or supervision.

While disability as defined medically is not the fault of the individual, it is the responsibility of the person with a disability to defer to the directives of health professionals and to be circumspect about the impairment. While medicine is not an exact science, analyses of disability that use a medical model tend to treat impairments as relatively straightforward scientific facts discernible by medical experts. Physicians are believed capable (and are given authority by the state) to objectively certify a person as "disabled." Today, the medical certification of disability is necessary to qualify for certain benefits and privileges.

Another definition of disability that has guided public policy and social interaction portrays disability as an economic incapacity. In this model, disability is associated with an inability to be economically self-sufficient, which leads to dependency on others or, ultimately, the state. Similar to the medical model, economically defined disability is an individual characteristic associated with incapacity, in this case, the inability to work. The federal census, for example, has defined as disabled anyone who reports being unable to work or keep house as the result of a physical or medical impairment. As with the medical definition, in this economic model, disability is a personal attribute associated with incapacity that can only be addressed by "fixing" whatever is wrong with that individual.

Higgins (1992) describes how medical and economic definitions individualize disability. One consequence of such individualizing is the social separation of those who do and do not have disabilities, a separation that may go so far as to socially define disabled people outside the human community. Another consequence of individualization is to place the burden of remedying problems associated with the disability on the disabled person. Such definitions neglect how the consequences of disability are the result of the interaction of an individual and the social environment. While many people with disabilities are isolated, critics of these models argue that such isolation is more the result of how others respond to disability than of a person's disability itself.

An alternative, writes Higgins (1992), is to "socialize" disability, to understand it as a social construct that is the product of a physical or mental condition and the social context for that condition. In this case, a condition (typically referred to in the literature as an *impairment*) becomes a disability only as the result of characteristics of the physical or social environment. For example, blindness can be a problem in reading a printed newspaper but not in listening to a recorded version of the same information. Using a wheelchair may be a disability when using a building equipped only with staircases, but not when using one that has incorporated ramps and elevators into its design. Such a social conception of disability turns our attention from an exclusive focus on the individual to a broader examination of physical and social environments.

Since the 1970s, a new and more political definition of disability characterizes it as the basis for a minority group. In this view, disability is a status comparable to race or gender that serves as the basis for exclusion and discrimination, and is best dealt with through enactment of legal rights. Arguing for this model, Paul Longmore (1985) wrote:

> Since World War II, and with accelerating momentum during the last decade, disabled persons in the United States and other developed countries have begun to identify themselves not as victims of disease and disablement in need of and dependent on benevolent oversight, but rather as a minority group, stigmatized, discriminated against, segregated, and denied the opportunity to participate equally in society for reasons not inherent to their medical conditions. . . . An emerging language, being developed by handicapped people themselves and particularly influenced by the disability rights movement, actively resists stigma and social subordination, seeks to create an opposing positive social identity, and, in some instances, affirms a minority group identity.

The minority group model makes a positive statement about the social status of people with disabilities. It has served as the basis for much of the federal legislation on disability of the past quarter century. The model explicitly builds on the assumption that people with disabilities are exposed to exclusion and unfair stereotypes—that their social standing is typically associated with social stigma.

DISABILITY, INTERACTION, AND STIGMA

Most people associate the term "disability" with incapacity, with those who cannot walk or see or hear. Such individuals are often thought to be unfortunate victims of bad luck. People with disabilities are thought to need special help to get around, assistance from their families or the government to support themselves, and special treatment because of their limitations. Disabled people are often congratulated for their bravery in being out in the world. Nondisabled people frequently speak to the disabled in a carefully upbeat manner, and may address a nondisabled companion rather than the disabled person herself.

When a child is born with a disability, many people feel sorry for the parents and may quietly be grateful there is no one with a disability in their own family. When a person with a disability is the subject of a news story, the account often emphasizes the person's courage in the face of the tragedy of a ruined life. In fictional accounts in films or books, people with disabilities are often angry and bitter about their lost opportunities, until they are helped to accept their situation by family members, health professionals, or social workers.

Erving Goffman uses the term "stigma" to characterize such views of disability (1963). Goffman refers to the spoiled identity of people with disabilities and suggests that their condition has discredited them socially. Those he calls "normals" may be uneasy around individuals with a disability and often react on the basis of stereotypes or avoid contact altogether. Even in situations where a person's disability is not directly involved, having a disability may become a master status that imposes general attributions of incapacity on the person with a disability. In some instances, individuals with disabilities may incorporate such negative stereotypes into their own self-image, reinforcing dependence.

The stigma associated with disability has created barriers to collective action, barriers that are exacerbated by the demographic dispersion of people with disabilities (Scotch, 1988). Nevertheless, the rise of a social movement of people with disabilities in the past 30 years has encouraged more positive images of disability and is leading to institutional change through government reform (Scotch, 1984). This movement has promoted independence through the removal of architectural, attitudinal, and institutional obstacles to societal participation. One segment of the movement has emphasized the promotion of independent living through self-help, peer support, and community-based services. The independent living movement dates to the founding of the first Center for Independent Living by Ed Roberts in Berkeley, California, in the 1960s and has grown to a national network of centers supported by federal rehabilitation funds. The other major component of the social movement of people with disabilities is the disability rights movement, which has organized at the local and national levels to seek legal prohibitions against discrimination on the basis of disability in schools, employment, transportation, and public accommodations. The greatest success achieved by this movement was the passage of the Americans with Disabilities Act of 1990.

PROBLEMS ASSOCIATED WITH DISABILITY

People with disabilities face a number of challenges in coping with social institutions that are often not designed to meet their needs. Throughout much of American history, many people with disabilities were denied access to public education or were shunted off to segregated programs that provided little beyond custodial care. As recently as the 1960s, over 1 million disabled children were not in school.

With the passage of the Individuals with Disabilities Education Act (IDEA) in 1974, public schools have been required to provide education and related services to all children with disabilities. Under IDEA, the federal government has required local school systems to place children with disabilities in regular classrooms when possible, and otherwise in as normal a setting as is consistent with their individual needs. This practice, often called "mainstreaming," has met with some criticism from teachers and parents of nondisabled children, yet it has opened up many opportunities to children who might otherwise have not received an education.

Once they leave school, many adults with disabilities face problems in finding employment. In a 1986 survey by Louis Harris and Associates of working-age people with disabilities, 66 percent of those not working said they wanted to work. While their disabilities were cited as the primary reason they were not working, 47 percent reported that employers would not recognize that they were capable of doing a full-time job, and 28 percent reported a lack of accessible or affordable transportation as important reasons they were not working. Twenty-five percent of the disabled respondents reported encountering job discrimination related to their disability.

For over 75 years, the federal-state vocational rehabilitation (VR) program has promoted the employment of people with disabilities through job counseling, skill acquisition, and the purchase of adaptive aids and devices. In its first half-century, the VR program concentrated on assisting people with less severe impairments, since they were thought to be most easily placed in paid employment. While successful in meeting this objective, critics of VR believed that the program was not assisting those who most needed its help.

Since the 1970s, the VR program has shifted priorities and is serving larger numbers of more severely disabled people. Although paid employment is still the primary goal of the VR program, it also supports independent living programs which allow people who may not be able to financially support themselves to live in the community as independently as possible. Federally supported centers for independent living operate in many communities and assist people with education and training programs, peer support, finding accessible housing, and arranging for the personal assistance needed by many to live on their own.

Employment issues for people with disabilities also include the problems of exclusion and discrimination. In 1973, the Rehabilitation Act prohibited discrimination by federal grantees and contractors, including most schools, universities, local and state governments, public transit systems, and health care facilities. The Americans with Disabilities Act of 1990 extended protection from discrimination to private employers and virtually all public accommodations. While neither law has led to massive changes in participation by people with disabilities, both have had important impacts in opening up institutions to disabled individuals who would otherwise have been excluded.

Another significant problem facing people with disabilities is access to health care. People with disabilities often require more health care services than those without disabilities, reporting on average two to three times more physician visits, six times more hospitalizations, and nearly three times longer hospital stays (DeJong, Batavia and Griss, 1989). People with disabilities often experience difficulty obtaining routine primary care and personal assistance in their homes, and long-term care facilities appropriate for working-age adults are also difficult to find. Moreover, there are tremendous barriers to purchasing needed private health insurance due to the exclusion from coverage of "preexisting medical conditions."

CONCLUSION

Disability is not in itself a social problem. However, people who have disabilities face a wide variety of problems in their daily lives that are the product of social forces. Isolation, expectations by others of incapacity, barriers to mobility and communication, and difficulties in obtaining jobs and health care are all related to how we respond socially to disabilities. Historically, people with disabilities have been offered modest financial support, but at the price of a dependence resulting from the difficulty of life in the mainstream of society.

In recent years, as the result of advocacy by the disability rights movement, efforts have shifted from supporting dependence to promoting independence through removal of disabling barriers and the creation of a more flexible society, and from educating disabled people how to accommodate themselves to prejudice to educating nondisabled people about the realities of disability. If this change is sustained, we can achieve what Irving Kenneth Zola (1989) has called a "universalized society," in which elimination of barriers is unnecessary because they are not constructed to begin with. At that point, disability may become an incidental personal attribute, rather than a handicapping condition associated with social problems.

REFERENCES

ALBRECHT, GARY L.
1992 *The Disability Business: Rehabilitation in America.* Newbury Park, CA: Sage.

BERKOWITZ, MONROE and CAROLYN GREENE
1989 "Disability Expenditures," *American Rehabilitation* 15: 7–15, 29.

DEJONG, GERBEN, ANDREW I. BATAVIA and ROBERT GRISS
1989 "America's Neglected Health Minority: Working Age Persons with Disabilities," *The Milbank Quarterly* 67 Supp. 2, Pt. 2: 311–351.

GOFFMAN, ERVING
1963 *Stigma: Notes on the Management of Spoiled Identity.* New York: Simon & Schuster.

HARRIS, LOUIS AND ASSOCIATES, INC.
1986 *The ICD Survey of Disabled Americans: Bringing Disabled Americans into the Mainstream.* New York: Louis Harris and Associates.

HIGGINS, PAUL
1992 *Making Disability: Exploring the Social Transformation of Human Variation.* Springfield, IL: Charles C. Thomas.

INSTITUTE OF MEDICINE
1991 *Disability in America: Toward a National Agenda for Prevention,* Andrew M. Pope and Alvin R. Tarlov, eds. Washington, DC: National Academy Press.

LAPLANTE, MITCHELL P.
1991 "The Demographics of Disability," in Jane West, ed., *The Americans With Disabilities Act: From Policy to Practice.* New York: Milbank Memorial Fund.

LONGMORE, PAUL K.
1985 "A Note on Language and the Social Identity of Disabled People," *American Behavioral Scientist* 28: 419–423.

SCOTCH, RICHARD K.
1984 *From Good Will to Civil Rights: Transforming Federal Disability Policy.* Philadelphia: Temple University Press.

SCOTCH, RICHARD K.
1988 "Disability as the Basis for a Social Movement: Advocacy and the Politics of Definition," *Journal of Social Issues* 44: 159–172.

VERBRUGGE, LOIS M.
1984 "Longer Life but Worsening Health? Trends in Health and Mortality of Middle-Aged and Older Persons," *Milbank Quarterly* 62: 475–519.

YELIN, EDWARD H.
1992 *Disability and the Displaced Worker.* New Brunswick, NJ: Rutgers University Press.

ZOLA, IRVING KENNETH
1989 "Toward the Necessary Universalizing of a Disability Policy," *The Milbank Quarterly* 67 Supp. 2, Pt. 2: 401–428.

EXERCISE 17

Name _____   Date _____

ID # _____   Class Time _____

I. *Media Scan:* Use the newspaper to collect three articles referring to persons with disabilities. The articles may be news stories, feature stories, and fictional depictions of persons with any disability.

    A. For each article, list the title, name of newspaper, and date of publication.

        1. Article 1:

        2. Article 2:

        3. Article 3:

    B. Are the images associated with disability positive or negative? For example, how independent or dependent is the person? What consequences of the disability are discussed? What emotional and/or character traits are attributed to the person(s) with disabilities, and what evidence is used to support the description? Briefly summarize your responses to these questions below.

        1. Article 1:

        2. Article 2:

        3. Article 3:

    C. What are the social consequences of the images you chose to examine—are they disabling in themselves or do they portray a positive message?

        1. Article 1:

        2. Article 2:

        3. Article 3:

II. *Environmental Scan:* Assume you know someone who uses a wheelchair and that you invited him or her to come to visit you where you live. The following questions ask you to evaluate the accessability of your own home for the person using the wheelchair.

    A. Could someone easily visit you? Stay overnight? Move in? Is the building fully accessible? Be sure to include the bathroom, kitchen, sleeping, and other areas of your residence in your discussion.

    B. What specific accommodations would need to be made to enable the person using the wheelchair to live in your home?

    C. Estimate the cost of each item identified in your answer to part B above.

III. *Family Scan:* As the essay states, one in seven Americans has a disability which limits that person in at least one major life activity.

    A. Create a family tree for your extended family (e.g., cousins, second cousins, intergenerational family ties, etc.), indicating the person's relation to you, his or her known disability (if any), and any limitations related to the disability. Remember to include chronic health conditions such as heart disease or asthma in addition to impairments that may limit physical activity, mobility, or communication. (Use a practice sheet to keep your tree within the space provided here if necessary).

    B. Given the age and social circumstances of your family members, does their particular disability status appear to be typical or atypical? Discuss below.

Name _____   Date _____

ID # _____   Class Time _____

IV. *Institutional Scan* (optional group project): As a class project, obtain a copy of any reports or plans your school has for compliance with the Americans with Disabilities Act of 1990. Answer the following questions about the report or plan:

A. How effective is it?

B. What resources are available for achieving compliance?

C. What priorities have been set?

D. How many students and employees with disabilities are at your institution?

E. How have the numbers of disabled employees changed in the past few years?

F. What recommendations would you make to improve the participation of people with disabilities at your school?

PART III

SOCIAL DEVIANCE

The selections in this part focus on behavior that violates important social norms and is, as a result, labeled problematic. The Robert L. Young essay explores a problem receiving much public and media attention today—criminal violence. The essay suggests that while rates of violence are indeed high in this society, the widely reported increases in overall rates of violent crime are a myth. A particular form of violent behavior, youth gang activity, is described in the selection by David MacKenna. Gregg Dockins explores chemical dependency and debates whether this form of deviant behavior is a disease or the symptom of other problems experienced by the individual. The connection between two forms of deviant behavior—mental illness and homelessness—is addressed by Dee Southard, who argues that rates of mental illness among the homeless population are exaggerated.

18

Is America Becoming More Violent?

Robert L. Young

The most important starting point in the study of any social problem is an accurate understanding of what the problem is. In some cases, a moderate amount of research may be necessary to reach that point, and once you have reached it you may find that your view of the problem has changed considerably and differs fundamentally from the view held by most others. A few years ago I was asked to attend and possibly contribute to the taping of a televised discussion of the problem of violence in America. The entire program was dedicated to trying to understand why the violent crime problem has gotten out of hand and seems to get worse every year. When the discussion moderator asked me to comment, I pointed out that, while violent crime is indeed a major problem in our society, the assumption that the overall violent crime rate is higher than in the past is simply false. I proceeded to support my claim with information similar to that which I will present here. As I expected, the producers of the program decided not to include my comments when the program aired. That decision did not surprise me for I knew that I had called into question a belief so broadly and deeply held that it has become almost impervious to counterfactual information.

The persistence of the belief in a constantly rising rate of violent crime, according to a number of authors, is a function of inordinate media attention devoted to the most gruesome acts of violence (Surette, 1994). Although some research can be found to counter such claims, there is mounting evidence that a disproportionate amount of media attention devoted to violent crime does influence public perceptions. Heavy television viewers, for example, appear to be more likely than those who watch less frequently to overestimate the amount of violence in society (Gerbner, Gross, Signorielli and Morgan, 1980) and to express greater fear of crime (O'Keefe and Reid-Nash, 1987; Sparks and Ogles, 1990). The pervasiveness of misconceptions about trends in violent crime, however, is due to more than simple media influence and is a topic worthy of considerably more attention than I can give it in this es-

say. Here I will limit my aim to presenting a clear and accurate picture of the current state of and recent trends in violent crime, and in so doing attempt to define more precisely the true nature of the problem.

THE REALITY OF VIOLENT CRIME

Public opinion polls consistently show that a substantial portion of Americans see violent crime as one of the most important problems facing our nation. Such concern is certainly not without warrant for America is perhaps the most violent nation in the postindustrialized world. Images of violence that appear so prominently in entertainment television and film are matched with alarming regularity by the real-life acts of violence we read about in our newspapers and see recounted on television news. In fact, the most logical conclusion to be reached by anyone who relies solely on media coverage is that the rate of violent crime is at an all-time high and continues to rise.

In fact, as an integral part of a complex and dynamic society, the face of crime in general and violent crime in particular has indeed changed, but are we really in greater danger of becoming victims of violent criminals now than we were a decade or two ago? Although few sociologists or criminologists would contest the claim that violent crime is a serious problem, a careful examination of the available data suggests quite strongly that the actual rate of most violent crimes has changed very little over the last 20 years.

The two most important and widely used sources of data on crime are the Uniform Crime Report (UCR), compiled by the Federal Bureau of Investigation, and the National Crime Victimization Survey (NCVS), conducted by the U.S. Department of Justice's Bureau of Justice Statistics. The UCR is actually a tabulation of reported crimes in that only those crimes reported to the police or other law enforcement agencies are included. The NCVS, on the

TABLE 18.1
Crimes of Violence per 100,000 Population

Year	NCVS Estimate	UCR Estimate*
1992	3210	301
1983	3100	221
1973	3260	187

*UCR estimates are based on data from Federal Bureau of Investigation, *Crime in the United States, 1992* (Washington, DC: U.S. Department of Justice, 1992).

SOURCE: Unless otherwise indicated, all tables in this selection are based on data from Bureau of Justice Statistics, *Criminal Victimization in the United States, 1973–1992* (Washington, DC: U.S. Department of Justice, 1992).

other hand, is a more comprehensive survey of crimes committed since it is based on a large representative sample of adult Americans who are interviewed about their experiences as crime victims. However, because it is based on reports of the victims themselves, the NCVS does not include homicide estimates. Finally, since many crimes are not reported to the police, with the exception of homicide, the UCR tends to underestimate—rather dramatically in some categories—the actual incidence of crime.[1] In order to adequately address the major question of this essay, we will examine data from both of these sources.

Because neither the UCR nor the NCVS is a perfect measure of the actual crime rate, both contain some degree of error. As a result, the reported rates of various crimes may vary substantially from one year to the next, even if the actual rate has changed very little. Therefore, we must look at those rates over an extended period of time in order to adequately assess meaningful increases or decreases.

Table 18.1 compares estimates of the overall violent crime rate for the years 1973 (the first year of the NCVS), 1983, and 1992 (the most recent year for which data are available at the time of this writing). Two things are obvious from an examination of this table. First, violent crime is grossly under-reported. In 1992, for example, it appears that there were approximately 10 violent victimizations for every one reported to the police (3210 victimizations versus 301 reported crimes per 100,000 population). Second, the two data sets suggest different answers to the question of whether violent crime has increased in recent years. While the number of reported violent crimes has in-

creased somewhat dramatically, according to the Uniform Crime Report (187 per 100,000 in 1973 to 301 in 1992), the National Crime and Victimization Survey suggests that the victimization rate has been extremely stable (3,260 violent crimes per 100,000 population in 1973 and 3,210 in 1992). The steady increase in reported crimes during a time when victimization rates seem to have been stable can be attributed to a number of factors, but two in particular. First, public expenditures on police protection increased by 416 percent from 1971 to 1990 and by 45 percent from 1985 to 1990 (Maguire and Pastore, 1994: 3). Larger budgets have allowed for the hiring of more police officers and the purchase of sophisticated technology. These changes in addition to other community-provided resources (e.g., 911 and other easily dialed emergency numbers) have allowed the police to detect and investigate more crimes than would have been possible in the past. Second, the widely held belief that the crime problem has worsened has probably encouraged citizens to report crimes they might not have reported in the past. Certainly reporting has been encouraged by neighborhood crime watch groups and police agencies as well. Because of the infrequency with which violent crimes are reported, the remainder of this analysis will focus primarily on data from the National Crime and Victimization Survey.

Even though the overall violent crime rate has been stable, it is possible that the rates of some types of crime have increased while others have decreased. If so, and if those that have increased are crimes that cause the most fear (e.g., homicide and rape), then public concerns about increases in criminal violence might indeed be justified. The data presented in Table 18.2, however, fail to confirm this hypothesis. If we examine the victimization rates for each category of violent crime, we discover that female rape and robbery decreased, while assault rose then declined to near 1973 rates, and homicide (i.e., murder and nonnegligent manslaughter) remained stable. Thus in no category of violent crime has the victimization rate increased appreciably over the past 20 years.

Although violent victimizations have remained steady for the population as a whole, it is still possible that the world has become more dangerous for certain segments of the population. Indeed, as Table 18.3 shows, overall violent crime has increased among young people (ages 12 to 24), especially during the past decade, and as Table 18.4 indicates there has been a similar increase among African Americans.

TABLE 18.2
Violent Victimizations per 100,000 by Type of Crime

Year	Female Rape	Robbery	Assault	Homicide*
1992	80	590	2550	9.3
1983	140	600	4210	8.3
1973	180	670	2490	9.3

*UCR estimate

TABLE 18.3
Violent Victimizations per 100,000 by Age of Victim

Year	12–15	16–19	20–24	25–34	35–49	50–64	Over 65
1992	7570	7790	7010	3760	2120	1000	480
1983	5130	6480	6010	4110	2040	900	550
1973	5560	6140	6430	3460	2160	1310	850

Thus it appears that among African Americans and young people an increased fear of violent crime is justified. In fact, victimization rates among African American teen-agers, both male and female, are the highest in our society. Given these facts, another group who can be justifiably concerned about recent trends in violent crime are the parents of teenagers, especially those in minority communities.

MORE VIOLENT OR MORE DEADLY?

As we saw in Table 18.3, although overall violent victimization rates remained essentially stable or actually declined between 1973 and 1992 among older groups, such victimizations increased rather substantially among teenagers (48 percent in the 12 to 15 category and 20 percent in the 16 to 19 category). Moreover, during that same period the homicide rate among teenagers increased even more dramatically. Among those age 14 to 17, for example, although the death rate from homicides remained stable among white females, it increased 77 percent among white males, 38 percent among black females, and 322 percent among black males (Maguire and Pastore, 1994: 386)!

How can we account for such dramatic increases in the homicide rate among young people? Perhaps the most important factor is the increased availability of lethal firearms. Although there are no reliable estimates of the number of firearms in the hands of teen-agers, an examination of the type of weapon used in murders reveals quite clearly that firearm deaths account for a rapidly increasing number of murders of teens. Table 18.5 shows trends in the use of various weapons in the murder of those from 15 to 19 years of age.[2] Note that the moderate decline in gun homicides from 1973 to 1983 was followed by a dramatic increase from 1983 to 1992. In fact, gun murders increased 273 percent during that period while murders

committed with other weapons actually decreased by 23 percent. Although not presented here, a similar but somewhat less dramatic pattern exists for the 20 to 24 age group. All other age groups show a much more stable pattern of weapons use.

CONCLUSION

So what do we conclude from all this? First, contrary to popular belief, the overall violent crime rate in this country is really no higher now than it was two decades ago. Assaults and murders have remained stable, while rapes and robberies have actually decreased. That, however, does not mean that the rate of violent crimes has been stable for all segments of the population. As we saw, violent victimizations of African Americans, teen-agers, and young adults have gone up. Moreover, as the data show, the higher murder rate among young people is directly related to the increased frequency of gun use among that group.

Ironically, the violent crime problem may have been fueled by government efforts to fight crime. Many criminologists believe that one of the unintended consequences of the government's succession of wars on drugs has been to drive up the profits of drug dealers without significantly reducing the supply (Kappeler, Blumberg and Potter, 1993). As both drug arrests and drug profits have gone up, so has the willingness of those involved to protect their investments with deadly force. At the same time, many law-abiding citizens have responded to the perception of an increasing violent crime rate by purchasing guns for protection. Some of these weapons are subsequently stolen and find their way into the hands of criminals or teen-agers who feel that they need them for personal protection. As the number of teen-age homicides has increased, so has the perception among teens that they need to arm themselves for protection, thus creating a vicious cycle of shootings, gun acquisitions, and more shootings. Conflicts among young people that previously would have been resolved with fists or knives are increasingly likely to be settled with high-powered and highly lethal firearms.

When we consider the overall trends in violent victimizations, it is hard to argue that America as a whole has become a more violent nation. However, when we look closely at the data, it is also hard to deny the fact that, among certain segments of the population, the violence that does occur has become more deadly.

TABLE 18.4
Violent Victimizations per 100,000 by Race of Victim

Year	White	African American
1992	2990	5040
1983	2990	4060
1973	3160	4170

TABLE 18.5
Murder Victims (15 to 19 Years Old) by Type of Weapon Used*

Year	Gun	Cutting/ Stabbing	Blunt Object	Personal	Other
1992	2433	230	40	34	114
1983	891	326	56	67	95
1973	1005	271	58	46	96

*UCR data used in this table.

NOTES

1. For those who are interested, a discussion of the strengths and weaknesses of each of these data sources can be found in most introductory criminology or criminal justice texts.
2. In Table 18.5, the use of the 15–19 age range, instead of 16–19, reflects the difference between reporting categories used in the UCR versus the NCVS.

REFERENCES

BUREAU OF JUSTICE STATISTICS
1973 *Criminal Victimization in the United States, 1973*. Washington, DC: U.S. Department of Justice.

BUREAU OF JUSTICE STATISTICS
1983 *Criminal Victimization in the United States, 1983*. Washington, DC: U.S. Department of Justice.

BUREAU OF JUSTICE STATISTICS
1992a *Criminal Victimization in The United States: 1973–92 Trends*. Washington, DC: U.S. Department of Justice.

BUREAU OF JUSTICE STATISTICS
1992b *Criminal Victimization in the United States, 1992*. Washington, DC: U.S. Department of Justice.

FEDERAL BUREAU OF INVESTIGATION
1973 *Crime in the United States 1973*. Washington, DC: U.S. Department of Justice.

FEDERAL BUREAU OF INVESTIGATION
1983 *Crime in the United States 1983*. Washington, DC: U.S. Department of Justice.

FEDERAL BUREAU OF INVESTIGATION
1992 *Crime in the United States 1992* Washington, DC: U.S. Department of Justice.

GERBNER, G., L. GROSS, N. SIGNORIELLI and M. MORGAN
1980 "Television Violence, Victimization and Power," *American Behavioral Scientist* 23: 705–716.

KAPPELER, VICTOR E., MARK BLUMBERG and GARY W. POTTER
1993 *The Mythology of Crime and Criminal Justice*. Prospect Heights, IL: Waveland.

MAGUIRE, KATHLEEN and ANN L. PASTORE
1994 *Sourcebook of Criminal Justice Statistics—1993*. Washington, DC: U.S. Department of Justice.

O'KEEFE, GARRETT J. and KATHALEEN REID-NASH
1987 "Crime News and Real World Blues: The Effect of the Media on Social Reality," *Communication Research* 14 (2): 147–163.

SPARKS, GLENN G. and ROBERT M. OGLES
1990 "The Difference between Fear of Victimization and the Probability of Being Victimized: Implications for Cultivation," *Journal of Broadcasting & Electronic Media* 34 (3): 351–358.

SURETTE, RAY
1994 "Predator Criminals as Media Icons," in G. Barak, ed., *Media, Process and the Social Construction of Crime*. New York: Garland.

EXERCISE 18

Name _____ Date _____

ID # _____ Class Time _____

I. By the time this book is published, more recent UCR and NCVS data will be available. Go to your library and update the statistics for the following five tables with the most recent data available to you. Record your results on the blank lines in the tables below.

TABLE 1
Crimes of Violence per 100,000 Population

Year	NCVS Estimate	UCR Estimate
1992	3210	301
1983	3100	221
1973	3260	187

TABLE 2
Violent Victimizations per 100,000 by Type of Crime

Year	Female Rape	Robbery	Assault	Homicide*
1992	080	590	2550	9.3
1983	140	600	2410	8.3
1973	180	670	2490	9.3

*UCR estimate

TABLE 3
Violent Victimization per 100,000 by Age of Victim

Year	12–15	16–19	20–24	25–34	35–49	50–64	65+
1992	7570	7790	7010	3760	2120	1000	480
1983	5130	6480	6010	4110	2040	900	550
1973	5560	6140	6430	3460	2160	1310	850

TABLE 4
Violent Victimizations per 100,000 by Race of Victim

Year	White	African American
1992	2990	5040
1983	2990	4060
1973	3160	4170

TABLE 5
Murder Victims (15 to 19 Years Old) by Type of Weapon Used*

Year	Gun	Cutting/Stabbing	Blunt Object	Personal	Other
1992	2433	230	40	34	114
1983	891	326	56	67	95
1973	1005	271	58	46	96

* UCR data used in this table.

II. Answer the following questions in the spaces provided.

   A. Do the trends in the estimates of violent crimes for the period 1973–1992 reported in Table 1 continue to hold in the years for which you collected data? If not, is there any reason to think the more recent data reflect a real change in the trends reported above as opposed to the normal fluctuation we might expect to find from one year to the next? If so, what might account for such a change?

   B. Do the trends in violent victimizations for the period 1973–1992 reported in Table 2 continue to hold as well? If not, is there any reason to think the more recent data reflect a real change in the trends reported above as opposed to the normal fluctuation we might find from one year to the next? If so, what might account for such a change?

   C. Do the trends for violent victimization by age for the period 1973–1992 reported in Table 3 continue to hold? If not, is there any reason to think the more recent data reflect a real change in the trends reported above as opposed to the normal fluctuation we might find from one year to the next? If so, what might account for such a change?

   D. Do the trends for violent victimization by race for the period 1973–1992 reported in Table 4 continue to hold? If not, is there any reason to think the more recent data reflect a real change in the trends reported above as opposed to the normal fluctuation we might find from one year to the next? If so, what might account for such a change?

E. Do the trends for murder for the period 1973–1992 reported in Table 5 continue to hold? If not, is there any reason to think the more recent data reflect a real change in the trends reported above as opposed to the normal fluctuation we might find from one year to the next? If so, what might account for such a change?

F. Given the information discussed in this chapter, what steps can we as a society take to reduce the threat of violent crime?

G. What are some of the key obstacles we face in reducing the threat of violent crime?

19

Delinquency and Youth Gangs

David MacKenna

Media and criminal justice agency reports convey to even the most casual reader that cities throughout the nation have experienced significant increases in juvenile crime during recent years. Police departments, especially those in metropolitan regions, consistently report annual increases in the number of adolescents taken into custody for status as well as serious, often violent, criminal offenses. Likewise, youth detention authorities across the country report that correctional facilities currently operate at their highest levels—some over full capacity.

To illustrate the seriousness of this national problem, the U.S. Office of Juvenile Justice and Delinquency Prevention (1993) reported that juvenile arrests for all violent crimes increased 41 percent during the years 1982 to 1991. For the crime forms of aggravated assault and murder, increases during this period were 72 and 91 percent, respectively.

Admissions to juvenile correctional facilities parallel these arrest trends, and the problem of overcrowding has become especially severe since 1984. At present, about 50 percent of confined adolescents are in institutions with an inmate population exceeding design capacity. This condition contributes to the longstanding national problem of housing juveniles in adult prisons. During 1984, youth admissions to adult institutions numbered 9,078, a figure which increased to 11,782 by 1990.

These rather dramatic arrest and incarceration increases closely parallel a period during which the media and criminal justice professionals have emphasized youth gang violence as a growing national problem. Of course, gang violence is not a new phenomenon in the United States. Sociologists and educators have maintained a special and continuing interest in the subject throughout this century. In fact, much of what we know about the origins of juvenile gangs and how they develop and function operationally is based on research initiated several decades ago in the pre-Depression era.

The following sections of this essay explore some

of this history and provide the background for a closer examination of certain modern-day factors which may contribute to the delinquent behavior of youth gang members. Late in the essay, some attention is given to behavior and attitude differences between gang affiliates and other adolescents. However, in considering the general issue of delinquency and youth gangs, the reader should recognize that no complete statistical profile exists to determine how much juvenile crime is a direct result of gang activity. No such categorization exists in the Uniform Crime Reporting Program. Even at the local police level, categorical distinctions are not normally made between the delinquent conduct of gang versus nongang members.

PROBLEMS OF DEFINITION

Frederic Thrasher (1927) was one of the first to conduct extensive research on youth gangs beginning his work during the 1920s, while a faculty member at Illinois Wesleyan University. His classic study, *The Gang: A Study of 1,313 Gangs in Chicago,* described these groups as the spontaneous efforts of young people to survive in a complex urban environment. He generally attributed their antisocial or illegal behavior to (1) the natural youthful desire for excitement and adventure in the company of peers, and (2) a decline in the influence of controlling institutions such as family, church, and schools.

After two decades in which national attention was largely directed to other forms of domestic and international violence, Albert Cohen's 1955 book, *Delinquent Boys: The Culture of the Gang,* renewed professional interest in closely examining this aspect of the delinquency question. With the work of Thrasher (1927) as a foundation, Cohen's efforts were followed by the extensive research of Walter Miller, which began in the 1950s and continued for some 20 years.

One of Miller's observations was the considerable

variation in definition used by public and private agencies for youth groups often described as "gangs." Through discussions with agency professionals and from his own research, Miller (1975) developed a formal definition of a youth gang as "a group of recurrently associated individuals with identifiable leadership and internal organization, identifying with or claiming control over territory in the community, and engaging either individually or collectively in violent or other forms of illegal behavior."

Miller and Thrasher generally agreed that true youth gangs reflect group solidarity, a measure of internal structure, leadership, and territoriality. Absent from the formal definitions of these early writers are certain later observations about gang membership such as having a group name, wearing distinctive clothing, having a regular meeting place, reflecting a particular group size or age range, and participating in certain ritualistic practices, especially as they would relate to joining or leaving a gang.

This issue of definition is important and basic to any realistic assessment of whether a community has a true "gang" problem, as opposed to a delinquent youth problem. And, differences in definition contribute to varied opinions among professionals as to the existence and seriousness of gang problems in many U.S. cities. In this context, Miller observed an interesting relationship between youth gangs and various adult agencies which respond to them. These groups include police, prosecutors, educators, and representatives of various social service agencies. Miller (1975) noted that agency personnel often present information about local gang activity in a manner that best serves organizational interests, rather than presenting an objective and accurate assessment of community gang problems. He further observed that this condition represented the "single most significant obstacle" to gathering sound, valid data on the nature and extent of true gang activity in any community.

Assessment problems are not unknown to present-day youth gang researchers. For example, in the 1990s, the Texas attorney general's office attempted to determine the nature and extent of youth gang activity in major Texas cities based on surveys of police agencies across the state (see Buhmann, 1991; 1992). After two years of research, the Texas attorney general's office personnel found the Texas gang issue complex and illusive. Staff difficulties in securing valid data from local police agencies prompted researchers to describe the gang situation in Texas during 1992 as a "moving target."

In their contacts with law enforcement, the Texas attorney general's office personnel became aware that definitions of "gang," as well as criteria for gang membership, vary greatly among agencies. Staff members ultimately concluded that while gangs are active in many Texas cities, there are no uniform criteria for identifying gangs and defining membership, nor are there broadly accepted procedures for maintaining records of gang-related incidents as distinct from other crimes committed by juveniles.

Some police departments responded to the Texas at-torney general's office surveys with data on what they termed "hard core" gangs, others on "aggressive" gangs, and still others on what were described as "criminal youth" gangs. Follow-up discussions with police representatives suggested to Texas attorney general's office personnel that the nature of these groups differed greatly from city to city. Obviously, a department which counts every juvenile identity group, or clique, as a gang will report more active gangs than those that report only groups that are highly organized, seen as a discrete unit in their neighborhood and/or school, and involved in serious criminal activity (Buhmann, 1991).

It has long been recognized that youth gangs normally have a core of committed members, some peripheral affiliates, and some that exist as a wider group of associates. Not only the degree of organization but also membership definition can affect the identification and labeling of gang crime as well as judgments about group size, permanency, and growth. In sum, how these issues are treated and presented by the police largely determines how the media portray community gang problems and, ultimately, how gang activity is perceived by citizens at large.

So, the better definitions of gangs would consider them as being rather well-organized youth groups with defined leadership, some degree of permanency, and participation in ongoing delinquent or criminal conduct. Operationally, juvenile delinquency is largely a group process. For example, research shows that up to 80 percent of delinquent acts are committed by youths who act collectively. And, as Figure 19.1 illustrates, about one third of the juveniles referred to Texas youth correctional facilities are considered gang members, and a similar percentage report a circle of friends who "at least sometimes think of themselves as a gang" (Buhmann, 1991).

Gangs, then, are present in some form in most medium and large Texas cities today. As is the case in other national regions, some are relatively harmless groups involved only on occasion in rather minor offenses. But even these juveniles can be driven by group identification, intergroup conflict, or peer pressure to more violent criminal activity.

FIGURE 19.1: Texas Youth Commission Referrals, 1990

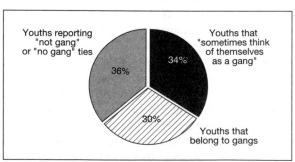

SOURCE: Elizabeth T. Buhmann, *Gangs in Texas Cities: Background, Survey Results, State-level Policy Options* (Austin: Office of the Texas Attorney General, 1991).

GANGS AND VIOLENCE

The previous observations illustrate that youth gangs are, in fact, conflict groups. Most true gangs will, at some point, become involved in violent activity. Violence is normally the most important public concern about gangs, and a concern about which there is often some confusion or misunderstanding. This condition may exist because (1) objective researchers are not normally present to accurately document gang event circumstances; (2) much information about gang violence is provided by members, individuals not noted for their veracity; and (3) close scrutiny of police records often reveals that some violent incidents attributed to local gangs are delinquent acts of unaffiliated youths, or individual actions of those with some gang relationship, but the acts may not be directly related to gang affairs. Martin Jankowski (1991) supports this view with his observation that many of the incidents for which gangs have been given credit are, in fact, the individual acts of members and, as such, are not in a strict sense "gang violence."

Gang members are defiant individuals. Both within and without the group, they struggle to survive and prosper in what most would consider a harsh environment. Numerous violent and criminal activities illustrate these points. A gang member, either alone or with an associate, may commit a street robbery, steal a car, or physically attack some rival over a girlfriend's affection. These acts may be criminal, but they may not always best be described as gang crime.

Yet, in their struggle to exist youth gangs do become involved in group-related violent actions. At times the issue is territorial. Groups fight to maintain neighborhood status, to maintain control over enterprise (possibly drugs), or they respond to some infringement on the well-being of a member. These struggles can have an "intra" as well as an "inter" gang character.

Because of the aggressive nature of gang members, violence may result from frustration, anger, or competition for positions of influence or leadership. As Jankowski (1991) states, "[a] gang member has to earn respect; it is not something everyone has. In addition, once a person has earned respect, he must be willing to protect it because a person's reputation depends upon respect, and reputation is an essential resource for success."

The general question of whether street gangs have become more violent in recent years is one which most law enforcement officials would answer with a resounding "yes." Unlike conditions in the 1950–1960s, today's gangs do not carry out aggressive acts with baseball bats or homemade zip guns; rather, their violence is frequently punctuated with sophisticated weapons ranging from sawed-off shotguns to quality automatic rifles and handguns. In the 1990s, these weapons are readily available, widely possessed, and are used by members in the normal course of gang or personal criminal affairs.

However, historic gang literature supports the contention that the violent use of commercially produced weapons has long been a part of gang culture. Thrasher's (1927) discussion of warfare between the Rats and the Jellyrolls in St. Louis during the 1920s is a case in point. It seems that a Rats gang leader was killed and a competitive group, the Jellyrolls, received blame. One of the Jellyrolls became especially vocal during this period of intergang tension and was found a few days later with 26 bullet holes in his body. The conflict escalated further when a Rats leader was later wounded by several Jellyrolls who fired at him in a car. Rats members could not immediately locate those they felt were responsible, so they shot up the home of a Jellyrolls leader. This early drive-by shooting is not dissimilar to some of the nightly events in major U.S. cities today.

Other researchers have likewise described and condemned the violence of gang members. Miller, Martin Haskell, and Lewis Yablonsky were three who did so during the 1970s. For a time during the 1960s, there was some diminution in gang violence, but in the 1970s Miller argued that violence had become more lethal than ever before. In this time period Haskell and Yablonsky (1978: 205) described the reactions of an East Los Angeles youth worker, Leo Cortez, who had been a gang member during his teen years. As he stated:

> Sometimes it really scares me because too many kids nowadays aren't following any of the old rules. In the old days gang members made certain that when they went on a retaliatory raid, they hit their enemy. But now they often are sloppy, or heedless, simply speeding by an enemy house at night and spraying it with bullets, regardless of who's inside.

> There was a time when small children weren't allowed to associate with gang members. But now I see little kids, 10 or 12 years old, wandering around with guns, . . . even 8-year-old kids are sniffing glue, paint, Angel Dust . . . even doing hard stuff.

Cortez also expressed the opinion that drug use is a major reason for this escalation in violence, coupled with a deeper sense of hopelessness. Gang members often feel that they have no future; in the case of Latinos, nothing but the barrio and their homeboys. Idle and in the company of peers, they set out to prove their manhood and in the process they are often either killing or being killed.

By the late 1980s, some teen-agers were embracing significantly more deviant and delinquent behavior, a trend which caused sociologist Wayne Wooden (1995) to brand a segment of juvenile extremists "Suburban Outlaws." Sometimes referred to as "Stoner youth gangs," these renegades often reflect an outlaw character and represent one form the gang phenomenon takes as it spreads from minority central city neighborhoods to Anglo-dominated middle-class suburbs.

"Stoners" are teen groups which may vary in size from 10 to 40 members and often congregate in video arcades or shopping malls. They are normally seen in some unique dress style, which in some regions includes biker-type or Doc Marten boots. Stoners frequently wear Tshirts, possibly decorated with some design associated with a heavy metal music group, or swastikas, hexagons, pentagrams, roach clips, and so on. Their tattoos or clothing sometimes reflect satanic or antireligious statements, and most members are Anglo males. These groups are structured much like traditional youth gangs; that is, they have unique names, leaders, colors, and similar dress. Skinheads represent one segment of those defined as Stoners, but hair length may vary depending on member interest or orientation.

Wooden (1995) suggests that members usually have a middle-class background and are often from broken homes where there may have been high incidence of illegal drug and alcohol abuse. Research suggests that the delinquent behavior of Stoner gangs includes drug violations, assault (especially involving females or parents), theft, racially oriented crimes, grave robbing, as well as the general desecration of cemeteries and churches. A spokesperson for the California Youth Authority (CYA), which closely monitors youth gang activity, estimates that 5 percent of that state's 1200 active youth gangs are Stoners. This movement seems to be growing not only in California but also in other national regions and is currently of special concern to law enforcement agencies.

DIFFERENCES BETWEEN GANG AND NONGANG YOUTH

Cohen and Miller have written extensively about some of the distinctions that can be drawn between the characteristics and background of gang versus nongang youth. Others that have explored this issue in various ways are Huff, Yablonsky, Herbert Bloch, and Arthur Niederhoffer. Huff (1990: 314) is in agreement that gangs are primarily a central city phenomenon attracting juveniles who are normally best characterized as being poor, disadvantaged, and culturally marginal. Some authorities have argued that gang involvement meets the status needs of lower-class youth as they confront middle-class values normally reflected in the American public education system. These lower-class values do not usually promote membership in the school band or the debate team. And it should be added that all boys do not have the physical attributes for athletics, a venue which saves some from the negative consequences of gang membership. So, for some adolescents gangs provide fellowship, excitement, and a measure of local recognition absent in the lives of those who, because of ability or class, do not socially integrate well into the public schools. Miller alleges that there is a definite lower-class culture with gang involvement a reflection or expression of that culture. This milieu can accept, if not promote, criminal behavior and will normally respect the independent, aggressive attitudes reflected by gang members. Miller views gangs as cohesive groups dominated by leaders who are generally more daring and charismatic than their followers.

Yablonsky has been largely concerned with violent or conflict-oriented gangs. Likewise, he suggests that such delinquent groups are products of the blighted and crime-ridden urban areas where they normally originate. He argues that conditions in these neighborhoods contribute to the development of youthful sociopathic personalities which often band together to act out aggressive behavior. Those inclined to such behavior recognize what they perceive as certain beneficial aspects to membership in a group that promotes and supports their delinquent or criminal conduct.

During 1993, this author participated in a federally funded research project in Fort Worth, Texas, which had as a primary goal the identification of basic social, familial and academic differences between youth gang affiliates and juveniles not so involved (Stevens and MacKenna, 1993). Project methodology included interviewing a number of gang and nongang youth representing various ethnic groups from different city sectors, in addition to administering a comprehensive "Youth Activities Survey" to 717 students rather evenly distributed over the eighth through twelfth grades in the local public school system.

Forty-five of the students participating in the school survey portion of the project reported that they had current or prior gang membership. Although much of the data collected in this overall research effort reaches beyond the scope of this article, some of the distinctions between gang and nongang student lifestyles, especially those concerning delinquent and criminal conduct, seem pertinent.

As might be anticipated, the reported record of arrest and confinement of survey respondents in the two groups differed rather significantly. Ninety-three percent of the nongang students indicated no prior arrests compared to only 51 percent of gang affiliates. Eleven percent of those with a history of gang involvement reported four or more arrests. Forty-one percent of gang members said that they had been confined in jail or a detention center at some time, compared to only 6 percent of nongang respondents.

Students were asked several broad questions concerning certain prior activities in which they might have been involved. One question asked whether, within the past year, they had participated in a range of socially negative or disruptive actions including theft, drug use, and arson. A second question presented a list of criminal and noncriminal activities often associated with youthful behavior. All items listed would meet some level of social disapproval, and students were asked to identify those in which they had some prior involvement. Table 19.1 summarizes responses to some of the listed items and serves to illustrate certain characteristic or lifestyle differences between those involved in gangs versus those not involved.

In addition to differences in conduct evident from the above data, survey results suggested various other distinctions between the two categories of youth. For example, nongang students reported more positive perceptions of education and personal academic performance than those in gangs. Gang affiliates placed less value on the im-

TABLE 19.1
Student Involvement in Selected Activities: Gang and Nongang Members

	Nongang Members	Gang Activity Members
Total Number of Respondents	672	45
Hanging out at malls	39%	49%
Drinking alcohol	11	36
Gambling	7	36
Smoking cigarettes	6	16
Using illegal drugs	3	16
Writing graffiti on public property	7	42
Involved in a shooting or stabbing	2	29
Stolen a car	1	27
Stolen something from a car	2	27
Stolen a purse or pocketbook	2	7
Setting fire to property	2	13

SOURCE: James W. Stevens and David W. MacKenna, *Kids Speak Out: Opinions and Characteristics of Fort Worth Gang and Non-Gang Members* (Washington, DC: Family and Youth Service Bureau, U.S. Department of Health and Human Services, 1993), pp. 127–128.

portance of education in successful life adjustment and were more inclined to feel that teachers lacked personal interest in them. Similarly, gang youth more often reported troublesome relationships at home; in fact, relations so poor that over 50 percent questioned whether they could expect any assistance from their parents if they became involved is some difficulty with the criminal justice system.

CONCLUSION

Results of the student survey provided considerable insight into youth gang issues in the city of Fort Worth, Texas, and suggest several reasons why these groups have become a permanent aspect of the social milieu. But Fort Worth, Texas, is by no means unique in this context; research in most major urban centers could be expected to produce similar results. Most metropolitan regions experience continual population growth and are increasingly multicultural and heterogeneous. And criminologists have long identified social heterogeneity as an important factor associated with the national increase in urban violence, whether perpetrated by juveniles or adults.

Not unrelated to this trend is the fact that economic conditions in most urban areas provide limited employment opportunities for juveniles, especially those with little education or vocational training. This problem is especially acute in minority neighborhoods where school dropout rates are high, and juveniles have little technical knowledge or work experience. With limited outlets for

time and energy, and often inadequate parental or institutional supervision, some individuals are attracted to youth gangs and the primary gang enterprise of the 1990s—drug trafficking.

The economic struggle of many families is likewise related to the limited parental guidance a number of adolescents receive. The continual increase in single-parent families has long been documented, and when coupled with the adolescent need for independence and peer association, children are distanced from parents and vulnerable to the negative street associations in their neighborhoods.

Making the gang problem even more serious in the 1990s is the increasing sophistication and ready availability of firearms. As long as automatic, military-style weapons can be readily purchased at gun shops, gun shows, local flea markets, and on the street, citizens can expect an ever-increasing number of young people and innocent bystanders to become victims of gang violence.

Finally, there are numerous other factors that allegedly contribute to the presence and growth of youth violence in American cities. These include (1) the social violence portrayed by television and other mass media, which may affect impressionable young minds; (2) a desire for material possessions beyond the reach of many teen-agers through normal employment opportunities; (3) the lack of a personal value system that promotes appreciation and respect for societal laws and mores; and (4) the extensive time available to unemployed, unsupervised, idle teens who spend a sizable portion of their time roaming about with peer associates of questionable character.

Many public institutions, especially schools and law enforcement agencies, struggle to meet their respective social responsibilities with limited fiscal and personnel resources. Other public and private organizations undertake to provide some limited response to community gang influences by employing a variety of diversion programs developed to occupy youth, especially during summer months. But again, resources available to these organizations (YMCA, city recreation centers, boys and girls clubs, Boy Scouts, religious groups, etc.) often fall short of community needs and the full range of diversion activities that might more effectively occupy potentially disruptive teens.

In the final analysis, however, diversion programs are weak substitutes for effective parental guidance and supervision, a force which many feel has been sorely lacking in the American society for some years. Unfortunately, there is little to suggest that this condition will change in the foreseeable future.

REFERENCES

BUHMANN, ELIZABETH T.
1991 *Gangs in Texas Cities: Background, Survey Results, State-level Policy Options.* Austin: Office of the Texas Attorney General.

BUHMANN, ELIZABETH T.
1992   *The 1992 Texas Attorney General's Gang Report*. Austin: Office of the Texas Attorney General.

COHEN, ALBERT
1955   *Delinquent Boys: The Culture of the Gang*. Glencoe, IL: Free Press.

HASKELL, MARTIN R. and LEWIS YABLONSKY
1978   *Juvenile Delinquency*. Chicago: Rand McNally.

HUFF, C. RONALD.
1990   *Gangs in America*. Newbury Park, CA: Sage.

JANKOWSKI, MARTIN S.
1991   *Islands in the Street: Gangs in the American Society*. Berkeley: University of California Press.

MILLER, WALTER B.
1975   *Violence By Youth Gangs and Youth Groups as a Crime Problem in American Cities*. Washington, DC: National Institute for Juvenile Justice and Delinquency Prevention, U.S. Department of Justice.

OFFICE OF JUVENILE JUSTICE AND DELINQUENCY PREVENTION
1993   *Comprehensive Strategy for Serious, Violent and Chronic Juvenile Offenders*. Washington, DC: U.S. Department of Justice.

STEVENS, JAMES W. and DAVID W. MACKENNA
1993   *Kids Speak Out: Opinions, Attitudes and Characteristics of Fort Worth Gang and Non-Gang Members*. Washington, DC: Family and Youth Services Bureau, U.S. Department of Health and Human Services.

THRASHER, FREDERIC
1963   *The Gang: A Study of 1,313 Gangs in Chicago*. Chicago: University of Chicago Press. (Originally published in 1927.)

WOODEN, WAYNE S.
1995   *Renegade Kids, Suburban Outlaws*. New York: Wadsworth Publishing.

EXERCISE 19

Name _____   Date _____

ID # _____   Class Time _____

I. As was suggested in the essay, juvenile involvement in violent crime has been increasing in the United States for some years. While it is not presently possible to determine how much of this increase can be directly attributed to youth gangs, one can examine the yearly changes in juvenile violence, of which gang violence is a part, by referring to arrest data available from the Uniform Crime Reports (UCR) published by the Department of Justice. These reports should be available in all college and university libraries.

To complete this exercise, select three years during the period 1980 to 1994. Complete the table by first identifying the years selected. Refer to the arrest tables in the copies of the UCR for these years. Identify the number of arrestees under age 18 for the crime forms listed in the table below. Next, record the total arrests for each crime form by year. Lastly, calculate the percent change for each crime form by comparing the annual arrest totals for the first and last years you selected. After completing the table, answer the questions that follow.

Juvenile Arrests for Violent Crime: Persons Under Age 18

Offense	Year ____	Year ____	Year ____	% Change
Murder				
Aggravated assault				
Rape				
Robbery				

A. Which crime form represents the greatest percentage change and the least percentage change?

B. Why do you think these two crime forms reflect the trends illustrated by your calculations?

C. List the societal factors or conditions that have, in your opinion, contributed to these trends.

D. What social policy changes do you think might be implemented to reduce juvenile involvement in violent crime?

20

Chemical Dependency:
Is It a Disease or Symptom?

Gregg Dockins

When I first began working in the field of alcohol and drug abuse,[1] I was confronted by colleagues regarding my perspective on chemical dependency. Metaphorically speaking, it was as though they were recruitment officers for one of two armies, and with new recruits there could be no mediocrity of middle ground. I was interested in this "either/or" mentality, and my experiences have led me to label this battle as "disease versus symptom." The "disease" camp consisted mainly of members of the fellowship of Alcoholics Anonymous who worked in the treatment field and argued that chemical dependency was a disease that could only be treated by those who had the same illness. The "symptom" camp was primarily made up of those who saw chemical dependency as a symptom of an underlying, or sometimes even an overt, problem. Advocates of the two competing perspectives on chemical dependency also prescribe different approaches to treatment.

Due to my educational background and an interest in systemic family therapy, my initial inclination was to support the symptom concept; but my personal experience of working in the field soon led me to believe that the disease concept also had merit. I came to conclude that neither concept, in and of itself, presented the complete picture. From every indication, it seems that a combination of the two perspectives is most fruitful. This chapter will examine both perspectives on chemical dependency, noting many linguistic parallels between the two views. A simple either/or mentality is challenged and I will show that the competing views are closer than they initially appear. This chapter begins by reviewing the underlying principles of each perspective, which will supply us with some working definitions and establish a framework from which to note the many similarities between the two perspectives. The outcome will be to highlight the compatibility between disease and symptom approaches and the complementary nature of these views.

CHEMICAL DEPENDENCY AS DISEASE

Although in years past, many believed chemical dependency to be a weakness, or character defect, the American Medical Association was noted for recognizing it as a disease in 1956 (Johnson, 1990). The term "disease" is defined in *Webster's Collegiate Dictionary* as "a condition of the body in which there is incorrect function resulting from the effect of heredity, infection, diet, or environment." By examining the concept of chemical dependency as a disease in light of this definition, one can see the vast expanse of explanatory possibilities that unfold. The acceptance of chemical dependency as an illness served to replace the stigma that the label of "chemically dependent," or more commonly, "alcoholic," once carried, allowing the alcoholic to seek medical assistance that was not previously available (Gorski, 1989).

A recent development in the definition of alcoholism as a disease came from the 1990 annual joint conference of the American Society of Addiction Medicine and the National Council on Alcoholism and Drug Dependence. As a result of this conference, a revised definition of alcoholism as a disease was published (American Society of Addiction Medicine [ASAM] and National Council on Alcoholism and Drug Dependence [NCADD], 1990), stating:

> Alcoholism is a primary, chronic disease with genetic, psycho social, and environmental factors influencing its development and manifestations. The disease is often progressive and fatal. It is characterized by continuous or periodic: impaired control over drinking, preoccupation with the drug alcohol, use of alcohol despite adverse consequences, and distortions in thinking, most notably denial.

The members of the organizations publishing this definition recognized that two of the most important changes

171

occurring were the acknowledgment of alcoholism as a primary disease, and the mention of denial as a criterion of the disease (ASAM and NCADD, 1990). These two additions alone caused the concept of disease to become a particularly interesting treatment issue among professionals, several of whom were associated with a longstanding organization which already recognized alcoholism and drug dependency as a disease, or illness. This organization was the fellowship of Alcoholics Anonymous (Anonymous, 1976). While we will not attempt to delve into the treatment aspect of alcoholism and drug dependency, it is important to examine the aspects of Alcoholics Anonymous that relate directly to the conceptualization of alcohol and drug abuse as a disease.

Alcoholics Anonymous was recognized by members of the medical community as an intricate part of the treatment of alcoholism as early as 1946 (Anonymous, 1976). The frustrations exhibited by medical professionals in their own inability to effectively treat alcoholism, provided a framework of support for the fellowship of Alcoholics Anonymous and their work with those suffering from the disease. One of the co-founders of Alcoholics Anonymous was not only an alcoholic, but a physician as well, lending additional credibility to the organization. Several other members of the medical establishment in the early 1940s, endorsed Alcoholics Anonymous as the most effective treatment modality of that time (Anonymous, 1976). This recognition and affirmation laid the foundation for more recent strides toward the acceptance of alcoholism as a disease (ASAM and NCADD, 1990).

With the concept of alcoholism as a disease so heavily tied to Alcoholics Anonymous, it is important to examine the underlying principles of the organization. Gorski (1989) defines Alcoholics Anonymous simply as "a worldwide fellowship of men and women who help each other to maintain sobriety by freely sharing their experiences with alcohol and drug use." This fellowship utilizes the Twelve Steps of Alcoholics Anonymous as the basics to recovery from this disease (Gorski, 1989). The goal of this approach is relatively simple, in that it encourages members to acknowledge the fact they cannot control their usage of the chemical; take responsibility for their behavior and actions in the past; change behavior in the future through healthy and responsible decision making; all the while, staying sober through accountability to other members of the fellowship via "sponsors." Due to the impact of these steps on the view of alcoholism as a disease, and the assistance they provide for recovery, many professionals have assigned *Twelve Steps and Twelve Traditions* and *Alcoholics Anonymous* as required reading (Gorski, 1989). The importance of Alcoholics Anonymous may have been best noted by Johnson (1990) when he stated, "chemical dependency is a treatable disease," whose "most easily available resource . . . is Alcoholics Anonymous" (17).

CHEMICAL DEPENDENCY AS SYMPTOM

The initial step toward understanding chemical dependency as a symptom of underlying problems from the perspective of systemic family therapy is to give a brief historical overview of the field of family therapy, including its theoretical orientations. The field of family therapy is understood here as viewing human interaction and behavior as based on the principles of general systems theory, as well as the family systems ideas of Bowen Theory (Kerr and Bowen, 1988). Although this is, admittedly, an overly simplistic description of the theoretical underpinnings of the field of family therapy, it is adequate for our purpose here—to better understand the "symptomology" of chemical dependency.

General systems theory (G.S.T.) is a relatively new approach to understanding behavior that developed in response to the lack of universality in the traditional scientific framework (Capra, 1982). This analytical approach involves breaking down of the *parts* to understand and define the *whole,* while acknowledging the interdependence and relationships that existed between the parts of a system. This problem, as it relates to human systems, was noted by Kerr and Bowen (1988), who stated, "our conceptualizations of human behavior have consistently de-emphasized the processes between people and focused on the process within people." The logic of systems theory involves a view of the individual as part of a greater whole, and not an independent figure who is subject to the laws of scientific, linear causality.

The nature of causality added an element of difficulty to the human aspect of the scientific theories in that "historically, theories about human behavior have reflected this individual emphasis in that they usually defined the 'cause' of behavior and clinical problems as existing inside the person" (Kerr and Bowen, 1988: 19). Further theoretical developments added the concept of defining behavior by relationships, broadening the application even more. With the application of cybernetic principles to the systems perspective, the modification made to causal relationships was the emergence of circular causality. This concept can be simplified by understanding "that A does not cause B, nor does B cause A, but rather that A and B are the cause of each other" (Constantine, 1986). This cybernetic maintenance, or regulatory feedback, is the principle which leads to the conceptualization of chemical dependency as symptom of a dysfunctional system. The most common example used by professionals is the "nag-drink" cycle. The example refers to a relationship where one spouse nags the other because of his or her drunkenness, and the substance-abusing spouse flees the nagging by going out to drink with friends. The first spouse clearly believes that it is the other's drinking that results in his or her nagging; whereas, the second spouse believes that his or her drinking is a result of the other's nagging. Both are correct. The alcoholic's drug use serves a function in maintaining the system through providing a balance, albeit negative in consequence, to the family, or interpersonal system. The application of the insights from systems theory results in the redefinition of chemical dependency as a symptom; however, it is fundamentally necessary to first define the word "symptom."

According to *Webster's Collegiate Dictionary,* a "symptom" may be defined as "a phenomenon that arises from and accompanies a particular disease or disorder and serves as an indication of it." When examining this definition in relation to the previous definition of disease, it becomes clear that these terms relate directly to the notion of causality and relationship issues. As evidenced in the aforementioned "nag-drink" example, one must acknowledge the relationships that exist in the context of a circular causality, as opposed to a cause-and-effect mentality. Since one of the key concepts in systems theory and family therapy is cybernetic maintenance, or regulatory feedback (Wiener, 1968), it becomes difficult at this point for a professional in the field of family therapy to accept chemical dependency as being caused solely by "heredity, infection, diet, or environment" [cited from the dictionary definition of "disease" given earlier in this chapter]. This act of accepting linear causality would be directly opposed to the fundamental principles of G.S.T. and family therapy. One study suggested that the alcoholic's behavior (i.e., drinking) may serve a function in the relationships within the family system that gives definition to the system (Frankenstein et al., 1985). The family systems model of drug abuse defines a family member's drug use as a symptom of the family dysfunction at the structural level of the system (Menicucci and Wermuth, 1989), for example; or dysfunctional intergenerational dyads, for example, mother-son enmeshment (Stanton and Todd, 1982).[2]

CONCEPTUAL PARALLELS

The most interesting aspect of this chapter comes in the form of the seemingly obvious similarities between the disease and symptom ideologies. There are several parallels between the two perspectives. Specific examples include:

Individuals. One focus in the field of family therapy is to concentrate on the individual in the context of larger systems or relationships, even when seeing an individual alone. Torgenrud and Storm (1989) found that many schools of family therapy may see individual clients, but the presenting problem is always addressed in the context of other family members or relationships. They acknowledge that changing one part of a system may not improve a system to a "healthy" level, but it will change the entire system—such is the nature of family systems theory. Going back to the "nag-drink" example, there are two possible points of intervention: getting the wife to stop nagging; or getting the husband to stop going

out to get drunk. The problem, however, is that if the nagging or the drinking stops, other elements of the relationship must be addressed, such as communication problems, common likes/dislikes, and so forth.

Interestingly enough, one of the professionals cited from the *disease* camp of chemical dependency, also views the individual in the context of families and larger systems (Johnson, 1990). Alcoholics Anonymous World Services, Inc. (1981) even discusses the fact that one of its Twelve Steps is specifically "concerned with family relations." Allen (1989) also discussed the fact that the renowned Twelve Step program has as its basic philosophy "treating the whole person," which includes working with alcoholics on many different issues (familial, educational, legal, recreational, etc.).

Family therapy schools argue the importance of treating individuals with any variety of dysfunctional symptomology (substance abuse included) by keeping them in the context of their family system or a larger system (Torgenrud and Storm, 1989). Similarly, the Twelve Steps of Alcoholics Anonymous are based on a systemic perspective of the individual, only in such a context it is called a "fellowship" (Gorski, 1989).

Dysfunctional Dyads and Codependency. As previously mentioned, there are several family therapy professionals who discuss the nature of chemical dependency in the context of dysfunctional relationships (Frankenstein et al., 1985; Madanes, 1981; Stanton and Todd, 1982). This would seem to indicate an emphasis on the relationship issues that contribute to the development and maintenance of the symptom, chemical dependency. One relationship element not yet discussed regarding the disease concept of chemical dependency, is that of codependency. Codependency has been defined by some as "being a partner in dependency" (Beattie, 1987). This idea appears to be very closely related to the notion of interdependence among members of a system. Johnson (1990) offered that "codependency implies that family members have their own 'something' to recover from." This is conducive to a conceptualization similar to that found in the ideology of chemical dependency as a symptom. More specifically, Madanes (1981) discusses a typical situation of the "symptomatic person" being in "an inferior position to the other spouse, who tries to help and to change him." Such reasoning suggests there may be an important overlap between the concepts of the dysfunctional family system and codependency.

Symptom and Disease. Madanes (1981) describes a situation in which some married couples seek out a symptom as a source of power in the relationship. She goes on to list some possible symptoms, one of which is alcoholism. The alcoholic will drink simply because the spouse cannot keep him or her from it. The irony is that the alcoholic soon finds him or herself unable to control his or her drinking, but continues in order to spite the spouse. This is a clear definition of alcoholism as a symptom; however, when the same relationship is examined in light of the disease framework, couples are found to engage in power struggles due to the disease process (Anonymous, 1976; Johnson, 1990). Both perspectives describe the same situation, uncontrollable drinking which destroys the relationships if left untreated.

CONCLUSION

The goals in this selection were to analyze two perspectives on chemical dependency—the disease and symptom models—and to show the parallels that exist between them. Additionally, I argued for the need to develop a framework in future studies which integrates the disease and symptom models. These two approaches are similar in nature and should not be considered in isolation any longer. Of course, these perspectives may be treated as mutually exclusive, yet to ignore the many ways in which they complement each other is to miss opportunities to better treat patients and help people solve real problems in their day-to-day lives. The question to be raised then, is not "Is chemical dependency a symptom *or* a disease?" Rather, the question should be "How can the field of chemical dependency utilize the concepts of both symptom *and* disease?" One possible approach would include physiological interventions to address the disease nature of chemical dependency, and psychological interventions to address the symptom nature. This would include a treatment which incorporates professional persons (e.g., doctors, therapists) and those who are recovering from alcoholism (e.g., counselors, sponsors, etc.). Gorski (1989) acknowledged that the Twelve Step approach from a disease framework should be done in conjunction with more traditional therapies (such as family therapy, rational emotive therapy, etc.) in order to be more effective. Allen (1989) also argues that if "treating the whole person" is the goal, then it should be done by implementing a variety of therapeutic techniques. Once the disease is acknowledged, it becomes the responsibility of the alcoholic/addict to act in ways which support and maintain sobriety. This responsibility may include counseling for related issues, such as marital discord, employment difficulties, or other situations. The implications of an integrated treatment framework could lead to changes which will affect not only the way chemical dependency is treated by professionals but also the way it is viewed by the larger society.

NOTES

1. Although there are differences in definition, in order to facilitate this effort, the terms "alcoholism," "substance abuse," "alcohol and drug abuse," and "chemical dependency" will be used interchangeably throughout this chapter.

2. For additional information regarding general systems theory and systemic family therapy, see Bertalanffy (1968; 1974), Minuchin (1980), and Schultz (1984).

REFERENCES

ALLEN, J.
1989 "Overview of Alcoholism Treatment: Settings and Approaches," *The Journal of Mental Health Administration* 16: 55–62.

AMERICAN SOCIETY OF ADDICTION MEDICINE and NATIONAL COUNCIL ON ALCOHOLISM AND DRUG DEPENDENCE (ASAM and NCADD)
1990 "Disease Definition of Alcoholism Revised." (Joint Press Release) Annual Joint Conference of the American Society of Addiction Medicine and the National Council on Alcoholism and Drug Dependence held in Phoenix, AZ.

ANONYMOUS
1976 *Alcoholics Anonymous.* New York: Alcoholics Anonymous World Services, Inc.

ANONYMOUS
1981 *Twelve Steps and Twelve Traditions.* New York: Alcoholics Anonymous World Services, Inc.

BEATTIE, M.
1987 *Codependent No More.* New York: Harper & Row.

BERTALANFFY, L. VON
1968 *General Systems Theory.* New York: George Braziller.

BERTALANFFY, L. VON
1974 "General Systems Theory and Psychiatry," in S. Arieti, ed., *American Handbook of Psychiatry,* 2nd ed. New York: Basic Books.

CAPRA, F.
1982 *The Turning Point.* New York: Simon & Schuster.

CONSTANTINE, L. L.
1986 *Family Paradigms: The Practice of Theory in Family Therapy.* New York: Guilford Press.

FRANKENSTEIN, W., P. E. NATHAN, R. F. SULLIVAN, W. M. HAY and K. COCCO
1985 "Asymmetry of Influence in Alcoholics' Marital Communication: Alcohol's Effects on Interaction Dominance," *Journal of Marital and Family Therapy* 11: 399–410.

GORSKI, T. T.
1989 *Understanding the Twelve Steps.* Independence, MO: Herald House/ Independence Press.

JOHNSON, V. E.
1990 *Everything You Need to Know About Chemical Dependency.* Minneapolis: Johnson Institute.

KERR, M. E. and M. BOWEN
1988 *Family Evaluation: An Approach Based on Bowen Theory.* New York: W. W. Norton.

MADANES, CLOE
1981 *Strategic Family Therapy.* San Francisco: Jossey-Bass.

MENICUCCI, L. D. AND L. WERMUTH
1989 "Expanding the Family Systems Approach: Cultural, Class, Developmental and Gender Influences in Drug Abuse," *The American Journal of Family Therapy* 17: 129–142.

MINUCHIN, S.
1980 "Structural Family Therapy." Workshop presented at the Family Institute, Berkeley, CA, February.

SCHULTZ, S. J.
1984 *Family Systems Therapy: An Integration.* New York: Jason Aronson.

STANTON, M. D. and T. C. TODD
1982 *The Family Therapy of Drug Abuse and Addiction.* New York: Guilford Press.

TORGENRUD, J. and C. L. STORM
1989 "One-person Family Therapy? An Analysis of Family Therapy Schools," *The American Journal of Family Therapy* 17: 143–154.

WIENER, N.
1968 "Cybernetics in History," in W. Buckley, ed., *Modern Systems Research for the Behavioral Scientist.* Chicago: Aldine Publishing.

EXERCISE 20

Name _____   Date _____

ID # _____   Class Time _____

I. This first exercise, a debate, is optional according to the preferences of the instructor. The topic of debate is "Symptom or Disease?"

    The individual exercises that follow can be supplemented by, or be substituted for, an in-class group debate in which members of the class debate the merits of the two approaches to chemical dependency. Your professor will divide the class into groups, preferably six to eight members each. One group will be assigned the task of supporting and defending the symptom approach. The other group will be assigned the task of supporting and defending the disease approach. Each group should develop several arguments to support its position, and prepare to present those arguments to the class. Each group will have fifteen minutes to argue in favor of its position. Next, each group will have a five- to ten-minute period for rebuttal. This will be followed by a two-minute final reply from each group to the other's criticisms. Obviously, the debate will not end with a clear winner, nor should it.

    Your argument should be carefully outlined and as detailed as possible. Use outside materials to support your position. Other textbooks (see the bibliography of this chapter for suggestions), newspaper/magazine articles, journal articles, or personal interviews with treatment professionals are all recommended outside sources.

II. With national health care reform at the center of public attention, there are many agencies and programs that will be affected. These groups typically endorse one or the other of the competing perspectives on chemical dependency (e.g., law enforcement entities, federal assistance programs [e.g., Medicaid], insurance companies, federally funded treatment centers).

    A. Identify the likely proponents of the "disease" definition (i.e., What groups or individuals might benefit most from having this view gain greater acceptance?).

    B. Identify the likely proponents of the "symptom" definition (i.e., What groups or individuals might benefit most from having this view gain greater acceptance?).

    C. What are the policy implications if chemical dependency is officially labeled a "disease" or a "symptom"?

III. Consider the following hypothetical situation and then reply to the questions below. A couple comes to the counseling center where you work requesting assistance with their marital problems. Upon completing an initial profile, you find that many of their relationship problems are due to the fact that they spend very little free time together. The husband regularly stays at his friend's house on the weekends to play poker and drink beer, sometimes leaving home Friday nights and not returning until Sunday. His wife has problems with his losing money and coming home drunk on Sunday afternoons.

    A. How might an understanding of chemical dependency as a disease help you as a counseling professional advise this couple?

    B. How might an understanding of chemical dependency as a symptom help you as a counseling professional advise this couple?

    C. How might a treatment be enhanced if the insights of both perspectives were combined?

IV. Consider another hypothetical situation. Members of a family come to your office to discuss the fact that their youngest daughter was expelled from school for smoking marijuana. The father refused to come to counseling, so the mother, oldest daughter, and younger daughter came without him, due to a mandate from the school counselor. In the initial session you find that the father is seldom home because he works for a company which requires constant out-of-town travel. The mother raises the daughters by herself during the week, relying on the father to return on the weekends to enforce discipline. The youngest daughter has been using marijuana on a daily basis for several years. The eldest has not had any disciplinary problems, performing at school as an A student. The mother feels that her youngest daughter's marajuana use is simply "acting out," although the daughter says that she can't stop using marijuana.

    A. From the disease perspective, how would you explain the youngest daughter's marijuana use, including the fact that she reports being unable to stop? What would you recommend?

    B. From the symptom perspective, what significance do you attribute to the father's scarce presence? What would you recommend?

    C. Which perspective would enable you to explain more of the family situation? And why?

21

The Myths and Realities of Homelessness and Mental Health*

Dee Southard

What is mental illness? Perhaps the most accurate and straightforward answer to this question is that mental illness is "whatever those professionals licensed to deal with the problem define as mental illness." Today, the psychiatric profession is the primary agent charged directly with the duty of defining and managing the mental health of the population. The fourth edition of the American Psychiatric Association's (1994) *Diagnostic and Statistical Manual of Mental Disorders,* otherwise known as *D.S.M.—IV,* contains the most commonly used official definitions of mental illness (at least among insurance companies who use it to determine reimbursement for psychiatric services and therapists who must use *D.S.M.—IV* code numbers for the illnesses they treat on insurance claim forms). Each of the several hundred disorders in *D.S.M.—IV* falls neatly into one of the following categories: (1) Disorders Evident in Infancy, Childhood, or Adolescence; (2) Organic Mental Disorders, (3) Psychoactive Substance Use Disorder; (4) Schizophrenia; (5) Delusional Disorders; (6) Mood Disorders; (7) Somatoform Disorders; (8) Dissociative Disorders; (9) Psychosexual Disorders; (10) Personality Disorders; and (11) Disorders of Impulse Control. Sometimes the decision to include or exclude one or another "disorder" in the *D.S.M.—IV* is highly politicized and reflects the influence of nonprofessional interests in the processes of defining mental health. One example of a "politically correct" illness included in the *D.S.M.—IV* is "post-traumatic stress disorder." Largely as the result of pressure from Vietnam veterans' organizations, this "condition" was included in the latest incarnation of the *D.S.M.* For similar political reasons, some conditions such as "self-defeating personality disorder" and "homosexual-

ity" are no longer considered mental disorders by the professional psychiatric community and are excluded from the *D.S.M.—IV.*

Less volatile than the definitions of many particular psychiatric disorders, cultural beliefs about mental illness as a "disease" have remained more or less the same for several decades. The mentally ill are "sick" people who need treatment and care "for their own sake" or "for the sake of society." These kinds of beliefs have legitimated a wide variety of individual practices and the official policies of governmental agencies and institutions charged with caring for the mentally ill. While the beliefs about mental illness have not changed much in recent years, in a number of cases, the social structures designed to care for those individuals in need of treatment have changed.

For the first half of this century, institutionalization in state mental hospitals was a routine form of treatment for many forms of mental illness. Thus, the number of patients in state mental hospitals rose steadily during the first half of the twentieth century to a peak level in 1955 of 558,922 (Blau, 1992). By the 1950s, state mental hospitals were overcrowded and expensive to maintain. In addition, some psychiatrists began to question the effectiveness of hospitalization for many forms of mental disorders. Moreover, investigative reports in the late 1950s and early 1960s exposed heinous living conditions within the facilities. Ken Kesey's (1962) popular book, *One Flew Over the Cuckoo's Nest,* revealed many of the problems of mental hospitals were experiencing as well as the more extreme treatments used in mental hospitals, such as frontal lobotomies and electrical shock therapy.

Thus, beginning in the mid-1950s many patients in the vast array of state mental hospitals were *deinstitutionalized* so that treatment of the mentally ill could be achieved in the communities in which the people lived. During the 1960s, the practice of using community-based treatment was extended to a wide range of illnesses for several reasons. Deinstitutionalization was in part a

* This material is based upon work supported by the National Science Foundation. Any opinions, findings, and conclusions or recommendations expressed in this material are those of the author and do not necessarily reflect the views of the National Science Foundation.

response to the vilification of the mental hospitals by the popular press. It was also due to the growing expense of the hospital system and the widened use of drug therapies for severe patients. State mental hospitals had also established more restrictive admissions requirements for involuntary commitment to institutions. By 1990 the number of institutionalized patients in state mental hospitals was only 92,000 (Jencks, 1994).

Deinstitutionalization was also supported by the expansion of community-based services programs designed to supply the mentally ill with medication and counseling services and in some cases residential care in the form of halfway houses. The 1963 Mental Facilities and Community Mental Health Centers Construction Act was projected to create 2,000 community mental health centers by 1980, but only 789 centers received funding (Blau, 1992). Consequently, in most communities a sufficient network of outpatient treatment services never materialized because of insufficient funding. Some of the former hospital inmates were released into the community with no money, with no place to go, or with no basic coping skills. The reality for some former mental patients was that one day they were in a place where all of their physical needs were met, and the next day they found themselves homeless and hungry on a city street.

THE MYTHS OF HOMELESSNESS IN THE UNITED STATES

In recent years, there has developed a widely shared impression that most homeless people are also mentally ill. Part of the reason for this particular misconception is what we might call "guilt by association." During the early 1980s researchers began investigating the dramatic rise in the number of homeless people in America. Researchers found mental illness to be higher among the homeless population than among the rest of the population as a whole. Several researchers asserted that the combined effects of the deinstitutionalization and the failure to provide adequate community-based mental health services were a major cause of homelessness in America. That some people who were homeless had once had careers as patients in mental hospitals was understood to mean that the pattern of deinstitutionalization of the mentally ill was a causal factor for homelessness. Rates of mental illness among homeless persons are also high because community-based care facilities for the mentally ill are typically located in central cities where the declining supply of low-income housing (i.e., rooming houses or single-room occupancy hotels) has resulted in few alternatives to the street.

We might also say the homeless are "guilty by attribution." In a society in which individual achievement and success is measured by material prosperity and possessions, it is not too surprising that the homeless person is stigmatized as deviant and defective. By all outward appearances the homeless disembody practically everything of value to "normal" people interested in "making it" and "getting ahead." By the standards of polite, middle-class culture, the homeless are people who do not want the "good things in life" and so they must be "sick" or incapable of achieving them because they are "ill." The homeless, then, become easily thought of as mentally ill because of deeply ingrained cultural beliefs that ask "who in their right mind would want to live on the streets?" Other popular beliefs about homeless people as "dangerous" or "crazy" or "nuts" only reinforce this dominant view. Indeed, it is almost taken as "common sense" that the homeless should be avoided whenever possible because they are so dangerous.

Among the most visible of the homeless population there are certainly those persons who manifest bizarre appearance and strange behaviors that reinforce prevailing beliefs. The stereotype of a middle-aged to elderly single male homeless person who spends much of his time shuffling between skid row and the drunk tank would be a fairly accurate description of the homeless in America in previous generations. The other widely recognized image, that of a "bag lady," is a forceful stereotype of homeless women. Yet, this well-known image of a dirty, disheveled, and mentally disoriented middle-aged woman who wanders aimlessly through the urban landscape carrying her belongings in shopping bags or pushing them along in a shopping cart is not so complete. Her "wandering about" the city is, in part, a strategy to avoid being charged with loitering by local authorities. It is also economic behavior—checking dumpsters and alleyways for recyclable or edible "commodities." Her unkempt appearance, while in part a result of her inability to find a regular and "affordable" cleaning station, is also part of a strategy to avoid violent confrontations with truly dangerous types on the street. Many homeless women indicate that they clearly understand their own predicament and articulate the strategies they use to survive in a homeless world. Some homeless women, for example, tell of how they deliberately wear many layers of clothing, not so much as protection from the weather, but to look as unattractive as possible to deter would-be rapists. What of the "bags" you might ask? Ask yourself this simple question. At the end of the day where do you leave the backpack, briefcase, or purse in which you carry your belongings? The homeless as a rule do not enjoy the security of the locked doors that separate you from the outside world. The stereotypes such as those just described do reflect the actual lives of some men and women who are homeless but they are not representative of the whole population. When taken to represent the population itself, stereotypical images distort our perceptions of the real situation.

The broad stereotypes of the homeless as people suffering from severe mental illness do not conform to the reality for the vast majority of people who experience homelessness. For example, in 1992 the Task Force on Homelessness and Severe Mental Illness estimated that approximately one third of the homeless, single adult population suffered from severe mental illness (Public Health

Service, 1992). Snow et al. (1986) found the figure to be close to 15 percent, with a small percentage having any history of psychiatric hospitalization. Most mentally ill people in the United States have housing (and occupations and careers) and most homeless people in the United States do not suffer from severe mental illness. As has been pointed out time and time again, mental illness and homelessness are reciprocal. If untreated mental illness can lead to homelessness; conversely, living on the streets as a homeless person can trigger mental illness.

The consequences of not having a home can be severe. Some of the effects are physical and some are mental. People who are homeless have little or no money, no secure place to sleep, and no access to a bathroom or a shower. They often go hungry and many go without needed medical or dental treatment for lengthy periods of time. They are often the victims of violent crimes such as assault or rape (much of which goes unreported because their encounters with police and other authorities are generally highly stressful situations that produce few results). Most of the people that are experiencing homelessness realize that life for a homeless person is fraught with personal danger. They understand that because they spend most of their time in public areas they are vulnerable to attackers and are relatively easy prey for robbers, rapists, and murderers. Some research has shown that homeless people are more likely to become crime victims than others in the population (Baum and Burnes, 1993). In the words of one homeless woman informant, *"You are crazy if you live on the streets and you aren't a bit paranoid!"* To most people who are not without a home, this woman's words would likely mean just one thing: *"You are crazy if you live on the streets."* People who live on the streets and who sleep in subway stations, out in the open, in doorways, in cardboard boxes, or in cars and vans, appear to manifest behavior that confirms mental illness. Yet, the fact may be that the homeless person is acting with rational self-interest in mind by avoiding the homeless shelters. Homeless shelters offer little solace because of the violence in them and degrading deference ceremonies one is put through to get a night's sleep indoors. While seeking to avoid romanticism, the research indicates that "homeless people display amazing adaptive skills, and that much of what they do *makes sense* if one views it from a perspective which takes into account the very unique nature of their situation" (Koegel, 1988: 14).

The homeless world is an *isolated* one. Somewhat paradoxically, however, the behavior of the individual who chooses the street and avoids the shelter contributes to problems stemming from social isolation. What the best research in recent years indicates is that the probability of experiencing homelessness increases if one experiences traumatic life events such as the loss of a job or a divorce and after one exhausts the support of family and friendship support networks. By the time an individual is faced with living on the street, more likely than not, they have become disengaged from all or nearly all the social supports they once enjoyed and depended upon. Because of this isolation, manifestations of mental illness become evident. The cycle of socially unacceptable or "deviant" behavior and isolation or growing "social distance" between the homeless individual and others becomes mutually reinforcing.

THE HOMELESS IN THE UNITED STATES TODAY

Who then are the homeless in the United States today? The face of homelessness has changed tremendously in just under a generation. While the middle-aged to elderly alcoholic male stereotype was a "good fit" with reality decades ago, it is no longer appropriate. The image of the bag lady is also erroneous because it distorts that many homeless women are in reality "heads of households" that are homeless. Still others manage to largely conceal their identity as a homeless person by maintaining some of the routines of the "legitimate" roles they once enjoyed. By the early 1990s, homeless families became the most rapidly expanding group in the homeless population. By some estimates, 40 percent of the homeless population were members of families that were homeless (Blau, 1992). There are hundreds of thousands of children who are homeless in the United States on any given night (U.S. Senate Committee, 1990). The phenomenon of homeless families is particularly disturbing due to its consequences for children. Research has shown that homeless children are more likely to suffer physical disorders from inadequate nutrition or untreated childhood illnesses than children who are not homeless (Molnar et al., 1990). Educators, clinicians, and researchers who work with homeless children report observing delayed development of language and motor skills, clinical depression, low self-esteem, and fear of separation from their parents. No longitudinal research has been conducted that focuses on the long-term effects of homelessness on children's mental health or on their ability to function in society; however, it is reasonable to extrapolate that many children who have experienced periods of homelessness will experience difficulties fulfilling adult roles in our society.

Although an accurate accounting of the nation's constantly changing homeless population cannot be obtained, most evidence suggests that the number of homeless persons swelled in the 1980s and continues to grow in the 1990s. Agencies that provide services to homeless people report that every year the number of requests for services continue to be larger than the year before (Goetz, 1993; U.S. Conference of Mayors, 1986). Interestingly, counting the homeless population became a controversy in its own right in the 1980s. As homelessness became a significant "public" issue in the early 1980s, the demand for accurate statistical measures of the homeless population grew, especially from advocacy groups and shelter providers who argued that there were over 2 million homeless persons in the United States. Finally agreeing to conduct a scientific study, the U.S. Department of Housing and Urban Development (1994) estimated that the homeless population was only about 250,000 to 350,000. Having an interest in finding a small population to justify further budget cutting for low-income housing programs, the government used measurement techniques that produced biased results. The most widely accepted estimates of homelessness range from about 750,000 to 1 million at any one time. The most recent research indicates nearly 7 million Americans experienced a period of homelessness at least once between 1985 and 1989 (U.S. HUD, 1994). Although the federal government spent $1.3 billion in Fiscal Year 1994 for homeless assistance programs (U.S. HUD, 1994: 44), homelessness continues to be a growing social problem.

REFERENCES

AMERICAN PSYCHIATRIC ASSOCIATION
1994   *Diagnostic and Statistical Manual of Mental Disorders: D.S.M.—IV,* 4th ed. Washington, DC: American Psychiatric Association.

BAUM, ALICE S. and DONALD W. BURNES
1993   *A Nation in Denial: The Truth About Homelessness.* Boulder, CO: Westview Press.

BLAU, JOEL
1992   *The Visible Poor: Homelessness in the United States.* New York: Oxford University Press.

GOETZ, EDWARD G.
1993   *Shelter Burden Local Politics and Progressive Housing Policy.* Philadelphia: Temple University Press.

JENCKS, CHRISTOPHER
1994   *The Homeless.* Cambridge: Harvard University Press.

KESEY, KEN
1962   *One Flew Over the Cuckoo's Nest.* New York: Viking Press.

KOEGEL, PAUL
1988   *Understanding Homelessness: An Ethnographic Approach.* Los Angeles: The Department of Geography, University of Southern California, The Los Angeles Homelessness Project.

MOLNAR, JANICE, WILLIAM RATH and TOVAN KLEIN
1990   Constantly Compromised: The Impact of Homelessness on Children," *Journal of Social Issues* 46 (4): 109–124.

PUBLIC HEALTH SERVICE
1992   *Outcasts on Main Street: Report of the Federal Task Force on Homelessness and Severe Mental Illness.* Washington, DC: Department of Health and Human Services.

SNOW, DAVID A., L. ANDERSON and M. MARTIN
1986   "The Myth of Pervasive Mental Illness Among the Homeless," *Social Problems* 33 (5): 407–423.

U.S. CONFERENCE OF MAYORS
1986   *The Continued Growth of Hunger, Homeless and Poverty in America's Cities: 1986.* Washington, DC: United States Conference of Mayors.

U.S. DEPARTMENT OF HOUSING AND URBAN DEVELOPMENT
1994   *Priority Home! The Federal Plan to Break the Cycle of Homelessness.* Washington, DC: U.S. Government Printing Office. HUD-1454-CPD, March.

U.S. SENATE COMMITTEE ON LABOR AND HUMAN RESOURCES
1990   "Homelessness: An American Tragedy." Hearings on September 29, 1989, and May 9, 1990 (S.Hrg. 101–806). Washington, DC: U.S. Government Printing Office.

EXERCISE 21

Name _____   Date _____

ID # _____   Class Time _____

I. This exercise asks you to imagine yourself in a variety of situations homeless people typically face and to note your reactions to these situations.

Imagine yourself as a person who has lost his or her job, used up his or her savings, sold his or her car, and has no source of income. Furthermore, you have been living on the generosity of friends and family members for some time, but the last of these has asked you to move on. Fortunately, a recent acquaintance promised you work in a nearby town and said he could put you up for a few days. You decide to go, but when you arrive neither your new friend nor the job is anywhere to be found.

Tonight is the first night that you have been literally out in the streets. Your clothing and your backpack and its contents are soaking wet from standing in line for three hours in order to get a place to sleep at the local shelter. As you enter you are not allowed to take your backpack into the sleeping area, instead it is locked into a storage area. You eat a cafeteria-style dinner and go into the sleeping hall which is a large room filled with cots that are spaced two feet apart. The room is noisy and you are unable to sleep soundly. By 5:30 A.M. the room is once again full of activity as all the people are preparing to leave. When you get dressed to leave, you realize that someone has stolen your coat right off the end of your cot as you slept. You complain to the shelter personnel. They tell you that its not even worth calling the police over; however, they do give you a used coat from the shelter clothing bin. The coat is too big and is dirty, but it is warm so you accept it. After eating a cafeteria-style breakfast you retrieve your wet backpack and head out to try to catch the 6:45 A.M. bus. The bus stop is located a block from the homeless shelter, in front of a busy mini-market. Across the street from the bus stop is a city park and a church. When the bus arrives you reach into the pocket where you were keeping your last seventeen dollars and your identification, but the pocket is empty. You have no money to get on the bus. You try to explain your predicament to the bus driver, but she tells you that she cannot let you on the bus without the fare and drives the bus away. You have an appointment to apply for assistance at the welfare office eight miles away at 8 A.M. The next bus will be arriving in fifteen minutes.

A. Briefly describe what would you do in such a situation.

B. Explain how any of the actions you described above could be considered "deviant" behavior?

C. Now turn to exercise VI in this section and complete the questions for scenario #1.

II. You have arrived at the welfare office; however, you arrived at 8:20 A.M. and your appointment was scheduled for 8:00 A.M. You are told that if you would like to you can wait for a "no-show," and if someone fails to show up for another appointment you can see a worker in that time slot. You decide to wait. Five hours later you are called to the front counter. The worker speaks to you from behind safety glass. The worker tells you that this is a prescreening session which is conducted prior to having you speak with an eligibility worker. You tell the worker that you want to apply for emergency cash assistance, food stamps, and housing assistance. The first thing the worker asks you for is your identification. You explain that it was stolen the night before. The worker tells you that you cannot receive aid without identification, and that your application cannot be processed at this time. The assistance the worker does give you consists of two bus tokens and a voucher referral form that is redeemable for a free box of food you can pick up at a church six miles away.

    A. Briefly describe what would you do in this situation.

    B. Explain how any of the actions you described above might be considered "deviant" behavior?

    C. Now turn to exercise VI in this section and complete the questions for scenario #2.

III. You have arrived at the church and present your voucher referral form from the welfare office to a person in the church's office. You are feeling hungry and are looking forward to eating. The church person explains that the church only passes out of boxes of food between the hours of 11 A.M. and 1 P.M. and encourages you to come back for your box of food the next day.

    A. Briefly describe what would you do in this situation.

    B. Explain how any of the actions you described above could be considered "deviant" behavior?

    C. Now turn to exercise VI in this section and complete the questions for scenario #3.

IV. You have used your last bus token to return to the homeless shelter that you slept in last night. It is 5 P.M. when you arrive. You wait in line outside of the building until 6 P.M., but you are too far back in line and all of the sleeping spaces have been given out before you enter. The shelter does, however, give you a warm evening meal before making you return to the street. It is cold and windy outside and you decide to go to the nearby city park. You find a footbridge that crosses a stream, and you go under it to keep dry. Underneath the foot-bridge you find that someone in the past had made a ring of stones for a fire pit. You look around and find a few dry sticks and twigs and make a small fire to stay warm by. About an hour later a city police officer comes by the edge of the footbridge and tells you that you must put out the fire at once and that you must move on. The park is closing and it is against a city ordinance to sleep in the park. You explain that you have no place to go and you are told that the police office cannot help you. Then you are told that if you are still there under the bridge in fifteen minutes when the police officer returns, you will be given a citation. You ask about being taken to jail for the night and the police officer simply tells you that you really don't want to make them do the paperwork to take you to jail because you will find it to be an unpleasant experience. The officer walks across the footbridge and on into the park.

    A. Briefly describe what would you do in this situation.

    B. Explain how any of the actions you described above could be considered "deviant" behavior?

    C. Now turn to exercise VI in this section and complete the questions for scenario #4.

V. An experienced homeless street person has observed your interaction with the police officer in the park. The street person approaches you and tells you about a doorway a couple of blocks away from the park which is deep enough for you to lie down in and be out of the rain, and where one of the mailbox slots is broken and warm air comes out of the building. The street person is going to go there and tells you that you can come along if you want to because the doorway is large enough for both of you to get some sleep in.

    A. Briefly describe what would you do in this situation.

    B. Explain how any of the actions you described above could be considered "deviant" behavior?

    C. Now turn to exercise VI in this section and complete the questions for scenario #5.

VI. Still imagining yourself as a homeless person, use the given scale to respond to the following questions about how you would feel in the previous scenarios.

1 "Not at all"
2 "A little bit"
3 "A moderate amount"
4 "Quite a bit"
5 "Very much so"

Scenario #1

_____ Do you feel safe?
_____ Do you feel optimistic about your future?
_____ Do you feel that your situation is improving?
_____ Do you feel that society is concerned about your personal well-being?

Scenario #2

_____ Do you feel safe?
_____ Do you feel optimistic about your future?
_____ Do you feel that your situation is improving?
_____ Do you feel that society is concerned about your personal well-being?

Scenario #3

_____ Do you feel safe?
_____ Do you feel optimistic about your future?
_____ Do you feel that your situation is improving?
_____ Do you feel that society is concerned about your personal well-being?

Scenario #4

_____ Do you feel safe?
_____ Do you feel optimistic about your future?
_____ Do you feel that your situation is improving?
_____ Do you feel that society is concerned about your personal well-being?

Scenario #5

_____ Do you feel safe?
_____ Do you feel optimistic about your future?
_____ Do you feel that your situation is improving?
_____ Do you feel that society is concerned about your personal well-being?

_____ Total the response scores.

```
    1       2       3       4       5
    |_____|_____|_____|_____|
```

_____ Divide the total by 20, then place that score on the number line below.

Social researchers sometimes use questionnaires like this one to assess homeless people's emotional wellness. What interpretation would you make of the score?

PART IV

GLOBAL SOCIAL PROBLEMS

Some global social problems result from the relations between societies. Other global social problems are the result of the actions of some societies which produce negative consequences for other societies or for the entire global population. In any case, collective responses to problems of a global nature are complicated by the large number of independent nation-states that must come to agree on the definition of and response to global problems. Due to vast inequalities between economic and geographic regions of the world, nations are unlikely to agree on what they define as a global social problems and the best way to respond to them.

In the essays in this part, these two features of the global system—political fragmentation and inequality among nation-states—are important reasons why such problems have persisted or emerged. Lloyd J. Dumas's selection on the proliferation of nuclear capabilities in the post–Cold War era is an excellent example of how the actions of individual states can create problems for other states and, in fact, change the entire system all together. The pollution of the environment, including the consequences for the world's supply of water, air, land, and other natural resources, is explored in Ray Darville's essay. The selection by Dana Dunn emphasizes the economic ties between nations and their consequences for women in developing societies. How women are utilized in the labor force, Dunn argues, has an important impact on their overall chances in life. In the final chapter, Elizabeth D. Leonard connects population growth and the massive urban upheavals in less developed countries to the systematic use of child labor.

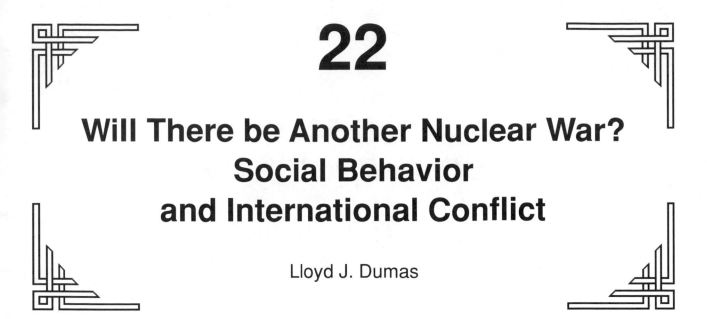

22

Will There be Another Nuclear War? Social Behavior and International Conflict

Lloyd J. Dumas

In the early morning of August 6, 1945, three American B-29 bombers appeared in the sky over the bustling port city of Hiroshima, Japan. One of them, the *Enola Gay,* dropped one bomb that obliterated the city. Three days later, a second atomic bomb demolished the city of Nagasaki. Soon the Japanese government surrendered. History's first nuclear war was over ... but the terror of nuclear weapons had only just begun.

Why were nuclear weapons designed and built? Was the nuclear age and the decades of danger that it has brought the result of some unstoppable process of scientific and technological development? Or has it sprung from deeper forces, forces rooted in human social behavior? Is it inevitable that there will be another nuclear war? Or has the end of the Cold War made the possibility of nuclear war a thing of the past? Will new technology or the understanding of social behavior be most critical to emerging from the nuclear age without the horror of another nuclear war?

WHY NUCLEAR WEAPONS?

From the beginning of human history, groups of people have wanted to influence the behavior of other groups of people. Long ago, people discovered that the threat or use of force could sometimes be effective in getting other people to do what they wanted them to do (or preventing them from doing what they didn't want them to do). The threat or use of deadly force is the most extreme example. Over the millennia of human history, the basic strategy has changed very little. We do not think any differently today than when we threatened each other with sticks and stones; it is our technical capability that has changed.

The development of the military as a social institution formalized the threat or use of mass organized force as a means of influencing behavior. In seeking to carry out their socially assigned task, militaries have always sought more effective ways of killing people or destroying property. As the centuries passed, more and more deadly weapons gave us the power to do increasing damage to one another. This led us from the most primitive clubs of prehistory to the most sophisticated high-technology weapons of today. The technology of violence has changed dramatically; the basic desire to control group behavior that motivates the threat and use of force is just the same.

Driven by our fears and our deep-seated need to protect ourselves, this strategy of force combined with our technological brilliance inevitably put into our hands superweapons whose wanton use could put an end to the human enterprise. With the advent of nuclear weapons in the middle of the twentieth century, we gained the capability to become the first species on earth responsible for its own extinction. As Albert Einstein, one of the greatest minds of the twentieth century, once put it, "The unleashed power of the atom has changed everything save our modes of thinking, and thus we drift toward unparalleled catastrophe" (quoted in Nathan and Norden, 1968).

SOCIAL FORCES AND THE NUCLEAR ARMS RACE

The development of nuclear weapons created an unexpected dilemma for the military. Finally, they had in their hands the ultimate weapon, a weapon so powerful that no more than a few hundred of them were needed to utterly destroy any opponent. The problem was that the weapon was so destructive that it did not fit into any traditional concept of warfare. They didn't want to let go of the weapon they had sought for so long, but they couldn't figure out how to use it as an effective tool of battle either. (To be sure, a number of battlefield nuclear weapons were developed, but they were never fired in combat, a fact which reinforces the argument being made here.)

The first solution to this dilemma was an updated version of the theory of deterrence, the formal theory which argued that social behavior can be controlled by the threat of force, rather than by its actual use. Simply put, the theory of strategic nuclear deterrence stated that war—or other violations of acceptable international social and political behavior—could be prevented by threatening nuclear annihilation of the offending society. When the United States was the only nation with nuclear weapons, the American government could credibly attach the threat of nuclear devastation to any behavior that seriously threatened what it perceived to be the interests of our society. But the American nuclear monopoly lasted only four years, and when it was gone, the situation was changed permanently.

As potential opponents gained the capability for retaliating with devastating nuclear force, America could only credibly attach the threat of nuclear attack to the most extreme situations, such as direct military attack against the homeland of the United States or its closest and most important allies. So the world settled into the balance of terror known as "mutually assured destruction," officially designated by the unusually appropriate acronym "MAD."

In the end, deterrence is not all that satisfying to political leaders and even less satisfying to action-oriented military forces. As nuclear arsenals grew, this combined with the fact that only a few hundred to a thousand of these weapons were needed for any rational deterrence strategy, pushed strategists to move from strict reliance on deterrence theory to the so-called "counterforce" approach.

Counterforce strategy stated that a nation should target its strategic nuclear arsenal against the nuclear forces and other military-related facilities of its opponent. Threatening military targets, it was argued, was more humane than threatening cities, and increased the chance that nuclear war might be kept limited. Attacking the opponent's strategic forces also had the advantage of limiting the damage they could do. Moreover, the improved accuracy of missile technology made the counterforce strategy seem feasible and had the military appeal of moving from the realm of pure threat into that of active warfare.

Counterforce strategy also legitimized the open-ended expansion of nuclear weapons arsenals. Only so many nuclear warheads could possibly be needed for deterrence, because only so many nuclear warheads were required to destroy a society (there are only so many cities). But with counterforce, every time an opponent built a weapon, you could justify building a few more of your own in order to be sure that it could be destroyed. As each side built more weapons, each side needed more weapons. There was no longer any apparent limit.

There are a number of problems with this approach. For one thing, the clear-cut distinction between military and civilian targets is more apparent than real. Many key military targets are in or near major cities (e.g., Kirtland Air Force Base is in Albuquerque, New Mexico; San Diego, California, is a major Navy port; San Antonio, Texas, is surrounded by five military bases). In fact, virtually every major city has a nearby airport large enough to serve as a military air base in the event of all-out war. They would all be on the target list. Secondly, it is very difficult to believe that either of two nuclear-armed opponents would surrender (or even back down) following a nuclear war with little enough destruction of population centers to leave much of its nuclear arsenal still intact. If it were ready to do that, why would it have attacked in the first place? When in history has any nation surrendered in a war while it still had devastating military capability available?

Most important, counterforce strategy undermines deterrence and increases the likelihood of nuclear war. Nuclear weapons accurate enough to be used in counterforce strikes are accurate enough to be used to try to destroy the opponent's ability to retaliate by striking first. If things got very tense, each side would have an incentive to start the war. A situation like this would make nuclear war more likely, and so make everyone less secure.

What about shooting down nuclear weapons after they have been launched? This approach also has the appeal of being more active, more like traditional warfare. In the 1960s and again in the 1980s, attempts were made to develop weapons systems with this capability. Some of this work continues today. These attempts triggered great national debates. The strategic defense initiative (known popularly as Star Wars) provides the best example. While the issue is a complex one, today, even the scientists and military organizations involved in this work do not believe that the country's population or industry can be shielded from large-scale nuclear attack in this way.

The problem is often stated as a technical problem of shooting down attacking missiles or planes. If it were a purely technical problem, it could eventually be solved. But the real problem is not purely technical; it is rather a military problem. The difference is straightforward. A technical problem is what could be called "a game against nature." Solving a technical problem is a matter of learning enough about the biological, chemical, and physical laws of nature and applying that knowledge in a clever enough way to accomplish a specific objective. For example, meeting President Kennedy's challenge to send someone to the moon and back by the end of the 1960s involved solving a series of difficult technical problems. In such a situation, the opponent—"nature"—is passive: It is not trying to prevent success. A military problem is a very different matter. It is a game against an opponent who is *actively* trying to thwart you, to stop you from succeeding; hence it is an infinitely more complicated situation.

When America was trying to put a person on the moon, no one was jamming communications systems, sabotaging launch vehicles, or trying to move the moon around. In contrast, an effective antimissile defense against nuclear attack must be able to contend with every obstacle that the attacker can put in the way. Given the enormous power of nuclear weapons, preventing the destruction of any given targeted city requires shooting down or deflecting *every* single incoming warhead. If only one warhead gets through the defense, the city is destroyed. Airplanes have been used extensively in warfare now for more than three quarters of a century. During that time, "shoot-down" anti-aircraft defenses have improved enormously. Yet because of great advances in the technology of attack aircraft, it is still not possible to guarantee that the latest state-of-the-art anti-aircraft systems will reliably shoot down all attacking aircraft. Why then should we believe that it would be any more possible to solve the more complex problem of antimissile defense?

At its base, the buildup of nuclear arsenals was never driven by technological imperatives. It is the result of social forces that shape the development and application of technology in the quest for an effective way of controlling human behavior.

HAS THE THREAT OF NUCLEAR WAR DISAPPEARED?

If, as has been demonstrated, the development of nuclear weapons technology and the buildup of nuclear arsenals are the result of social forces, rather than technological imperatives, then should not the path to the elimination of the threat of nuclear holocaust ultimately lie in the arena of social behavior, rather than in science and engineering? The search for a technical solution to the problem of nuclear war is foolish and futile. We must look for a solution in the realm of behavioral science.

At the very beginning of the nuclear arms race, with its nuclear advantage intact, the United States made an extraordinary proposal. In June 1946, in what came to be known as the Baruch Plan, it proposed to permanently renounce nuclear weaponry if other nations would do the same and to destroy its existing nuclear weapons, after the nations had put in place a worldwide system to detect and punish violations. Within days, the Soviet Union put a similar proposal on the table. A critical difference was that the Soviets called for existing weapons to be destroyed first, and violation control systems to be put in place last. The United States would not agree to the Soviet approach, the Soviets would not agree to the U.S. approach, and no negotiated middle ground was reached. In these early fateful days of the nuclear era, the world lost perhaps the best opportunity it ever had for abolishing nuclear weapons and eliminating the threat of nuclear war in its infancy.

With the loss of the American nuclear monopoly, the arms race was underway. Soon, Britain, France, and China would join the "nuclear club." From 1946 to 1986 many arms-control agreements were made, many treaties were signed, but *not a single nuclear weapon was ever destroyed or even moved as a result of any of them*—until the mid-1980s. In 1987, the landmark Intermediate-range Nuclear Forces (INF) Treaty was signed. It broke through two important barriers: The Soviets officially agreed to

"on-site" inspection for the first time, and the treaty called for the actual destruction of some 4 percent of the huge nuclear arsenals of both sides. It was a small start but an important one. In the years since INF, additional agreements were reached for large-scale arms reductions.

Because of such progress in arms reductions agreements, and because of the end of the long Cold War, many people believe that the threat of nuclear war has all but disappeared. Unfortunately, nothing could be farther from the truth. Clearly, the nature of the threat has changed, but the dangers posed by nuclear weapons are still all too real and perhaps even more difficult to control.

The threat of an all-out nuclear war between the superpowers has certainly been sharply reduced, but that is not primarily because of progress in arms reductions. Both the United States and Russia still have enormous arsenals of nuclear weapons, a small fraction of which could destroy any nation on earth. Yet because of the dramatic improvement in relations between the United States and Russia (as well as with the other nuclear-armed successor republics of the former Soviet Union), the outbreak of intentional nuclear war is much less likely today than at any time since the beginning of the nuclear age. Although the threat of accidental nuclear war is also very real, its probability has dropped sharply as diminished international tensions have moved military nuclear forces to lower levels of alert. What has caused these changes? Technology? Science? No, the progress that has been made toward a reduced nuclear threat has been in the realm of improved social and political relations.

The breakup of the former Soviet Union, followed by very hard economic times and political turbulence in its successor republics, has increased other dimensions of the nuclear threat. More nations now have nuclear weapons, and there is some indication that control over nuclear arsenals, weapons designers, and nuclear materials is less certain. The proliferation of nuclear weapons to other countries has always been a serious part of the nuclear nightmare because it is harder to prevent nuclear war when there are more "fingers on the button." More decision makers in control of more arsenals of nuclear weapons make their use in regional nuclear conflicts more likely.

Looser controls also raise the probability of nuclear terrorism. The purpose of political terrorist activity is to apply pressure on decision makers in order to achieve some particular goal. Terrorists often try to affect the political process by demonstrating that the authorities cannot protect the public, and so force the authorities to concede to their demands. To achieve their objectives, terrorists use shock and terror. What could be more shocking or more terrifying than threatening to blow up a city with a nuclear weapon? Today, it easier for a terrorist group to steal, to buy on the black market, or to build one or more nuclear weapons than at any time since their creation.

Nuclear weapons and related systems are designed,

built, and operated by people organized through bureaucracies. One thing we know about people, singly or in groups, is that they make mistakes. The safety of the entire nuclear system ultimately rests on the reliability of fallible human beings. Nothing can be done to eliminate the risk of human error and unreliability. Giving control to computers or other technical systems raises other nightmarish possibilities and will not eliminate this risk. For who will design and build the computers and who will write their programming? Even having futuristic computers and robots design and build other computers and robots cannot solve the problem because these reproducing machines must originally have been designed, built, and programmed by fallible human beings. The only way to eliminate the nuclear threat and put an end to the possibility of nuclear devastation is to abolish nuclear weapons.

CAN NUCLEAR WEAPONS BE ABOLISHED?

Nuclear weapons arsenals did not come into being by accident. The design and construction of the first atomic bomb was the result of one of the most intensive and costly scientific projects in history, lasting years and involving some of the world's best scientific minds. Over the past half century, the buildup of nuclear military forces to their present size, variety, and destructive capability in all nuclear-armed nations was also the result of a conscious and expensive process. There is little or no prospect of eliminating nuclear weapons unless we can address the social and political forces underlying this process.

At its most basic level, the nuclear arms race has been driven by the idea that the threat and use of force is an effective and appropriate way of influencing the behavior of groups of people. In a world of actual and potential enemies, real or imagined, this belief has been bound up with the idea that security is best achieved by carrying and sometimes openly threatening to use a very big stick. There is no doubt that security is a powerful and legitimate concern for everyone. If we are to find our way to a world without the threat of nuclear war, we must find our way to a world without nuclear weapons. If we are to find our way to a world without nuclear weapons, we must find another, more effective and less dangerous way of achieving security by influencing the behavior of others.

Humans are inherently social beings. Most people today live in highly interdependent and complex societies. On a daily basis, we rely on one another for a whole series of things that are critical to our physical survival and emotional well-being—from food, clothing, and shelter to approval, affection, and support. Yet, when you think about it, we rarely use force or the threat of force to get others to do what we need them to do. Instead, for the most part, we influence their behavior through positive incentives, often by creating situations of mutual benefit.

For example, when we need food, we typically go to a grocery story or restaurant and pay the grocer or restauranteur money, which they want, in exchange for the food that we want. They have done all the things we needed them to do to see to it that the food was available for us, not because we threatened to beat them up or kill them if they did not, but because they correctly believed that we would pay them for the food and their effort in getting it to us. We have influenced their behavior not through the threat or use of force, but by setting up and participating in a system of voluntary mutually beneficial exchange. Clearly, it is possible to buy dinner this way, but is it also possible to prevent war and achieve security this way?

Consider the case of Western Europe. France, Germany, Italy, the Netherlands, Belgium, Spain, Britain, and so forth have fought countless wars with one another over the centuries. They lit the fire for the two worst wars in human history during this century, wars which took the lives of more than 50 million people and injured countless millions more. Now they are members of the European Common Market, a web of voluntary, mutually beneficial economic exchange relationships. And today, if you were to ask citizens on the streets of any major city in any of these countries what they thought the chance was of their country going to war with any other Common Market country you chose to name, they would laugh at the question. The citizens of these countries and their governments still have many conflicts and disagreements. They debate, they argue, they shout—but they no longer even think of shooting at each other (or of threatening to use nuclear weapons to resolve their disagreements). The change in their social, political, and economic relationships has created a remarkable change in their social and political behavior. They no longer feel the need to use force or even the threat of force to influence one another's behavior. As a result, they are all much more secure.

Perhaps there is a lesson in this. Perhaps in this situation lie the seeds of a much less costly, more effective, and less dangerous system of international security, emphasizing the use of positive incentives rather than threats of violence to achieve security and prevent war. Violations of the accepted norms of international behavior by renegade nations could more easily and effectively be punished by the use of wide-ranging multilateral economic sanctions. In such a world, nuclear weapons would be useless, counterproductive, and hopelessly out of place. In such a world, we might indeed be able to abolish nuclear weapons and emerge from the nuclear age without the horror of another nuclear war.

SUGGESTED READINGS

CORTRIGHT, DAVID and GEORGE LOPEZ, eds.
1995   *Economic Sanctions: Panacea or Peacebuilding.* Boulder, CO: Westview Press.

DUMAS, LLOYD J.
1986 "Realities of the Nuclear Age: Growing Sources of Threat," *International Journal of Mental Health* 15: 16–39.

DUMAS, LLOYD J.
1993 "Organizing the Chaos," *Bulletin of the Atomic Scientists* 49: 46–49.

SCHELL, JONATHAN
1982 *The Fate of the Earth*. New York: Avon Books.

SCHELL, JONATHAN
1984 *The Abolition*. New York: Alfred A. Knopf.

WESTON, BURNS, ed.
1990 *Alternative Security: Living Without Nuclear Deterrence*. Boulder, CO: Westview Press.

REFERENCES

NATHAN, OTTO and HEINZ NORDEN, eds.
1968 *Einstein on Peace*. New York: Schocken Books.

EXERCISE 22

Name _____   Date _____

ID # _____   Class Time _____

I. Imagine that you are a foreign policy advisor to the President of the United States. The larger and more militarily powerful of two less developed countries has just invaded a disputed region that has been part of its smaller neighbor for 50 years. In the space provided below, write a memo to the President presenting at least two suggestions for resolving this crisis *without* the threat or use of military force.

MEMORANDUM

TO: The President of the United States
FROM:
SUBJECT:

II.   Look through one week of international news reports in your local newspaper or a major metropolitan newspaper such as *The Washington Post* or *The New York Times*. Find every article that deals with a dispute between two or more nations or subnational political groups and record the information requested in the blank spaces below. Then select two of the articles—one in which the conflict involves at least one nuclear-armed nation, and another article about a situation in which force or the threatened use of it is described. Provide brief summaries of the two articles in A through C below.

_____ Newspaper name

_____ Week of observation

_____ Number of articles located

_____ Number of conflicts involving at least one nuclear-armed nation

_____ Number of cases in which force is being used or threatened

_____ Number of cases in which conflict is resolved primarily through nonviolent means

A.   Attach a copy of an article describing conflict involving at least one nuclear power and summarize briefly the conflict situation.

B.   Attach a copy of an article in which the use of force or the threatened use of force is involved in some conflict situation. Summarize briefly the conflict situation.

C.   Compare the conflicts in which force is being used or threatened to those in which peaceful resolution is being used. What do you think accounts for the difference? Explain your answer in a brief essay below.

23

The Environment as a Social Issue

Ray Darville

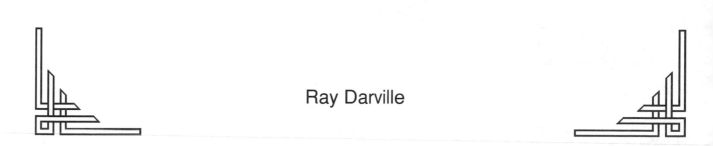

Why is the environment considered by many to be a serious social problem, and, more specifically, why should you be concerned about your environment? Quality of life, in fact life itself, is substantially affected by the condition of the environment. Environmental problems contribute not only to ill-health and mortality for individuals but also to mental health and emotional problems. Studies show that those who spend a great deal of time outside in natural areas report that they feel better about themselves, happier and more at peace. John Muir once said: "Climb the mountains and get their good tidings. Nature's peace will flow into you as the sunshine into the trees. The winds will blow their freshness into you, and the storms their energy, while cares will drop off like autumn leaves" (quoted in Miller, 1993).

Environmental problems are costly to individuals and society. A significant share of our tax dollars pay for maintaining and cleaning the environment and preventing future environmental problems. Billions of dollars are spent each year on the environment. This investment is viewed by many as a legacy to our children who will inherit the environment we leave behind.

SELECTED ENVIRONMENTAL CONCERNS

One of the greatest environmental concerns is that of population growth. According to the Population Reference Bureau, world population size reached 5,607,000,000 in 1994. The Bureau indicated that world population will increase to over 7 billion people by 2010. At present rates of growth, world population will double in 43 years, resulting in a population of over 11 billion people before many of you retire.

One reason for concern over population growth is the stark difference between developed and developing countries. Developing countries are by definition poorer and have higher birth rates and population growth rates than more developed countries. For example, their rate of natural population increase is six times that of developed countries. The doubling time for the population of developing countries is only about 36 years and these countries contain almost 80 percent of world population. In developing societies, the average woman has almost four children compared to two children for women in developed societies.

A central notion in the discussion of environmental problems and population growth is that of carrying capacity, which is the "number of people that can be supported in an area given its physical resource base and the way those resources are used" (Miller, 1993). Some scholars (Meadows, Meadows and Randers, 1992) argue that the world has already reached carrying capacity and that environmental systems are already beginning to deteriorate. The following equation can be used to describe the environmental impact of population size:

$$
\begin{array}{c}
\text{Number} \\
\text{of people}
\end{array}
\times
\begin{array}{c}
\text{Number of} \\
\text{resource units} \\
\text{consumed} \\
\text{per person}
\end{array}
\times
\begin{array}{c}
\text{Environmental} \\
\text{degradation and} \\
\text{pollution per} \\
\text{resource unit used}
\end{array}
=
\begin{array}{c}
\text{Environmental} \\
\text{impact}
\end{array}
$$

This equation suggests that while developing countries contribute to environmental problems through their overpopulation, developed countries contribute through their overconsumption. On average, developed countries have a standard of living 18 times that of the developing countries. The Population Reference Bureau (1994) estimates that per capita income in less developed countries is $950 while the statistic is $16,610 for developed countries. While scholars often talk about the carrying capacity of the world, we do not have a world government in place that can effectively coordinate population size and consumption rates. Instead, we have some 200 sovereign nations that must address this issue, and they often do so independently and in a competitive fashion. This national "self-interest" does not contribute to the maintenance and improvement of the global environment and may in fact detract from it.

Keating (1993) argues that "the major cause of the continued deterioration of the global environment is the unsustainable pattern of consumption and production, particularly in industrialized countries." He suggests that excessive demand by rich societies, including the United States, places great stress on the environment. This creates unnecessary pollution and greatly depletes natural resources in these countries. He indicates that policy makers should reexamine their production and consumption patterns and individuals should be educated as to the environmental impact of their own behavior. Developing countries, in contrast, should promote sustainable consumption as they create new economies. Can you identify changes you might consider making in your own behavior to reduce consumption and diminish pollution? Can you identify policy recommendations you might make concerning production, consumption, and pollution?

Another serious environmental problem is the degradation and loss of natural resources. Air pollution continues to be a major problem, both indoor and outdoor. Outside air pollution comes from various sources including burning of fossil fuels in power and industrial plants and in motor vehicles. A problem associated with air pollution is acid deposition, better known as acid rain. Acid rain can damage buildings, kill fish and aquatic life, create regional haze, weaken or kill trees, stunt the growth of crops, and aggravate human respiratory diseases. Recently, the Environmental Protection Agency (EPA) argued that indoor air quality is the "most significant environmental issue we have to face" (Miller, 1993). In a report, the EPA estimated that perhaps 26,000 people die annually as a direct result of indoor air pollution; the World Health Organization (WHO) states that 1.25 billion urbanites are exposed to indoor pollutants (Miller, 1993). Do you ever question the quality of the air you breathe? Remember—as a college student, you spend most of your time inside, not outside.

Water is a finite resource. Some problems with water include too little water in some geographic areas (droughts, normal rainfall patterns), too much water (floods, monsoon season) in others, water sources that are too distant from people, contaminated drinking water, and wasteful water consumption. Within the United States, the East has enough water but the West is in constant need of water. In the western United States, some 85 percent of the water is used by the agricultural industry for crop irrigation (Miller, 1993). The problem of water supply is an international issue as well. Worldwide, droughts cause more economic damage than any other natural hazard (Miller, 1993). In fact, Miller argues that the availability of water and "water-rights" will be a prominent foreign-policy concern of many countries into the twenty-first century. Have you ever wondered what causes flooding? Flooding is not simply a problem of there being too much water in one place at one time; rather the problem stems from the interaction of such climatic factors with uniquely human

ones such as the overcultivation of land, deforestation, overgrazing, mining, and urbanization.

Water pollution may come from point and nonpoint sources. Point sources involve such entities as factories, sewage treatment plants, mines, and oil wells. This pollution is easy to identify, monitor, and regulate, yet the costs associated with doing so are often high. Nonpoint sources include runoff of chemicals into surface water from various places such as urban areas, logged forests, croplands, and roadways. These nonpoint sources of water pollution are more difficult to locate and control.

Global warming is another environmental issue receiving much attention today. Have you ever parked your car for several hours in hot temperatures and returned to what feels like an oven? This represents the greenhouse effect in that heat is trapped and cannot dissipate. Scientists generally agree that concentrations of greenhouse gases are rapidly increasing, that humans are the primary cause of these gases, and that the resultant rapid climate change can be disastrous for both ecosystems and human society. A rise in the world's temperature would cause sea levels to rise, thus flooding coastal wetlands, barrier islands, croplands, and coastal cities. Depletion of the ozone layer allows more ultraviolet-B radiation to reach earth, which increases the incidence of eye cataracts and skin cancer and decreases the yield of food crops.

The loss of wildlife and biological diversity (biodiversity), in general, is an additional environmental problem. Biodiversity is important for many reasons. These reasons include evolution and the maintenance of life-sustaining systems throughout the world. Plants, for example, provide food for animals in the food chain that later provide humans with food. Plants provide substances in about half of prescription and one fourth of nonprescription drugs. Wildlife provides recreational opportunities including hunting, fishing, bird watching, and photography. The major threat to most wildlife species is the destruction, fragmentation, and degradation of their habitats. These problems destroy not only habitat but also food, shelter, migration routes, and breeding areas. Loss of habitat has been difficult particularly for bird species—including the American bald eagle, California condor, whooping crane, and Atwater's prairie chicken. Henry David Thoreau once remarked: "In wildness is the preservation of the world" (quoted in Miller, 1993). While the extinction of some species is natural, humans have greatly accelerated the extinction of others.

Nonrenewable energy resources present a significant environmental problem for our society. Two thirds of known oil reserves are located in only five countries: Saudi Arabia, Kuwait, Iran, Iraq, and the United Arab Emirates (Miller, 1993). Despite the price of gasoline, oil continues to be a relatively cheap form of energy and can be transported easily. Yet, when burned carbon dioxide gas is released into the atmosphere, it creates air pollution and contributes to changes in the global climate. If current government subsides were removed and the price of oil included cleanup of all of the harmful environmental effects of using oil, the price of gasoline would be far too expensive for most people to use. Oil companies have known for some time that our oil reserves are being depleted and have begun diversifying into different industries. At current rates of consumption, world oil reserves may be depleted (for economical reasons) in 35 years (Miller, 1993). Our automobile companies have increased fuel efficiency (miles per gallon), but this serves only as a Band-Aid, not as preventative medicine to cure the problem. Despite pollution and the knowledge of reserve depletion, millions of people are in a sense "addicted" to oil and gasoline consumption. Many are calling for increased research and product development of alternative forms of energy, particularly solar energy to operate not only our vehicles but also our homes and businesses. The U.S. Solar Research Institute estimates that solar energy could provide as much as 50 percent of our energy needs now and for the next 50 years (Miller, 1993).

THE TRAGEDY OF THE COMMONS

Garrett Hardin, a biologist, helped to develop the notion of the "tragedy of the commons" that appeared first in the work of William Lloyd in 1833 (Hardin, 1994). The scenario follows. A community has a pasture ("commons") open to all people. Herders use the commons to feed their cattle. One could reasonably expect that each herder would attempt to keep as many cattle as possible on the commons in order to maximize gain. Either implicitly, or perhaps explicitly, each herder considers the utility of having one more animal in the herd to be fed at the commons. One more cow would increase profits (a positive utility of one). However, this might lead to overgrazing. Since all herders would potentially overgraze, however, they all share the consequences of this decision (a negative utility of less than one, a fraction of one). The herder would conclude that more utility is gained than lost from adding another animal to the herd. Since more animals add to utility, each herder would make the same decision. "Each man is locked into a system that compels him to increase his herd without limit—in a world that is limited. Ruin is the destination toward which all men rush, each pursuing his own best interest in a society that believes in the freedom of the commons. Freedom of the commons brings ruin to all" (Hardin, 1994).

Hardin goes on to point out that we have a number of important commons in the world. These include land, water (including oceans), and air. Perhaps nowhere is this concept best illustrated than with our national park system. Currently, the system has over 300 units, covering 80 million acres, which range from national battlefields and monuments to national parks. In 1950, the National Park Service recorded a total of 33 million visits to national park service areas (U.S. Bureau of the Census, 1993). By 1990, only 40 years later, national park visits totaled almost 260 million, an eightfold increase. Other threats, beyond the numbers of visitors, include air pollution (particularly at Shenandoah National Park in Virginia), extensive development in Florida (Everglades National Park), copper smelters near Glacier National Park (Montana) that cause fluoride contamination, and noise pollution resulting from helicopter flights in and around the Grand Canyon National Park (Arizona). Other problems the national parks are experiencing include poaching, traffic jams, crime, drugs, and vandalism. These problems are so serious there are now reports that park visitors are asking for refunds of entrance and other fees (Miller, 1993). Perhaps due to overcrowding, crime is climbing dramatically in national and state parks. In 1990, for example, these parks recorded 16 murders, 44 rapes, 147 armed robberies, and 207 aggravated assaults (Miller, 1993). Park rangers are spending more of their time in law enforcement instead of park management and environmental education. The greatest danger to these parks is human activities outside the parks themselves. Mining, timber-harvesting, grazing, water diversion, and urban development encroach on park boundaries and wildlife increasingly.

The National Park Service is attempting to develop policies that both protect the parks and serve the needs of visitors. Some suggestions include restricting access by limiting the number of people and automobiles, restricting the types of activities, and reevaluating the role of concessions (i.e., restaurants, gas stations) within park boundaries. Park personnel are beginning to use local people to aid in these policies. Rocky Mountain National Park (Colorado) now has an active volunteer organization which performs many duties in place of rangers who must attend to other duties. These actions provide an example of constructive measures that can be implemented to protect our environment and minimize the many social problems which result from environmental degradation.

REFERENCES

HARDIN, GARRETT
1994 "The Tragedy of the Commons" in Donald VanDeVeer and Christine Pierce, eds., *The Environmental Ethics and Policy Book: Philosophy, Ecology, and Economics.* Belmont, CA: Wadsworth Publishing.

KEATING, MICHAEL
1993 *The Earth's Summit's Agenda for Change.* Geneva, Switzerland: The Center for Our Common Future.

MEADOWS, DONELLA, DENNIS L. MEADOWS and JORGEN RANDERS
1992 *Beyond the Limits: Confronting Global Collapse, Envisioning a Sustainable Future.* Post Mills, VT: Chelsea Green.

MILLER, G. TYLER
1993 *Environmental Science,* 4th ed. Belmont, CA: Wadsworth Publishing.

POPULATION REFERENCE BUREAU
1994 "1994 World Population Data Sheet." Washington, DC: Government Printing Office.

U.S. BUREAU OF THE CENSUS.
1993 *Statistical Abstract of the United States, 1993.* Washington, DC: U.S. Government Printing Office.

EXERCISE 23

Name _____   Date _____

ID # _____   Class Time _____

I. Miller (1993) argues that individuals count—that it is the actions of billions of individuals that create environmental problems. If so, then the actions of billions of individuals can help solve environmental problems as well. List below any actions that you are now taking to solve environmental problems. Then list three actions that you *could* take to solve these problems.

    A.

    B.

    C.

    A.

    B.

    C.

II. The notion of the "tragedy of the commons" is important to consider when studying environmental problems. Answer the following questions about the tragedy of the commons.

    A. List three such commons.

        1.

        2.

        3.

    B. Explain why each of these commons is important to society and to you.

        1.

        2.

        3.

    C. Identify some steps which our society can take to minimize the problems caused by the tragedy of the commons.

    D. Do the policies or actions suggested in part C above require government intervention or do they depend on individuals? Explain why one or the other would be preferable.

III. Locate a recent newspaper or news magazine article concerning an environmental problem. Attach the article to this page and answer the following questions.

   A. What is the exact nature of the environmental problem described in the article?

   B. How does this problem directly or indirectly affect you?

   C. What or who is identified as the "cause" of the problem?

   D. How extensive is the problem? Are many people affected or just a few?

   E. What could you do to address this problem?

   F. What should our society do to address this problem?

IV. You are mayor of a small town called Watertown with a population of about 5,000. Your city has a low crime rate, good schools, and a pleasant environment. It is located along a scenic, free-flowing river that provides recreational opportunities and drinking water for residents. A manufacturing company has proposed building a production facility just outside town. The plant will produce personal computers and other electronics such as fax machines. The facility will take two years to complete with a life expectancy of 30 years, while providing 500 much needed jobs for Watertown.

   However, the facility will result in the loss of habitat for wild animals such as deer, birds, and small mammals. There is the potential of air and water pollution that can affect plants, animals, and humans. Because many new "outsiders" will be moving into the community, new housing must be built to accommodate them. A new school may need to be built to educate workers' children. The manufacturing company, you discover, has a prior history of air and water pollution, including citations from EPA and state agencies. The citations involve organic chemicals such as oil and cleaning solvents which threaten humans and aquatic life; water-soluble inorganic chemicals such as acids, salts, leads, and mercury; and inorganic plant nutrients that deplete water of oxygen and can kill fish and damage humans, especially children.

   The company says it complies with all government environmental regulations and will be a "good neighbor" in the community. Its jobs and tax money are needed to finance improved streets and roads, schools, and other public buildings.

   Your assignment is to decide if you want the company to build its facility in your community. Write a summary of the argument for your position.

   (As an alternative exercise, the class can divide into four groups—city council, company representatives, local environmental group, and local chamber of commerce—and debate the issue before the city council. Each group should prepare a brief oral presentation that summarizes its position on the plant proposal and reflects its own interests. Then, each of the three other groups gets a maximum of five minutes to present its case before the city council. The city council then has five minutes to debate and decide the fate of the manufacturing plant.)

24

Gender Inequality in Developing Societies

Dana Dunn

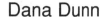

World system theory, a relatively recent perspective on the sociology of development, offers insight into the development process in less developed countries—insight that is lacking in the more traditional, modernization theory. Modernization theory views development as the panacea for the economic and social problems of less developed countries (LDCs). Walt W. Rostow (1960), a prominent modernization theorist, identifies several stages through which all developing countries should pass. These stages resemble the stages of development of the United States and other industrialized nations. The final stages are characterized by increases in overall economic growth as well as a reduction of income inequality within the developing country. The ultimate result of development, then, is an increase in the standard of living for the entire population of the developing nation (Chilicote and Johnson, 1983).

Modernization theories have become less fashionable and are often criticized today for their inability to explain the development process and its outcomes. The tendency to equate development with "progress for all" leads to a distorted picture of social reality. In particular, modernization theory predictions of increasing equality among people in LDCs as a result of economic growth simply have not been realized. The reality is that many countries experience overall economic growth, yet the distribution of income within these countries undergoes little change. To the extent that redistribution occurs, wealth simply becomes more concentrated in the hands of a small elite class while the majority of the population experiences a decline in standard of living (Bornschier and Ballmer-Cao, 1980; Evans and Timberlake, 1980; and Rubinson, 1976).

World system theory addresses many of the shortcomings of the modernization perspective. Case studies of developing countries, indicating deteriorating social and economic conditions, precipitated the increasing accep-

tance of world system theory, which offers explanations as to why inequality often increases in developing countries. World system theory posits an international division of labor, within which certain wealthy, powerful countries (core countries) exploit poor, less powerful countries (peripheral countries). Core countries expand into the noncore countries in search of cheaper raw materials, cheaper labor, and less regulated industrial environments. The peripheral countries become dependent upon the core countries for economic and technical assistance necessary for industrialization and economic diversification. Once industrialized, the noncore countries become even more dependent on core countries as markets for export goods. Often the subsistence economy of the noncore countries is severely disrupted as a result of the industrialization process. Thus, the income from exports becomes critical for the noncore countries. As a result, dependence becomes even more embedded in the relationship between the two sets of countries. Exploitation often results as the interests of the core countries and the upper classes of the noncore take precedence over the socioeconomic needs of the majority of the noncore countries' population (Bollen, 1983; D'Onofrio-Flores, 1982; Portes, 1978; Wallerstein, 1974; Ward, 1983).

World system theory acknowledges that LDCs will *not* follow the development paths of more developed countries (MDCs) due to the exploitative nature of the relationship between the two sets of countries. In other words, the disadvantaged, dependent position of the periphery is thought to distort the typical consequences of socioeconomic development. This distortion is portrayed as taking the form of lowered economic growth, an increase in income inequality, labor displacement, and unemployment. In summary, dependence is described as having negative effects for LDCs and resulting in a decline in standard of living for a significant portion of the population.

THE EFFECTS OF DEVELOPMENT ON WOMEN

The focus of this chapter is on the extent to which development affects the distribution of resources *across the sexes*. Accumulating evidence concerning the relationship between development and the status of women suggests that development often stimulates and reinforces the oppression of women. In other words, the socioeconomic status of women within developing countries declines relative to that of men as a result of development (Blumberg, 1981; McCormack, 1981; Ward, 1983). Development affects the lives and well-being of women in LDCs primarily through changes in the nature of work, in terms of what is produced, how it is produced, and for whom it is produced. For many women, development and industrialization result in displacement from the rural sectors of the economy and a shortage of jobs in the urban industrial sector. A common result of changing the predominant mode of production from agricultural to industrial is an increase in the number of people migrating from urban to rural and rural to urban areas searching for subsistence (Boserup, 1970; Loutfi, 1980; Tinker, 1976). First attention will be focused on the problems and displacement of women from agriculture as a result of development, then on the poor or nonexistent job opportunities for women in the industrial sector.

WOMEN IN AGRICULTURE

Women produce the majority of the world's food, yet as a result of development, they often lose control of the agricultural means and fruits of production previously at their disposal. Blumberg (1981) posits that women's control over the means of production relative to men's is a strong indicator of their status. Agricultural development in LDCs has often operated to reduce women's control over resources and thus their status (Boserup, 1970). The erosion of women's control over the agricultural means of production began as early as the colonial period. It was common for colonial policy to require the issuance of legal land titles. These titles, in most cases, were given to males, despite the fact that women often controlled the land prior to the issuance of titles. In many respects, this can be viewed as the more developed country passing on its discriminatory beliefs and practices to the developing country. As a result, women became mere laborers on land controlled by men (Blumberg, 1981).

In addition to transferring the ownership of land to men, development within the agricultural sector gives men access to information and training services that are often denied to women. Once again the biases and sex-based division of labor of the core is imposed on the LDC. Despite the fact that women's role in agriculture is greater than men's, training programs and agricultural assistance is offered to men. Training, if available for women, is usually focused on domestic tasks such as cooking and sewing (Boserup, 1970; Loutfi, 1980; Tadesse, 1982; Youssef,

1974). Men also have privileged access to credit and loans in developing countries; thus, they are able to invest in fertilizers and herbicides while women are not. Some studies reveal that despite these advantages men's agricultural production does not exceed that of women's (Blumberg, 1981).

Women's access to new agricultural technology is also extremely limited. Women's participation in agriculture is inversely related to regional development; that is, in areas where new technology is prevalent, one finds a low percentage of women. It appears that technology imported from developed countries brings with it a preference for male employees. In areas where new technology is introduced, female labor is often displaced in the long run. For example, in many LDCs the introduction of high-yield varieties of crops caused an increase in the demand for female labor in the short run due to high yields and intense cultivation. Later on, the introduction of fertilizers, weedkillers, and other mechanical labor-saving technology led to a substantial decrease or displacement of female labor (Loutfi, 1980; Tadesse, 1982).

The changing nature of women's relationship to the means of production does not mean that women are no longer active workers in agriculture. In fact, the work of women often increases as a result of agricultural development. Thus, women's control over resources decreases as the amount of work increases. This occurs because developed countries encourage LDCs to devote most of their efforts to the production of export crops which are often inedible. Because the wages received from the production of export crops are often insufficient for subsistence, women are forced to engage in subsistence farming. Thus, women labor on male-controlled land by day to produce export crops and "moonlight" by gardening on small, inadequate plots of land in order to feed the family. This subsistence agriculture is almost always considered the responsibility of women (Loutfi, 1980; Tinker, 1976).

When agricultural development is accompanied by industrial development in urban areas, the work of women often increases even further. This occurs because men migrate to the urban areas for the scarce manufacturing jobs. Women are then forced to take over the tasks traditionally regarded as males' tasks, such as care of livestock. This adds to the already overwhelming workload of women for they become responsible for traditionally male tasks as well as cash crop production and subsistence farming (Boserup, 1970).

Men are, of course, more successful than women in finding employment in the industrialized sector, yet the wages obtained from such employment are usually insufficient for supporting the family. In virtually all countries where women grow food for family consumption, the wages paid to male industrial workers are reduced to a minimum. This situation allows the employer to reduce the wages of the male below a level necessary for the reproduction of the worker and his family (Tadesse, 1982).

It becomes obvious that the consequences of agricultural development are often quite negative for women.

It is relevant at this point to ask about the impact of these development consequences for the population a whole. One might assume that the introduction of new technology and foreign dollars increases the standard of living for the average family unit in LDCs despite the negative effect upon women. This is, however, a faulty assumption. Several factors operate to actually reduce the standard of living of the total population, and they are, in part, a direct result of the situation of women in LDCs.

For example, the problematic situation of women in LDCs often results in an increase in malnutrition in these countries. The time constraints women face as a result of increasing workloads leads to their rejecting food crops that require a high labor input and offer low yields. Often the substituted low labor crops have inferior nutritional value. The end result of switching to low labor, high-yield crops is often malnutrition for a significant portion of the population (Blumberg, 1981; Tadesse, 1982). A specific example can be seen in the case of an African country which, for reasons mentioned above, replaced yam production with cassava production. Cassavas have a much lower nutritional value and lack the vitamins and minerals necessary for a reasonably balanced diet. The result was a serious malnutrition disease which affected large numbers of children.

Another way in which the negative consequences of agricultural development for women may be extended to the rest of the developing countries' population is related to different spending patterns among males and females. Some studies indicate that men and women in LDCs spend income in quite different ways. Men (particularly those physically separated from their families as a result of urban migration for employment) tend to spend income on drink, travel, transportation, and female companionship, while women tend to use income for improving the standard of living for the family (Blumberg, 1981). To the extent that this holds true in LDCs, transferring resources to males will only result in an increase in their individual welfare, whereas increasing the resources of females will have a positive effect on the welfare of the family unit as a whole (Loutfi, 1980).

Changes in the workload of women resulting from dependent development may also result in a significant reduction in the quality of child care in LDCs. Overburdened women in developing countries do not, in almost all cases, have access to child-care facilities. If women in LDCs cannot adequately care for their children as a result of their increasing workload, their only option is to leave the children in the care of unemployed, older children (primarily of ages 7 to 10) or the elderly (often physically impaired) (Youssef, 1974).

WOMEN IN THE FORMAL LABOR MARKET

Development in the industrial sectors of LDCs results in numerous problems for women in the formal labor market. Women's participation in the wage labor market in de-

veloping countries is characterized by the following: occupational segregation by sex, inadequate wages, and the displacement of women as a result of the introduction of labor-saving technologies. Thus, the status of women in the formal labor market often declines as a result of the development process (Mitra et al., 1980; Organization for Economic Co-operation and Development, 1980; Tadesse, 1982).

In developing countries, as well as in the United States and other developed nations, women are segregated into relatively unskilled, low-reward sectors of the economy. In developed countries a variety of social institutions reinforced this sex-based division of labor. Developed countries, through their role in the development of LDCs, often impose their institutionalized system of occupational sex segregation on the LDCs (Barnet and Muller, 1974). The cost of this sex-based occupational segregation or discrimination is great for any society in that such arrangements place artificial limitations on the structure of the work force. Approximately one half of the population (women) is denied access to certain types of work. In many cases, those denied access to jobs are better qualified than those currently holding such jobs. Thus, a potentially productive worker is refused employment, as a result of sex discrimination, while an unproductive worker remains on the job. Wealthy nations can afford to indulge in this form of discrimination. It is likely that LDCs will be unable to prosper under such arrangements, for their economic base is not strong enough to waste potential talent in the manner described.

Many "logical" explanations are offered for the segregation of women into less favorable jobs in LDCs. It should come as no surprise that they often resemble those explanations commonly used in the United States. The most common explanations are women's lack of education and training relative to men's, and potential conflict between wage work and domestic roles (Tadesse, 1982). Given existing social arrangements, these arguments may be valid; however, the traditional arrangements can easily be modified so as to nullify these arguments. For example, training and education can be provided for women as well as men. If a limited capacity for training exists in LDCs, it would be most efficient to offer training to those with the most ability rather than strictly to men. The potential conflict between work and domestic roles could be addressed by the provision of child-care facilities. Staff for these facilities would be abundant because of the oversupply of labor in LDCs.

The changes mentioned above are beginning to be recognized in MDCs, but the likelihood of implementing such changes in LDCs remains slim. Changes in social structure are most likely to occur when actively pursued by organized groups. Organized women's groups have existed in developed countries for some time and have been responsible for many positive social reforms for women. Such groups are less common in developing nations because overburdened women have little time for political activism. Lack of education is also a factor preventing women from collectively pursuing their interests in the political arena. Until women can overcome these obstacles and organize in pursuit of reform, occupational sex segregation is likely to remain prevalent.

Occupational sex segregation often results in women becoming concentrated in the newly developing tertiary sector of the economy. Dependent development distorts the labor force in LDCs by creating an oversized tertiary or service sector (Evans and Timberlake, 1980; Ward, 1983). Some of the newly created tertiary occupations are clerical. These clerical positions are typically held by women and, as a result, pay extremely low wages. Despite the inadequate remuneration, clerical jobs are highly prized by women and constitute only a small percentage of the jobs in the tertiary sector. The majority of the jobs within the newly created tertiary are domestic. Women are commonly employed as maids, cooks, housekeepers, cleaners, and sweepers. Employed in occupations such as these, women have no access to information, training, and technology that is prevalent in the manufacturing sector (Tadesse, 1982).

The segregation of women into the tertiary sector is primarily responsible for the large wage differentials between the sexes. Jobs typically held by women, such as domestic tasks, are assigned lower rates of pay. This occurs because the men, not women, are viewed as the breadwinners and responsible for the maintenance of the family.

More problematic than either occupational segregation or low wages is the issue of declining employment in the wage labor market for women. The early stages of industrialization create an increase in the demand for both male and female labor. Yet when industry becomes further mechanized, women tend to be replaced by machines or men operating machines. The lack of labor absorption of women in the manufacturing sector of LDCs is a reflection of the fact that development has occurred as a result of the use of imported technology that decreases the demand for unskilled labor. Global technology often has a devastating effect on the Third World economies in that it destroys jobs (D'Onofrio-Flores, 1982; Evans and Timberlake, 1980).

Industries adopting capital-intensive technology typically displace or stop hiring women rather than men because women have not had the training or education necessary to operate the new equipment (Tadesse, 1982). As indicated earlier, men in LDCs are given exclusive control over resources (new technology), and control over resources results in numerous advantages for the controllers. Women, deprived of technical knowledge and training, are often unemployed or underemployed.

In some instances the decline in women's employment is partially offset by a new source of employment. Multinational corporations (MNCs) often locate subdivision of their manufacturing processes in developing countries (Tadesse, 1982). Traditionally, these are high concentration areas of women in manufacturing, that is, textiles, electromechanical products, and clothing. These jobs are exported from the developed countries because they are low-paying, routine, and often hazardous. The LDC is seen as a source of cheap and willing labor. Given the virtually unlimited supply of female unemployed labor, women typically perform these jobs. Because of their inferior status, women employees provide the perfect solution for the MNCs' problem of labor costs. This practice of exporting jobs is probably the most direct example of the developed country exploiting the developing country, and women in particular.

CONCLUSION

In this selection I have summarized the negative effects of development for women in LDCs. The structure of the world economy—in particular, the relationships between developed and developing nations—has negative consequences for women. Clearly, the status of women relative to men in LDCs declines as a result of the position of these nations in the world economy. The status of women, due primarily to a loss of control over economic resources, is linked to the declining well-being of the total populations in LDCs.

REFERENCES

BARNET, RICHARD T. and RONALD E. MULLER
1974   *Global Reach: The Power of Multinational Corporations.* New York: Simon & Schuster.

BLUMBERG, RAE LESSER
1981   "Rural Women in Development," in Naomi Black and Ann Baker Cottrell, eds., *Women and World Change: Equity Issues in Development.* Beverly Hills, CA: Sage.

BOLLEN, KENNETH
1983   "World System Position, Dependency and Democracy: The Cross-National Evidence," *American Sociological Review* 48 (4): 468–479.

BORNSCHIER, VOLKER and THANYH-HUYEN BALLMER-CAO
1979   "Income Inequality: A Cross National Study of the relationship between MNC-Penetration, Dimensions of the Power Structure and Income Distribution," *American Sociological Review* 44 (3): 487–506.

BOSERUP, ESTER
1970   *Woman's Role in Economic Development.* New York: St. Martin's Press.

CHILICOTE, R. H. and D. JOHNSON
1983   *Theories and Development: Modes of Production or Dependency.* Beverly Hills, CA: Sage.

D'ONOFRIO-FLORES, PAMELA M.
1982   "Technology, Economic Development and the Division of Labor," in Pamela M. D'Onofrio-Flores and Sheila M. Pfafflin, eds., *Scientific-Technological Change and the Role of Women in Development.* Boulder, CO: Westview Press.

EVANS, PETER B. and MICHAEL TIMBERLAKE
1980   "Dependence, Inequality, and the Growth of the Tertiary: A Comparative Analysis of Less Developed Countries," *America Sociological Review* 45 (4): 531–552.

LOUTFI, MARTHA F.
1980   *Rural Women: Unequal Partners in Development.* Geneva, Switzerland: International Labor Office.

McCORMACK, THELMA
1981 "Development with Equity for Women" in Naomi Black and Ann Baker Cottrell, eds., *Women and World Change: Equity Issues in Development.* Beverly Hills, CA: Sage.

MITRA, ASOLK, LALIT P. PATHAK and SHEKHAR MUKHERJI
1980 *The Status of Women: Shifts in Occupational Participation.* New Delhi, India: Abhinar Publications.

ORGANIZATION FOR ECONOMIC CO-OPERATION AND DEVELOPMENT
1980 *Women and Employment.* Paris: OECD.

PORTES, ALEJANDRO
1978 "On the Sociology of National Development: Theories and Issues," *American Journal of Sociology* 82 (1): 55–85.

ROSTOW, W. W.
1960 *The Stages of Economic Growth.* Cambridge: Cambridge University Press.

RUBINSON, RICHARD
1976 "The World-Economy and the Distribution of Income Within States: A Cross-National Study," *American Sociological Review* 41 (4): 638–659.

TADESSE, ZENEBEWORKE
1982 "Women and Technology in Peripheral Countries: An Overview," in Pamela M. D'Onofrio-Flores and Sheila M. Pfafflin, eds., *Scientific-Technological Change and the Role of Women in Development.* Boulder, CO: Westview Press.

TINKER, IRENE
1976 "The Adverse Impact of Development on Women," in Irene Tinker, Michelle Bramsen and Mayra Buvinic, eds., *Women and World Development.* New York: Praeger.

UNITED NATIONS
1980 *Report of the World Conference of the United Nations Decade for Women: Equality, Development and Peace.* New York: United Nations.

WALLERSTEIN, IMMANUEL
1974 *The Modern World System.* New York: Academic Press.

WARD, KATHRYN B.
1983 "The Economic Status of Women in the World System: A Hidden Crisis in Development," in Albert Bergesen, ed., *Crises in the World System.* Beverly Hills, CA: Sage.

YOUSSEF, NADIA HAGGAG
1974 *Women and Work in Developing Societies.* Westport, CT: Greenwood Press.

EXERCISE 24

Name _____   Date _____

ID # _____   Class Time _____

I. Worldwide, approximately 105 males are conceived for every 100 females. The "oversupply" of males is short lived, however. Biology favors women in that they are hardier and more resistant to disease. As a result, in societies where girls are treated much the same as boys, there are about 106 females for every 100 males. If both sexes receive similar nutrition and health care, women live longer. This leads to a "life expectancy gap" between the sexes. In the United States this gap is such that on average women live about seven years longer than men.

The story changes, however, when the sexes do not receive equal treatment. In many Asian and North African countries, for example, fewer female than male children survive due to unequal treatment. In developing countries where the benefits of development are not distributed equally across the sexes, men live longer, on average, than women.

A. Collect information on life expectancy for men and women for the countries listed in the table below. Many sources contain this data. The following organizations commonly publish life expectancy data: the World Bank, the United Nations Development Program, and the Population Reference Bureau. Record the data in the table. Calculate the life expectancy gap for each country (female life expectancy minus male life expectancy). Positive numbers indicate that, on average, women outlive men. Negative numbers indicate that women die earlier than their male peers.

	Female Life Expectancy	Male Life Expectancy	Life Expectancy Gap
Bangladesh			
Bhutan			
Germany			
India			
Nepal			
Pakistan			
Sweden			

B. Drawing from the essay, list five factors that may contribute to men's longevity in the countries with a negative number in the "Life Expectancy Gap" column.

1.

2.

3.

4.

5.

II. The table below provides information on female education and literacy, fertility, and infant and child mortality. Use the information to answer the questions below.

Region	% Female Ages 15–19 in Secondary School	% Female Adults Literate	Total Fertility Rate	Infant Mortality Rate	Child Mortality Rate
World	36	56	3.6	81	10
Developed	87	97	2.0	18	(.)
Developing	28	43	4.2	90	—
North America	96	99	1.8	10	(.)
Latin America	44	77	4.1	62	6
Western Europe	79	97	1.8	12	(.)
Eastern Europe	—	97	2.3	28	1
Middle East	33	36	5.8	96	12
South Asia	18	19	4.9	120	13
Far East	38	58	2.7	45	6
Oceania	71	85	2.7	39	3
Sub-Saharan Africa	12	29	6.4	113	22
Northern Africa	35	23	5.8	91	16

SOURCES: Population Reference Bureau (1985) *World Data Sheet and The World's Women: A Profile*; World Bank (1985), *World Development Report*: United Nations (1985) *State of the World's Children*.

(.)   Approaching 0.
—   Data unavailable.

A.   What is the relationship between education/literacy for women and fertility?

B.   What is the relationship between education/literacy for women and infant mortality?

C.   What is the relationship between education/literacy for women and child mortality?

D.   Explain why these relationships exist.

25

Global Population, Poverty, and Child Labor

Elizabeth Leonard

For most of human history the world's population increased very slowly as human societies worked a delicate balance between high birth rates and high death rates. Global population began a noticeable rise in the seventeenth century and virtually exploded in the nineteenth century with the advent of the Industrial Revolution. Advances in agriculture, medicine, and sanitation greatly reduced death rates across all age groups. World population reached 1 billion around the year 1800 and its second billion by 1930. Only 30 years later (1960) the population reached 3 billion and 1 billion more were added to total 4 billion just 15 years later (1975). In 1987, the global population grew to over 5 billion. Today, the world's population stands at more than 5.5 billion persons.

Where is all this growth occurring? Early on, most of the growth in population occurred in the industrialized countries of Western Europe. Since World War II, most of the growth has occurred in the less developed nations of Asia, Latin America, and Africa. About 40 percent of the population in these countries is under 15 years old, suggesting that much of the future growth in world population will be concentrated in areas of the world already struggling to provide for their inhabitants.

Continued population growth has significant and far-reaching consequences. One such consequence is the ongoing expansion of cities. In fact, a major demographic trend of the late twentieth century is the increase of the world's population that lives in urban areas. Experts project that by the year 2000, 3 billion people will live in urban areas, three fourths of them in developing nations (Moffett, 1994). Much of the rapid urban growth is the result of high birth rates in the cities. However, a substantial portion of swelling urban populations is caused by extreme rural poverty. Rural residents are "pushed" from their land and into the cities by systemic changes in agricultural production: the mechanization of production, environmental degradation, and increasingly concentrated ownership of land by the wealthiest members of society.

The exodus from rural to urban areas occurs within countries and crosses international borders as individuals and families seek to escape poverty and find work that will sustain them. To the rural poor, the cities offer a better chance for survival. Unfortunately, their hopes are dashed quickly. Migrants to urban areas in less developed countries are much more likely to be poor and unemployed than city natives (Harrison, 1979). Cities are unable to keep up with the service demands of their burgeoning populations—demands for clean water, sanitation, electricity, housing, transportation, employment, education, and public health and safety. For many urban poor, life can be harsh, harsher in some respects than life in the countryside. Yet, the lack of opportunities outside the city to earn enough to get by and the hope to do at least that in the city causes life at the bottom of the urban hierarchy to remain attractive to those migrating from rural areas.

CHILDREN AND WORK

In the countryside, large families and high birth rates put growing pressure on arable land which, in turn, may act as a catalyst for rural-urban migration. In fact, one of the underlying causes of poverty in developing nations is large family size. Yet, having a large family is also a widely used survival strategy for many households. Paradoxically, the large family is, simultaneously, a cause of and a response to poverty. Rather than more mouths to feed, additional children are viewed as more hands to be put to work and as potential sources of social security in old age.

Recent immigrants to urban areas settle in urban slums, on the streets, or in squatter settlements. Such areas are the fastest growing sections in the large cities of newly industrializing nations. In Calcutta, India, for example, one third of its 10 million inhabitants live in slums and 500,000 are homeless. Half the populations of Manila, Delhi, and Nairobi are slum dwellers; families set up households in the garbage dumps of Mexico City; and 20 million homeless roam the streets of Latin American cities. In Cairo, nearly 5 percent of the population lives in the "City of the Dead"—a group of adjacent cemeteries and one of the world's largest squatter towns (Moffett, 1994). Throughout the developing world, poverty, rapid urban growth, exploding populations, and the deterioration of family networks combine to create hordes of street children, partially or totally abandoned, and living under conditions of extreme deprivation. The magnitude of the problem is great. UNICEF, for example, estimates the number of street children worldwide to be 80 million (Fyfe, 1989).

The unemployment encountered by many families forces them to scratch out a living with marginal, unsteady work often in the informal sector of the economy. While many poor families do not send their children out into the labor force, child labor does appear to be on the rise in developing countries as a great number of children are forced prematurely into the labor pool in order to help their families survive (Moffett, 1994). Eighty percent of the world's children now live in developing countries and 97 percent of children who work do so in these nations (Bouhdiba, 1982). Not all work activities performed by children are considered "child labor." In many societies, children participate in work with family members, such as domestic or subsistence chores; it is an integral part of their socialization for adulthood. Children who work alongside their parents in rural or agricultural settings work as an extension of the household division of labor. This kind of child labor is of a very different nature when compared to the work performed by children in industrial settings who sell their labor to employers. In the cities of less developed countries, recent migrants account for a high percentage of child labor (Rodgers and Standing, 1981). While most working children perform agricultural work organized through households that are outside of formal labor markets, rapid urbanization and the growth of child labor in factory production in the less developed countries is increasing.

To be sure, "work" may be a positive component of a child's development. The work of children itself is not the issue, rather its abuse and the conditions under which it is performed are in question. How then may we distinguish between acceptable or tolerable work activities of children and exploitative child labor? One attempt to make such a distinction comes from the International Labour Organization (ILO). The ILO relates child labor to "diverse forms of exploitation, in which the beneficiaries are members either of another class or of another generation" (Rodgers and Standing, 1981). Another distinction made by the United Nation is found in Bouhdiba (1982), who describes child labor as work undertaken by a child at too early an age which is ill-suited to his or her physical constitution and capacity; thus, it has a negative impact on the child's mental and psychosocial equilibrium. Such child labor is clearly exploitative. In sum, when the work children undertake seriously impairs their physical and/or mental well-being, it becomes exploitative and, as we shall see, it contributes to the very cycle of poverty that generates it. Most nation-states today have laws that prohibit the exploitative use of child labor. Despite such formal regulations, the use of millions of children as workers continues to occur in developed and developing countries. Bouhdiba (1982) notes that the United Nations' International Covenant on Economic, Social and Cultural Rights acknowledged the problem and established the following guidelines regarding the employment of children:

> Children and young persons should be protected from economic and social exploitation. Their employment in work harmful to their morals or health or dangerous to life or likely to hamper their normal development should be punishable by law. States should also set age limits below which the paid employment of child labor should be prohibited and punishable by law.

The exploitation of child and even infant labor is not uncommon to the process of industrialization (see Smelser, 1959). Extreme abuses of child labor occurred in the course of Europe's early industrial development and in America decades ago. The issue of children's rights was first seriously examined during the Industrial Revolution. Interestingly, when the early nineteenth century English Parliament passed child labor laws to limit a child's workday to a maximum of 12 hours, it was the parents of child laborers who opposed the law most vehemently (Smelser, 1959). In England, the Factory Act of 1802 was the first act of legislation aimed at improving the well-being of children. There have been many measures to restrict the use of child labor by industrial firms since these early efforts.

The utilization of children in labor markets outside of the household economy occurs for many reasons. The isolation of new immigrant families in urban areas from the social support of extended family networks increases the vulnerability of their children to exploitation as workers. For such families children do not decide independently of parental influence whether or not they work; even less do they decide where and under what conditions they will work. In extreme cases, parents may commit their children to years of servitude to pay off debts; sometimes parents sell their children outright. Structurally, the decision to have children work is much like having children work within the structure of the household economy—additional productive hands increase the economic well-being of the entire family. The crucial difference of course is that the work of children now takes place (formally or informally) in the labor market. The utilization of children in one or another labor market is not confined to the past of already industrialized countries. The problem is a systemic one because wherever there are impoverished families, rural or urban, confronting the stark reality of their survival, children are vulnerable to exploitation. And of course, children without families, especially those in urban areas, are also vulnerable to exploitation.

The utilization of children as workers also is appealing to many employers. Unscrupulous employers find children to be the most easily exploited of all labor groups. Children constitute a work force that is cheap, renewable, docile, flexible, and unorganized. Generally, children are unaware of rights and protection that the law may afford them, and they lack any real economic, physical, or social power.

Many of the same factors that make child labor appealing to some employers may also make some states and their decision makers turn a blind eye to instances of childhood labor. On the one hand, the utilization of children in the work force can be an economic asset, especially if the supply of such children is great and if the state is particularly concerned with the broader, more macroeconomic and social issues of rapid economic development. States have other interests of their own in not noticing children in the work force. Children who work are not on the street contributing to other problems such as crime and they are not demanding expensive services such as formal education. On the other hand, the utilization of children in the work force can serve to displace adult workers.

Gender inequality is a well-known influence on fertility practices around the globe and such inequality also influences the work roles assigned to children. Many cultures, especially ones with large rural populations, place a higher value on male offspring than on female ones. Thus, the practice of having many children until the desired number of male children is reached is not uncommon. Where the supply of female children is greater than desired, female children are particularly vulnerable to exploitation. As Bouhdiba (1982) notes, "It is girls who are most readily, but not exclusively, made use of improperly as servants. They may be put out to work, fictitiously adopted, or simply sold."

Child labor practices may also reflect racial and class biases. For example, "fair-skinned" families in Bolivia and Colombia "adopt" little Indian girls as young as three years of age and put them to work as domestic servants (Bouhdiba, 1982). In both rural and urban areas of South Africa, generations of whites have exploited the labor of "colored" children along with their parents. Despite laws to the contrary, as late as the 1980s, a child could still be born a slave in parts of Algeria, Burkina Faso, Cameroon, Chad, Guinea, Ivory Coast, Mali, Mauritania, Niger, Nigeria, Senegal, and Sudan (Sawyer, 1988). In India, fathers over 40 years old in debt bondage to employers (i.e., working to pay off debt rather than receive wages) may be released from servitude by having one of their children, some as young as five years of age, work off a debt; and in some cases such practices span multiple generations (Rodgers and Standing, 1981).

HOW MANY CHILDREN WORK?

How many children throughout the world labor for their survival or for their families' subsistence? And what kinds of work do they perform? A complete tally of the number of children in the world's labor force cannot be estimated reliably; however, the extent of exploited child labor that has been documented suggests a problem of staggering proportions. The best estimates give a range of anywhere from 50 million to 300 million children worldwide (Rodgers and Standing, 1981; Berger, Belsey and Shah, 1991). Statistics indicate that 5 million children between the ages of 5 and 14 account for 19 percent of the total labor force in the Philippines (Rialp, 1993). Among Western European countries, Italy is thought to have the largest number of working children, 1.5 million (Fyfe, 1989). India has the world's largest child labor force with estimates ranging from 15 million to 45 million (Rodgers and Standing, 1981; Sawyer, 1988). Bouhdiba (1982) notes that in Pakistan, the carpet manufacturing industry alone employs 1.5 million children, many of them from the age of 6; that 3 million children work in Colombia; and some 16 million African children under age 13 work. By comparison, in the United States, approximately 800,000 children work in the agricultural industry alone (Sawyer, 1988).

Children who work often are shielded from public view so it is impossible to reliably describe all of the kinds of work they perform. Yet, there are some general factors which increase the likelihood of children working in certain industries. Since much of the labor of children is informal, nearly invisible to outsiders, marginal, and often illegal, some industries are less likely than others to utilize child labor. Most white-collar work, for example, does not utilize child labor. Capital-intensive industries, in general, also are less likely to seek out children as laborers.

While children are employed in virtually every occupation, labor-intensive industries are the sites where most working children are likely to be found. Domestic work industries employ the greatest number of children. Frequently, this takes the form of impoverished girls from rural areas fictitiously adopted into urban homes in less developed countries. Elsewhere, working children are employed as shepherds in Italy working 14-hour days, farm workers in the United States, sweatshop workers in the United Kingdom and the U.S. garment industries, plantation workers in Malaysia, armed soldiers in Rwanda, mine workers in Colombia, matchstick makers in India, who breath sulfur fumes for 11 to 12 hours a day, tobacco workers in Thailand, shirt makers in Guatemala, street beggars in Calcutta, coral divers plunging without equipment to depths of 100 feet from Philippine fishing boats, and in the carpet industries of Morocco, Pakistan, and India that employ children who regularly work 72 hours a week.

Due to the often clandestine conditions of child labor, the conditions of work are frequently substandard or hazardous: poor ventilation, heating, and lighting; excessive crowding; long hours without sufficient rest periods; and repetitive tasks performed in one position. Because children are still undergoing physical development, their vulnerability to many hazards is particularly troublesome.

Children employed in industrial occupations suffer from high rates of asthma, silicosis, tuberculosis, lead poisoning, polyneuritis, and paralysis. Children employed in jobs that require them to hold the same position for hours on end or carry loads too heavy for their small frames, often experience stunted or malformed growth. One recent study showed that in some instances the rural children in Africa's Sahel region perform work considered much harder than the work performed by adults (Fyfe, 1989). In recent years the number of labor standards violations involving children in the United States has been considerable. Citing statistics compiled by official sources, Dumane (1993) reports that across all industries approximately 300 children have been killed and 70,000 injured on the job since 1980.

The most distressing and dangerous of all forms of child exploitation, child prostitution and pornography, are also on the rise worldwide. Child prostitution is demeaning, oppressive, and dangerous. The explosive increase in child prostitution in some areas of the developing world is related directly to severe poverty. Thailand has the highest proportion of child prostitutes in Asia; prepubertal young girls from impoverished villages are exported to Germany, or sent to Bangkok brothels, having been sold or leased through agents (Sawyer, 1988). Researchers document similar scenarios involving boys and girls in Macao, Istanbul, Bombay, Paris, Brazil, and resort cities in the Philippines (Bouhdiba, 1982; Rialp, 1993). Children exploited by prostitution and pornography are especially vulnerable to physical as well as psychological pain and injury, and exposure to disease and to sadistic customers. One study of Thai brothels in a popular tourist province found that 44 percent of underage prostitutes tested positive for HIV (Hiew, 1992). It is important to remind ourselves that child sexual exploitation is not restricted to the developing world. Aiding and abetting in the worldwide sexual exploitation of children, it is the people of affluent countries primarily that make child pornography a multibillion-dollar industry.

CONCLUSION

The tremendous expansion of global population during the past few decades and the factors that forced rural residents to migrate to heavily populated urban areas in the less developed countries have created an available pool of child labor, which many employers find so hard to resist. The exploitation of children in the work force is likely to continue as long as it is an integral part of the economy, whether it be at the local or global level. The practice of utilizing child labor is entrenched most deeply where the impoverished economies of developing countries intersect with the affluence of the developed world, especially in industries where the labor content of the goods that are produced is high.

REFERENCES

BERGER, LAWRENCE R., MARK BELSEY and P. M. SHAH
1991   "Medical Aspects of Child Labor in Developing Countries," *American Journal of Industrial Medicine* 19: 697–699.

BOUHDIBA, ABDELWAHAB
1982   *Exploitation of Child Labor.* New York: United Nations.

DUMANE, BRIAN
1993   "Illegal Child Labor Comes Back," *Fortune* April 5.

FYFE, ALEC
1989   *Child Labour.* Cambridge, UK: Polity Press.

HARRISON, PAUL
1979   *Inside the Third World.* London: Penguin Books.

HIEW, CHOK C.
1992   "Endangered Children in Thailand: Third World Families Affected by Socioeconomic Changes," in George W. Albee, Lynne A. Bond and Toni V. Cook Monsey, eds., *Improving Children's Lives.* Newbury Park, CA: Sage.

MOFFETT, GEORGE D.
1994   *Critical Masses.* New York: Viking Press.

RIALP, VICTORIA
1993   *Children and Hazardous Work in the Philippines.* Geneva, Switzerland: International Labour Office.

RODGERS, GERRY and GUY STANDING
1981   *Child Work, Poverty and Underdevelopment.* Geneva, Switzerland: International Labour Office.

SAWYER, ROGER
1988   *Children Enslaved.* London: Routledge.

SMELSER, NEIL J.
1959   *Social Change in the Industrial Revolution.* Chicago: University of Chicago Press.

EXERCISE 25

Name _____   Date _____

ID # _____   Class Time _____

I.   As you have seen, global population has increased sharply in recent decades. This exercise asks you to gather data on population projections for the world and regions of the world through the year 2020.

   A.   Complete Table 1 below by gathering the appropriate data. (*Hint:* The U.S. Department of Commerce regularly publishes *World Population Profile,* which includes the relevant population projections including the 1990 baseline data below. If your library does not have this publication, use others; and if the years for the projection data do not match the dates provided, indicate what years you used.)

TABLE 1

Region	Population (in millions)			
	1990	2000	2010	2020
World	5,329			
Developing	4,117			
Developed	1,213			
Developing Asia	2,868			
Latin America	449			
Sub-Saharan Africa	541			

   B.   Answer the following questions about the future of the world's population from the data you have collected.

   1.   What percentage of the world's population lived in developed countries in 1990? What is the projected figure for the year 2020?

   2.   Which regional populations are projected to grow fast and which ones slowly?

   3.   Which region has the greatest rate of projected growth from 1990 to 2020?

II.   This exercise asks you to gather data on the projected growth of the urban population for the world and regions of the world through the year 2020.

   A.   Complete Table 2 below by gathering the appropriate data. (*Hint:* The United Nations publishes *Prospects of World Urbanization,* which includes the relevant population projections including the 1990 baseline data below. If your library does not have this publication, then use others; and if the years for the projection data do not match the dates provided, indicate what years you used.)

TABLE 2

Region	Urban Population (in millions)			
	1990	2000	2010	2020
World	2,260			
Less-developed	1,385			
Developed	876			
Asia	931			
Latin America	324			
Africa	223			

B. Answer the following questions about the future urban growth from the data you have collected.

1. What percentage of the world's urban population lived in more developed countries in 1990? What is the projected figure for the year 2020?

2. Which regional urban populations are projected to grow fast and which ones slowly?

3. Which region's urban population will increase the most by the year 2020?

III. Make comparisons between the two tables:

A. Explain why the data in the two tables you just completed are not directly comparable. (*Hint:* Pay more attention to the ways in which the regions are "defined" rather than slight differences in the years for which data were collected.)

B. Despite the limitations with the data you just discussed, indicate below at least two main trends concerning population growth *and* urban population growth derived from these tables.

Name _____   Date _____

ID # _____   Class Time _____

IV. Find a recent newspaper or magazine article concerning the use of children in the labor force.

    A. Attach a copy of the article to this exercise and provide the following information.

        1. Article title:

        2. Author:

        3. Date of publication:

        4. Name of newspaper or magazine:

    B. Identify the industry in which children are utilized.

    C. What reasons are noted in the article which explain why children are utilized as workers? (If none are specified then supply your own.)

    D. List specific advantages employers receive by using child labor.

CONCLUSION

ADDRESSING SOCIAL PROBLEMS

We chose a format for this volume that would stimulate your thinking about a wide range of social problems. Working though the exercises should have sensitized you to many of the social factors that contribute to the emergence and maintenance of social problems. Having now read the selections in this text, you should also have a strong sense of the complexity of social problems. It is our hope that you are beginning to see why it is often difficult to develop and implement satisfactory solutions to most social problems. If so, then you should also understand that there is no "one right way" to "solve" a particular social problem.

In this concluding chapter we review briefly some of the factors that make social problems complex so as to bring attention to the difficulties in public policy efforts for addressing these problems. In addition, we examine the implications of these issues for the role of social activism in bringing about social change.

In the introduction to this volume we emphasized that many social problems are enduring features of social organization and that other social problems are emergent phenomena. One reason for this is that social problems are complex, multidimensional phenomena. Social problems do not simply "fail to go away" or "endure" because we do not have the right technology to solve them or because we as a society are not wealthy enough to change the conditions which give rise to them. Social problems usually affect the lives of many people in society. The selections by Ray Darville on environmental problems, Leonard Beeghley on poverty, and Robert A. Hanneman on health care exemplify this feature of many social problems. Clearly, there are likely to be many people and groups that have interests at stake when problems come to be addressed as matters of public policy. The extent to which groups may be aware of such interests will in large measure affect their resistance to, or support for, policies that address issues defined as social problems.

The fact that social problems may persist for a long period of time brings attention to another aspect of their complex nature: Different people and groups do not necessarily see the same phenomena as equally problematic. It is, for example, widely agreed (at least among economists) that very high inflation is not good for an economy—prices spiraling upward, people unable to afford services and goods, and so forth. But what about periods when inflation is routinely low, such as in the United States since the mid-1980s? During these more normal periods, expert and popular opinion is less uniform. Lower levels of unemployment are usually associated with higher levels of inflation as low unemployment tightens up labor markets, resulting in higher wages and prices. Ramona Ford's essay on the problems of the working class addressed this kind of issue in great detail. The question this example raises for us concerns the definition of the problem. There is always a question of "who stands to gain?" when a situation is defined as problematic or not. The answer to this question usually depends upon whom one asks. The selection by Joel Best emphasizes this constructed aspect of social problems definition in greater detail than any of the other selections in the text. Jonathan H. Turner's selection concerning the politics of welfare reform also taps into some of the dynamics that are involved in defining what is and is not a problem in the process of reforming the current welfare system in the United States.

Many of today's longstanding social problems of inequality and social institutions are similar in nature to the inflation-unemployment example: Pressing social issues do not *directly* affect everyone. Today, inflation and unemployment fluctuations are closely monitored by the government because they are seen as one of the most important indicators of the overall health of the economy. For many people, however, the situation is not problematic because they are not significantly affected by the issue. Relatively secure upper-middle-class professionals are largely immune to the effects of these indicators because their employment status is not connected to the price of labor in the same way as is the case for entry level workers. For others, the problem is very significant. For example, low unemployment is an economic problem for some segments of society (e.g., business persons wanting to pay low wages for entry level jobs), but not for other segments (e.g., the working poor seeking jobs to support their families).

Even though socially advantaged segments of the population may not be *directly* affected by a particular social problem, when the problem is of a sufficient scale they are likely to be *indirectly* affected over the long run. For example, economically advantaged professionals may not experience financial strain resulting from relatively minor fluctuations in unemployment or inflation, but they will be affected by the likely increase in crime that is associated with the economic dislocation of low-income workers and an increase in poverty. These unanticipated consequences of social problems result from the interconnected nature of social groups, processes, and institutions. Many selections in this text highlight this feature of social problems: the discussion of educational assessment by Dorothea Weir, Elizabeth Leonard's discussion of youth employment, Dana Dunn's discussion of gender inequality, and Jan W. Weaver and Steven R. Ingman's discussion of elder care.

Many social problems are similar to the unemployment-inflation issue in yet another respect: Over time, attempted solutions to problems can come to be defined as problematic in and of themselves, such as government efforts to rectify society's problems. This "solutions-as-problem" feature of many social problems exists, in part, because our attempts to "solve" social problems reflect the negotiated efforts of many interested parties. The problem of economic inequality, for example, has largely been addressed through the taxation system. It is not surprising then that the relative distribution of "tax burdens" is usually at the heart of political debates year after year. Virtually all enduring social problems are, in effect, old problems complicated by our collective efforts to improve upon them. What is a solution to a problem at one time, later may be viewed as an emergent problem all its own, especially if the structural conditions which gave rise to it in the first place are not addressed adequately. The current debate over "welfare reform," as discussed by Jonathan H. Turner in this text, focuses attention on this problematic aspect of public social issues.

Earlier we also stressed the value of analyzing social problems from both the macro- and micro-levels. This dualistic nature of social reality is a feature of all societies. In the United States, for example, we routinely experience social reality through the micro-lens as private, individual experiences and troubles. Only occasionally do we really seek to understand ourselves or interpret the events in our lives in terms of the macrostructural, "big picture" problems. Indeed, there are usually moral prescriptions against doing so because we would have to swim against strong cultural currents that reward "individualism" and invite

the stigma of personal "irresponsibility." Recall, for example, the handy labels so widely used to describe recipients of public welfare that were discussed in Jonathan H. Turner's essay on inequality and stratification. So often such labels reflect a pattern of "blaming the victim," which ignores the social structural contributions to the problem. Note too the problems raised in the discussion of spouse abuse by Linda Rouse, teen-age pregnancy by Monica A. Longmore, mental-health and related problems discussed by Dee Southard and Gregg Dockins, respectively, sexual orientation by Kenneth Allan, and poverty by Leonard Beeghley. A common thread running through these selections is that micro problems have a structural context.

The complexity of social problems has many sources. The enduring quality of many social problems, the divergent interests among the many subgroups of the population, the problem of definition, and the near moral imperative to view social problems in terms of individual responsibility are among the most important sources of this complexity. These factors must be considered when attempting to forge satisfactory solutions to social problems as matters of public policy.

Developing satisfactory solutions to contemporary social problems is also a complex process because issues that come to be defined as social problems are often costly and involve large numbers of people. The magnitude of problems such as inequality (see for example, Elizabeth M. Almquist's discussion of gender inequality, and Dana Dunn and David V. Waller on the feminization of poverty) and deviance (see, for instance, Robert L. Young on crime rates and David MacKenna on youth gangs) reflect these facts. Because of their scope, solving social problems requires the coordinated efforts of many groups. Sometimes markets can solve social problems by getting services or resources to consumers at affordable prices. In many instances, however, markets appear to be incapable of providing goods and services due to the risks some actors would have to take. The building of the interstate highway system illustrates these points nicely. After World War II there were clear uses for the establishment of a national highway system. Considering the cost of the interstate highway system, what investor(s) would build such a costly system without guarantees on the return of investment? Thus, for matters of efficiency many social problems are best addressed as matters of public policy. Usually, this entails an important role for the federal government because it is most capable of organizing the complex interests and activities needed to address important public issues.

When social problems become matters of public policy, the efficiency consideration just discussed is quickly relegated to the background. Once issues become defined as social problems, groups that were not interested in the issue before may develop an interest and a desire to participate in the policy formation process. The desire of many groups to have an impact on policy decisions can slow down the process by which social problems are solved, but it also creates the potential for reaching satisfactory solutions that multiple interest groups can live with. Thus, the complexity of solving social problems means that such solutions are always going to be negotiated and, by definition, *imperfect*. In other words, in virtually every case there is *no one right way* to solve a social problem because for each set of interests there is a different solution.

With the issues and limitations of public policy formation we have just discussed in mind, how then can sociology's tool kit best be utilized to develop viable policies for addressing pressing social problems of the day? This question has long interested practitioners within the discipline as well as many policy makers and interest groups outside the discipline. Should we employ sociological insights to advocate in favor of an oppressed class interest, as some would have us do? Are we doomed to serve the interests of the dominant class or those of the state, as some others have suggested? We believe that there are two ways in which sociology's tools can best be utilized to positively affect public policies addressing social problems. First, theory and method can be employed to inform policy makers about the consequences of implementing alternative "solutions" to problems. Secondly, sociological analysis can sensitize policy makers to the complexities of problems and their solutions. Social problems are foremost experienced as individual, micro-level phenomena, but they are always based in the social structural arrangements within which individuals are located. Failure to account for this dualism of social life will result in policy choices that only naively address the surface level of problems.

SOCIAL ACTIVISM

In addition to public policy formation, individual action is also an important vehicle for addressing social problems. Here we are concerned with the extent to which people become *involved* in efforts to affect change when confronted by social problems. Sometimes people react to social problems by seeking change within themselves as a means of coping with the problem. For example, a widespread and diverse form of social activism is socially conscious shopping—a strategy which involves supporting organizations whose practices the individual judges to be socially responsible and boycotting irresponsible

organizations. Of more concern to us here, however, are the conditions which lead people who join or support voluntary organizations that attempt to influence public policy to change social arrangements defined as problematic.

The willingness to participate in collective efforts to affect change, while not unique the United States, does occur at higher levels in the United States than in many other countries of the world. The extent and nature of people's attempts to affect social change will be influenced by many factors, not the least of which is their access to those resources needed to influence others and policy makers. Because valued resources are distributed unequally in society, some social classes or segments of society are inherently more organized and less fragmented than others. For the vast majority of persons in the United States, the resources needed to change social arrangements, even those arrangements widely defined as problematic, are beyond their reach. For persons rich in resources who are well connected to policy makers, the situation is vastly different. For them, the $1,000-a-plate dinner honoring their congressperson is, for all practical purposes, the functional substitute for the average person's attendance at a political rally.

The fact remains that millions of people seek to change social arrangements by participating in grass-roots organizations as well as in established, national-level social movements. These are the best available means for individuals to become personally involved and be personally responsible for their own lives. Despite the vast differentials in power and influence among segments of society, there have been tremendous gains over the decades by those who have had to overcome the difficulties involved in engaging in collective efforts to address social problems. Charles Case's selection on changing race and ethnic relations in the history of the United States documents such progress, and Janet Saltzman Chafetz's essay on work-family conflict reflects similar changes for women. If history can serve as a teacher of the effectiveness of social activism, then the lesson needed to be relearned is that change and "progress" are possible, but these are only temporary, constantly negotiated definitions of social reality. While it is true that there is no one right way to solve social problems, this fact only points to the need to participate, however possible, in efforts to construct satisfactory solutions to today's enduring and emerging social problems.

NOTES

NOTES

NOTES

NOTES

NOTES

NOTES

NOTES

NOTES

NOTES

NOTES

NOTES